DP ARCHITECTS ON ORCHARD ROAD

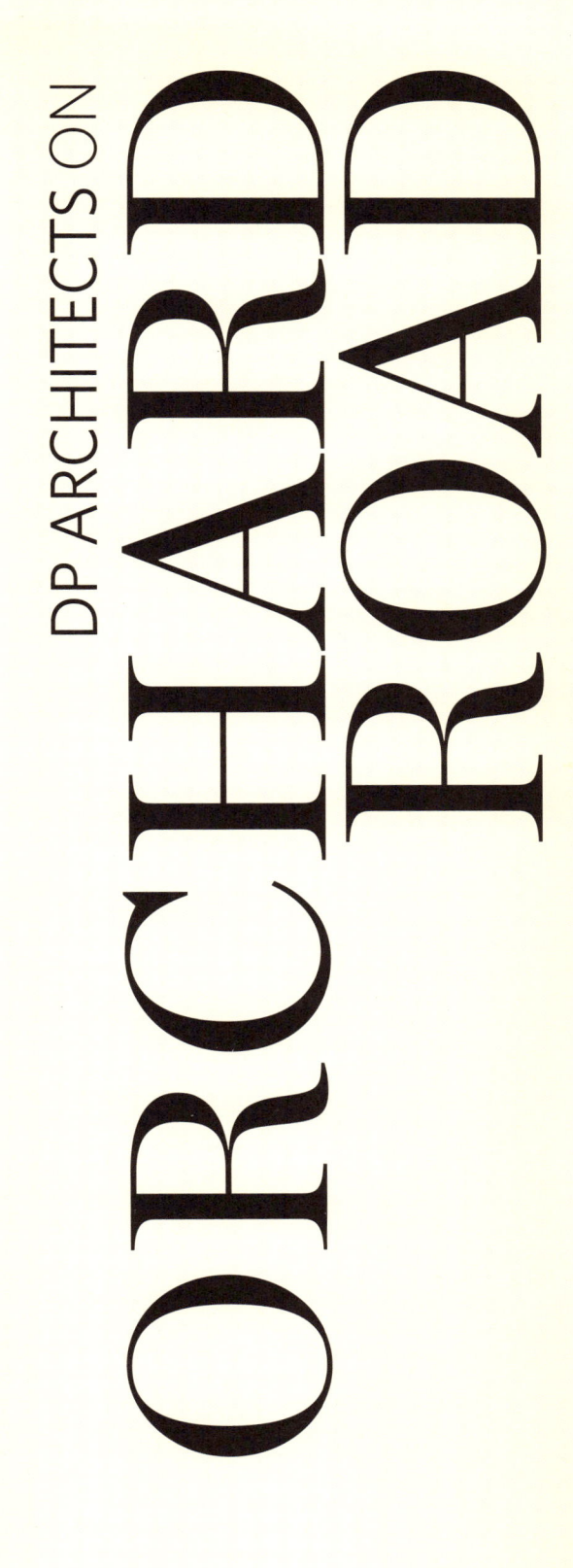

EVOLUTION OF A RETAIL STREETSCAPE

Collin Anderson
Preface by Fumihiko Maki
Foreword by Kenneth Frampton

images
Publishing

Published in Australia in 2012 by
The Images Publishing Group Pty Ltd
6 Bastow Place, Mulgrave, Victoria 3170, Australia
Tel: +61 3 9561 5544 Fax: +61 3 9561 4860
books@imagespublishing.com
www.imagespublishing.com

Copyright © The Images Publishing Group Pty Ltd 2012
The Images Publishing Group Reference Number: 977
ABN 89 059 734 431

National Library of Australia Cataloguing-in-Publication entry:

Author	: Anderson, Collin
Title	: DP Architects on Orchard Road: Evolution of a Retail Streetscape / Collin Anderson
ISBN	: 978 1 86470 462 4 (hbk.)
Subjects	: Orchard Road, Singapore. Architecture, Modern—20th century—Singapore.
Dewey Number	: 725.21095957
Contributor	: Kenneth Frampton, Columbia University
Edited by	: Debbie Ball, The Images Publishing Group
Graphics	: Fu Tingting
Illustrations	: Anusan Angkuna, Eugene Foong, Lek Chalermchart Noonchoo
Design Consultant	: The Press Room

Pre-publishing services by United Graphic Pte Ltd, Singapore
Printed by SC (Sang Choy) International Pte Ltd, Singapore on 140 gsm Golden Sun Woodfree paper

IMAGES has included on its website a page for special notices in relation to this and our other publications. Please visit www.imagespublishing.com.

All rights reserved. Apart from any fair dealing for the purposes of private study, research, criticism or review as permitted under the Copyright Act, no part of this publication may be reproduced, stored in a retrieval system or transmitted in any form by any means, electronic, mechanical, photocopying, recording or otherwise, without the written permission of the publisher.

Every effort has been made to trace the original source of copyright material contained in this book. The publishers would be pleased to hear from copyright holders to rectify any errors or omissions.

The information and illustrations in this publication have been prepared and supplied by DP Architects. While all reasonable efforts have been made to ensure accuracy, the publishers do not, under any circumstances, accept responsibility for errors, omissions and representations express or implied.

CONTENTS

PREFACE
2   *Fumihiko Maki*

FOREWORD
4   The Presence and Potential of Orchard Road - *Kenneth Frampton*

INTRODUCTION
10   DP Architects on Orchard Road

PART 1 - A CONTEXTUAL HISTORY

CHAPTER ONE
22   Situating Orchard Road's Malls: A History of Retail Form

CHAPTER TWO
32   A Comparison: Global Retail Streetscapes

CHAPTER THREE
46   A Contextual History of Singapore

CHAPTER FOUR
54   The Evolution of Orchard Road

PART 2 - CONTRIBUTIONS OF DP ARCHITECTS

CHAPTER ONE
72   Designing Orchard Road's Street-Integrated Malls

CHAPTER TWO
84   DP Architects Feature Projects

86   Wisma Atria
102   Paragon Shopping Centre
116   Grand Park Orchard
128   Mandarin Gallery
142   The Heeren
152   TripleOne Somerset
164   Orchard Central
180   The Centrepoint

186   *A Global Presence:* Retail Projects Worldwide

188   Our People

190   Endnotes

192   Credits

193   Contact Details

Preface

Fumihiko Maki

When I first visited Singapore, Orchard Road was still lined with many small- to-medium-sized buildings. However, it was also dotted with larger, mixed-use buildings, suggesting that this street would eventually become the most important spine of Singapore. Towards the southern end of Orchard Road, there was the Old Raffles Hotel, where I stayed for a few days. From the window of the hotel bar, one could appreciate the seashore within reach. With a glass of martini in my hand, I savoured the idle ambience of the tropical evening. That was 1959.

Ten years later, DP Architects came to my attention when their ambitious Golden Mile Complex proposal was announced, not too far from Orchard Road. The project was not only establishing high standards for the modern architecture movement in Singapore, but was also one of only a few truly heroic architectural ventures in the whole of Asia at that time.

Since then, DP Architects has become one of the most respectable architectural firms in the region. In the last two decades, the firm has been a creative catalytic force for the development of the Orchard Road corridor, working closely with the Urban Redevelopment Authority (URA). Together, they have transformed Orchard Road into one of the world's most recognisable shopping districts. By developing and implementing various guidelines over time, they have successfully fused street life with activities on multi-level retail floors within.

As an overseas advisor to the URA in recent years, I hold fond memories of how the organisation always regarded Orchard Road as the backbone of Singapore, and an inspiration to shape the entire country. I therefore hold in high esteem the efforts of DP Architects and its collaboration with the URA, as we continue to experience the fruitful transformation of Orchard Road.

While this book represents the history of DP Architects and its contribution to the enrichment of the Orchard Road corridor, it also serves as a record of my intimate memories of the past half-century.

Fumihiko Maki is the 1993 Pritzker Architecture Prize Laureate, and a Principal at Maki and Associates, Tokyo. He has served an advisory role to Singapore's Urban Redevelopment Authority, and has taught at Washington University, Harvard University and the University of Tokyo.

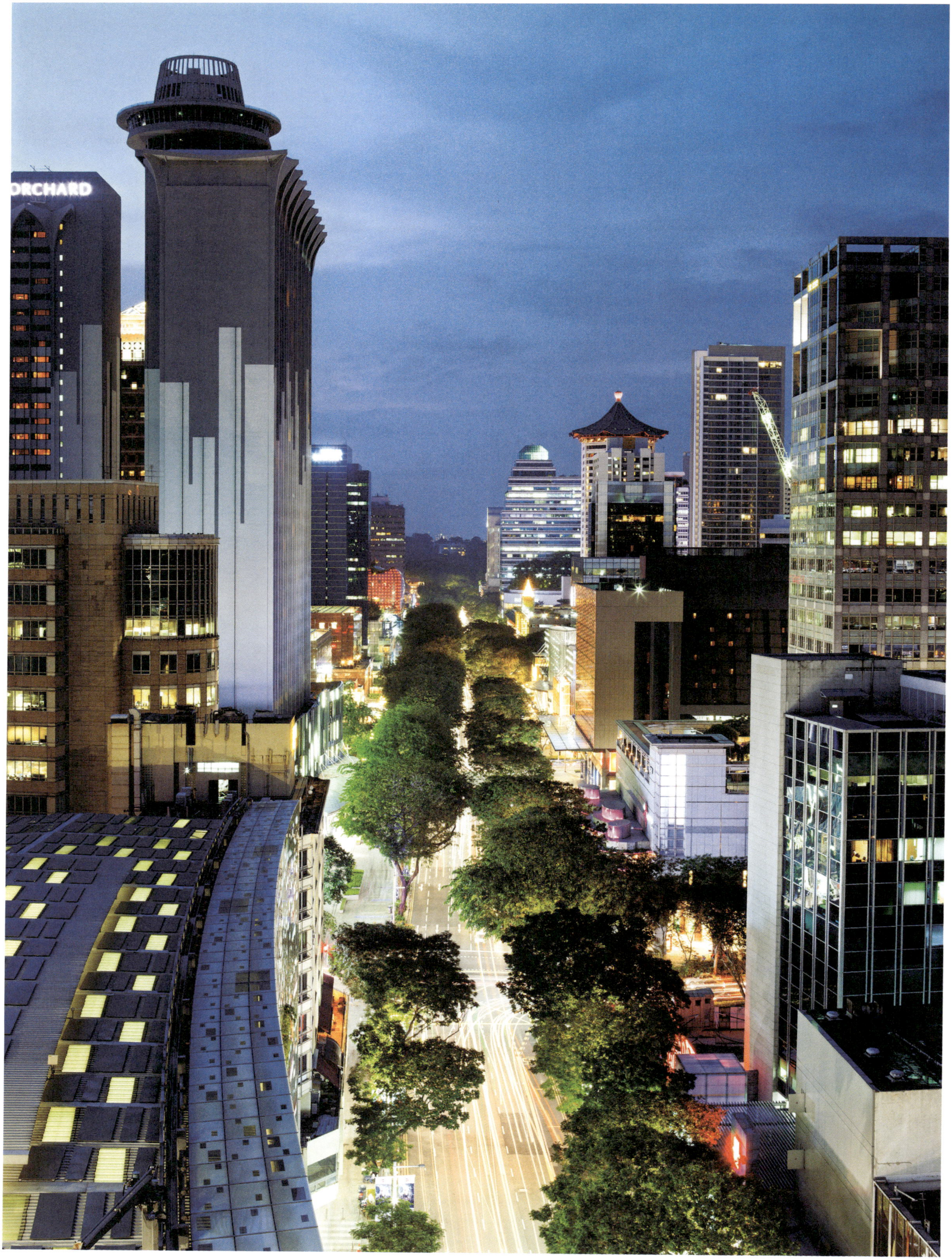
ORCHARD

Foreword

The Presence and Potential

of Orchard Road

Kenneth Frampton

With the exception of the multi-level pedestrian infrastructure of downtown Hong Kong, there is perhaps no other single commercial street where such a consistent effort has been made to augment the shopping frontage and surface of the street through multiple levels and the gradual widening of the carriageway together with its attendant sidewalks over time. Although the discrepancies in scale and context are such that it would be preposterous to compare Singapore's Orchard Road to the format of the Hausmannian boulevard, we may nonetheless argue that the Parisian boulevard and the café terrace have been, however remotely, the model for the development and reworking of Orchard Road by DP Architects over the past forty years. In pursuit of this goal the firm has even been able to remake the frontage of an entire block in less than a decade.

While the department store has long since been superseded as a commercial paradigm by the top-lit, big-box mall, the unifying potential of the arcaded street-front remains variously combined along Orchard Road interspersed with the occasional café terrace and accompanied by a continuous allée of shade trees bracketed at intervals by glass canopies and by the occasional use of escalators to give easy access to additional elevated shopping frontage running parallel to the street.

Along with the provision of a fire lane and a 30-metre-wide carriageway, what is crucial in this street section, is the standard 10-metre wide promenades to either side of the road. This normative shopping boulevard section has been put in place along Orchard Road by the Urban Redevelopment Authority (URA) through the mandatory imposition of setbacks as the road has been developed over the past four decades. This has surely encouraged the expansion of sidewalk frontages via elevated shopping decks let into the face of the average five-to-six-storey commercial podia that have invariably been erected beneath high-rise slabs made up of either office or hotel accommodation. An essential precondition for the optimisation of such elevated commercial facilities has been the perfection of the open-air, weatherproof escalator as a device to ensure the continuity of pedestrian flow up to the raised levels.

DP Architects has been continuously involved in the design and re-design of some 20 major retail facilities across the 2.2-kilometre extent of Orchard Road. To find a comparably consistent typological

OPPOSITE
Orchard Road at night, Angsana canopy aglow. View westbound from Orchard Central.

development of a single street, one has to go back a long way, perhaps even as far as the palazzo-lined Strada Nuova, Genoa, built over the space of some 200 years between the 16th and 18th centuries. In addition to a US$26 million renovation of the promenades in 2009, DP Architects and the URA have been involved in the transformation of Orchard Road into a boulevard lined with Angsana shade trees since 1970. This ambitious civic programme will now be taken further, in part through a master plan study developed by DP Architects in association with The Jerde Partnership and the Rotterdam-based Office for Metropolitan Architecture (OMA).

This overall joint effort envisages the further evolution of what we may now recognise as the standard Orchard Road section, in which the received contemporary commercial type of the big-box shopping mall entered through a top-lit atrium escalator hall, is enlivened on the street through urban verandahs of a standard 7.5-metre depth, let into the face of the first, second and third floors, while maintaining the continuous shopping arcades at grade along with outdoor refreshment areas, situated along the frontage between the arcades and the shade-trees.

DP Architects has characterised this section as a combination of the conventional introverted mall with the extroverted tropical mall. In this hybrid street form, horizontal movement is fused with vertical movement as multi-storey podia become increasingly activated at the sidewalk level and above. This invention of a totally new urban typology was an integral part of the URA development plan and was backed by state subvention and by the further decision on the part of the Singapore Tourist Board to expand the existing elevated pedestrian decks so as to create in addition to commercial space, so called 'green rooms' for the accommodation of art exhibitions and other public cultural events.

In a didactic graphic comparison DP Architects has shown how the typical Orchard Road section of the 1990s was transformed over the past two decades so as to incorporate and enliven the promenade section, either by virtue of inclined 'billboard', curtain-walled façades or by suspended glass canopies. This spatio-functional integration was augmented by substantial cantilevered urban verandahs at the second floor. Escalators have been integrated into this augmented section so as to provide immediate ease of access from the sidewalk to the first and second floors.

The various Orchard Road interventions by DP Architects may be generically separated into works where its main task was either to alter the overall form through additions and alterations or alternatively to create new commercial blocks from the ground up. Among the interventions they have completed to date, the Wisma Atria complex, dating from 1984, was transformed by the same firm, barely two decades after its realisation, into a six-storey orthogonal urban verandah with escalator access to its third floor. This dramatic sectional change was animated further through supergraphics and LED display lighting.

Close to Wisma Atria, the same architects were to transform the pre-existing bunker-like Mandarin Gallery taking up some 150 metres of the prestigious frontage in proximity to the Somerset MRT station. This entailed the creation of a four-storey retail podium out of what had previously been a rather secluded hotel lobby. Here the architects played with an appliqué, 'deconstructed' glass façade, equipped with deep cantilevered glass canopies and decks; the latter being provided in order to incorporate escalator access to the first-floor frontage and thereby tie in the rest of the mall with the street. By removing a vehicular lane the architects were able to incorporate a series of bays, which simultaneously enclose the internal space and encourage further pedestrian penetration.

In the so-called TripleOne Somerset development, further to the east on the same side of Orchard Road, the shopping complex is set back from the main thoroughfare by an entire block. In this instance DP Architects had the opportunity of re-working an existing five-storey podium beneath an elegant high-rise structure dating from the 1970s. Initially designed for the Public Utilities Board this 24-storey building is near to the Somerset MRT which currently antedates by a decade. The main strategy here was to sustain the rhythmic modularity of the high-rise form and to transform the entirety of its five-storey undercroft, into a top-lit, big-box shopping mall; a major modification which entailed the destruction of a public auditorium located within the body of the structure. Aside from adding shops to the street frontage, the main strategy here was to treat the new curtain wall envelope, as discreetly as possible. Here all the mechanical movement takes place inside the building rather than on the street.

To find a comparably consistent typological development of a single street, one has to go back a long way, perhaps even as far as the palazzo-lined Strada Nuova, Genoa, built over the space of some 200 years between the 16th and 18th centuries.

ABOVE
Views of the Orchard Road pedestrian promenade.

Equally powerful in terms of its pre-existing high-rise form, the Paragon Shopping Centre is a block that has been through multiple incarnations since it began life as a site for a General Motors car showroom in the mid-1950s, only to become Singapore's first supermarket a few years later. In the 1980s this volume was converted into the Promenade Shopping Centre, which was later expanded into the 18-storey Paragon Shopping Centre in 1997. Following the 2002 URA zoning amendment, DP Architects added a four metre deep projecting glass façade and a glass canopy which cantilevered an additional two metres beyond the new face of the building. Among the more striking aspects of this development is the six-storey top-lit galleria/atrium, penetrating the block in depth with escalator access at its ends, together with a continuous curtain wall along Orchard Road and decorative lighting on the upper reaches of the building.

Originally built in 1997 as a six-storey retail podium, expressly designed to appeal to young people, the Heeren block was transformed in 2010 through the addition of an elaborate curtain wall to a building which had previously served as the blank container of a totally introverted atrium shopping mall. The additional rhetorical element here is a four-storey 'baroque' front, suspended in front of the existing podium, which is otherwise left virtually untouched. Articulated by covered walkways, billboards and escalators this addition incorporates, at different levels, an urban verandah, a covered walkway and a small outdoor refreshment area.

As in the TripleOne Somerset block, Grand Park Orchard is a retrofit of the podium of a pre-existing modern building dating from the 1980s. This is a rather unusual 11-storey hotel with a stepped section of stacked individual rooms occupying one wing of the building. This complex, now known as the Park Hotel, is in effect a *bâtiment d'angle*, with a 28-metre-high LED media screen cutting across the diagonally clipped corner of the plan at this point.

The only block to have been designed by DP Architects from scratch in the last 25 years, is the Orchard Central development of 2009, in which the main mass-form is an 11-storey block covered in a metal sun-screen. Here, the main façade fronting onto Orchard Road is entirely glazed and intercepted by escalators, which dramatically ascend to the top of the building. The escalators cut across the surface to pass behind gigantic glass planes, which are canted out slightly above the street front.

The provision of open-air escalator access cutting across the front of a big-box commercial space attains its apotheosis in this building. Here escalators rise diagonally across the curtain wall to provide a continuous link from the street to as far up as the sixth and eleventh floors. This circulatory *tour de force* is seems to owe something to Piano and Rogers' winning competition entry for the Centre Pompidou, Paris, built in 1972. As in the Centre Pompidou, one of the reasons for conducting pedestrians across the face of the building by escalator has been to provide a panoramic view over the city. This dynamic belvedere terminates, as in Paris, in a landscaped roof deck.

This is the first, truly 'high rise' shopping mall along the Orchard Road corridor and as a result, it posits a new, somewhat extravagant type-form. In addition to continuous escalator access, the upper floors of the building are also served by a carpark on the roof to which access is gained via a spiral ramp in the southeast corner of the block. There are many aspects of this work that seem to stem from the early fantasies of Archigram, only here the sun-screening of the façade has been affected by a 'deconstructivist' aesthetic, which so far seems to have fallen short of a satisfactory resolution. One of the most unusual features, is the way a kind of 'trans-programming' has been allowed to infiltrate the work in the form of a five-storey rock climbing wall, which occupies one side of the central atrium opposite a bank of glass elevators. This innovation combined with an extended form of escalator access suggests the evolution of a more diverse kind of commercial facility in which many different programmatic functions are brought together under one roof, as in the Changi Airport Terminal 3 opened in 2008 in Singapore's International Airport, to the designs of SOM and Gensler Associates. Here, aside from the usual 'duty free' marketing space and diverse restaurants, the new terminal also includes a swimming pool, a gymnasium, cubicle sleeping facilities, showers, a cinema, a 12-metre-high indoor slide, an entertainment deck with play stations, an interactive art zone, a pharmacy and photo kiosks.[1]

The second emerging syndrome that the roof garden of Orchard Central brings to mind is the possibility of greening the entire glass façade of a shopping podium so that the urban verandahs may enrich and protect from the sun by automatically irrigated vegetal sunscreens. Such suspended vegetation can be found in Geoffrey Bawa's Kandalama Hotel, built in Damballa in Sri Lanka, dating from 1994. Here one approaches a level of sustainability which is literal as well as cultural, going beyond the so-called 'green rooms' envisaged by the Singapore Tourist Board 'green façades' of suspended plant material having an enormous potential for reducing the heat gain on the surface of a building.

Finally there remains the potential for opaque or partially opaque façades of top-lit, big-box shopping facilities to serve as gigantic information screens, both externally and internally, equally capable of both enlivening the street and animating the interior. In this regard, Times Square in Manhattan has been the model for a form of light-architecture since the 1920s. One recalls in this connection such precedents as the diminutive Pravda newspaper building projected for Moscow by the Vesnin Brothers in 1923 or Oscar Nitzchke's much more sophisticated Publicity Building designed for the Champs Élysées in Paris in 1936. In both instances, the building was conceived as a media-machine and we may surely find the continuation of this tradition in the contemporary use of giant plasma screens within the interior of Terminal 4, at London's Heathrow Airport recently completed to the designs of the Rogers Partnership. This plus the well-established technique of rolling 'ticker-tape' news headlines running continuously across the façade of an otherwise neutral form remains, as a civic trope, which is still full of potential. In this regard, despite all our technical prowess, it remains questionable as to whether we are yet able to illuminate buildings at night in a manner that is as sophisticated as that which was achieved in Berlin and New York in the 1920s and 1930s. This still elusive potential brings to mind the all but unlimited and sophisticated possibilities of today's LED technology, as well as the opportunities involved in illumination of large-scale buildings.

In addition to these considerations, there remains the perennial challenge posed by single-usage zoning, for despite the presence of the occasional downtown hotel, Orchard Road would appear to be devoid of residential accommodation connected directly with the main commercial corridor. Thus unlike Paris, where both the galleria and department store were accompanied by residential fabric, Orchard Road as it currently stands, is devoted exclusively to the passing customer.

Kenneth Frampton is the Ware Professor of Architecture at Columbia University's Graduate School of Architecture Planning and Preservation. He was born in the United Kingdom, 1930, and trained as an architect at the Architectural Association in London. His publications include Modern Architecture: A Critical History *(1980),* Studies in Tectonic Culture *(1995),* Le Corbusier *(2001) and* Labor, Work & Architecture *(2003).*

NOTES:

1 I have in mind the 480-metre-long digital sound and light display known as the Freemont Street Experience. This kinetic covered street lined with 12 million LED lights was first created in 1992 by the Jerde Partnership.

The idea of trans-programming was first consciously elaborated by Bernard Tschumi when he entered the competition for the National Library of France (TGB) in Paris in 1989.

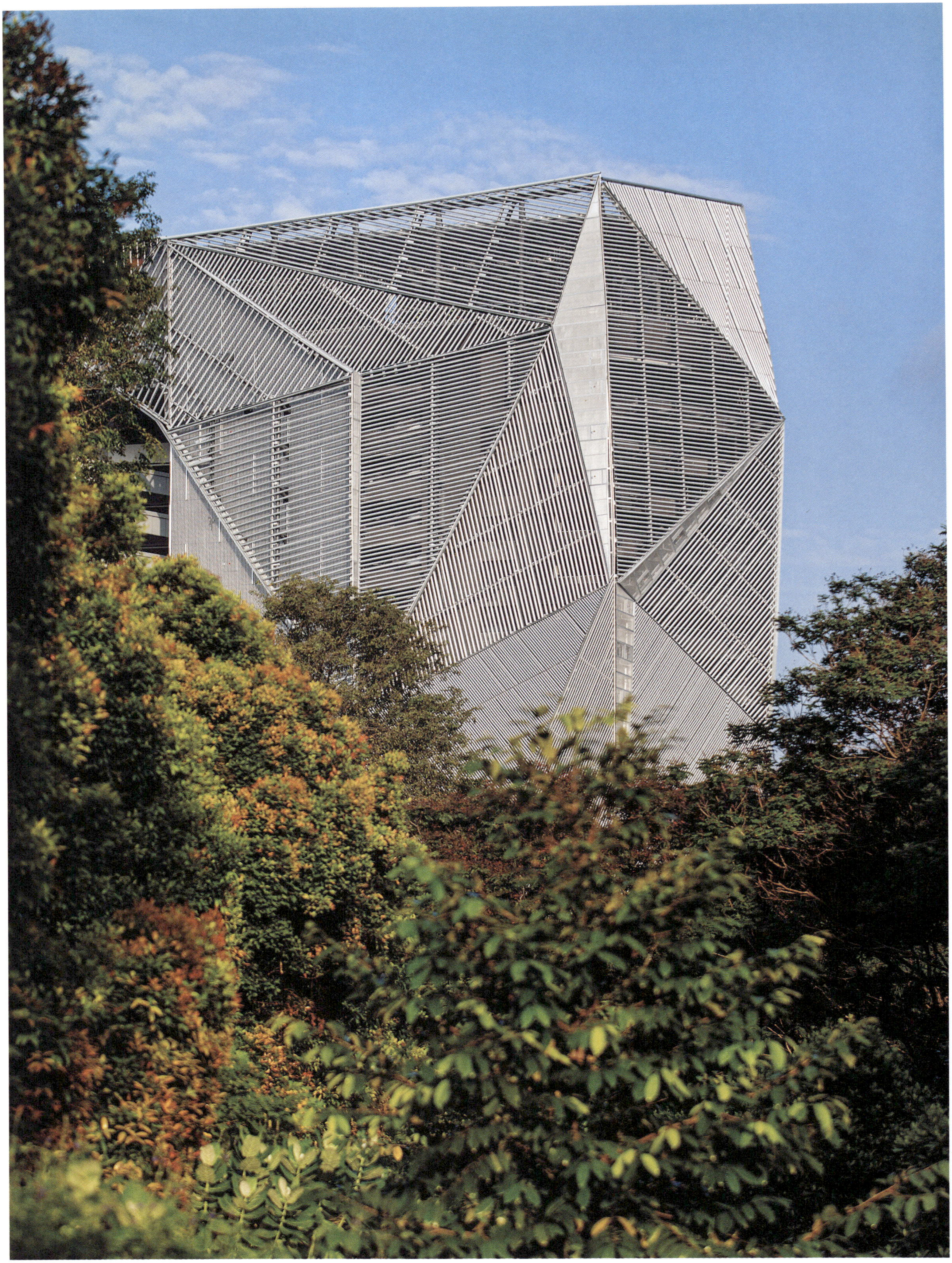

Introduction
DP Architects
on Orchard Road

In the last three decades, DP Architects has reinvented some twenty buildings along Orchard Road – Singapore's foremost retail and fashion corridor – in an ongoing endeavour to marry public street space with commercial retail space. In doing so, the practice has helped to spawn a new retail building typology, a positive contribution to Singapore's city fabric as a generator of connectivity: the street-integrated urban mall, representative of a set of design strategies that respond to urban, climatic and social conditions.

Spaces of shopping lie at the heart of urbanism in Asia. Arguably the most public of spaces, they serve as a stage for the largest range of human activity and perform as a point of convergence for social and cultural exchange. The shopping centre today is a site where visitors congregate, eat, drink and become absorbed in an environment of unbounded recreation and consumption.

The Orchard Road corridor is an accumulation of large-scale commercial malls that work in conjunction with the pedestrian streetscape as an integrated civic space – one of the most important urban elements in the composition of contemporary Singapore. Orchard Road concentrates an astonishing 20 per cent of the country's privately owned, leasable retail space.[1] This commercial-building string functions as a centre of gravity around which satellite developments in office, hotel and residential programmes revolve.

This book explores the forms of Orchard Road's individual shopping centres, as well as its comprehensive form as a public shopping streetscape. It does so by tracing relations between global architectural history and the urban history specific to Orchard Road.

Mall Space. Street Space.

Street space is integral to the form of a city. Pedestrian streets – shopping streets in particular – serve to fuel city life as connective social elements that oppose the barriers of vehicle-only roadways. The extent to which urban planning methods accommodate pedestrian patterns of movement greatly contributes to an urban region's long-term health and sustainability.

But the functions of pedestrian streets and shopping malls have historically contradicted one another. Whereas the 'streetscape' purposefully connects

OPPOSITE
Orchard Central as viewed westbound and from Istana Park.

> Orchard Road concentrates an astonishing 20 per cent of the country's privately owned, leasable retail space. This commercial building string functions as a centre of gravity around which satellite developments in office, hotel and residential programmes revolve.

multiple regions of a city, the 'mall' building type evolved in complete isolation from the city's fabric – a direct result of the automobile's decentralisation of cities worldwide over the course of the 20th century. Malls were initially designed for the very purpose of recreating the density of the traditional town centre amidst suburbs, and were in built with networks of 'pedestrian streets' that efficiently organised commercial shops for customers travelling by foot. Due to the tendencies for these buildings to inherit introverted forms and be serviced by vast, asphalt-covered car parks, mall designs generally yielded loose site relationships. Echoes of this harsh disconnect became especially clear once closed-form malls were constructed within the heart of urban centres, at variance with their locations and neglectful of context.

Following Orchard Road's initial maturity characterised by a concentration of two and three-storey rows of shophouses built over the course of the 19th century, its commercial shops progressively amassed as a collection of large-scale shopping malls, erected from the 1950s onwards. Aside from the international proliferation of the mall and perhaps the more obvious and direct forces of land-zoning policies, it is necessary to credit both Singapore's equatorial climate (unforgiving to the outdoor pedestrian), and the geographic location of Orchard Road within the city as engines for the development of 'one-stop shopping' malls that catered to customers arriving by vehicle. Prior to the implementation of public transit infrastructure in the late 1980s, the anatomy of Orchard Road did not promote pedestrian mobility.

In its work on Orchard Road, DP Architects has striven to reverse these development patterns. Working with local building codes – most importantly a set of incentives implemented beginning 2002 to establish greater architectural variety amongst storefronts – DP Architects has implemented a number of design strategies to reinforce the relationship between the streetscape and the individual mall. These include: the use of external escalators to unify the sidewalk promenade with multiple storeys of retail shops; the reconstruction of façades with transparent frontages to furnish a level of openness; and the articulation of façades with new geometries and material patterns, for increased visual engagement. Each of these techniques is intended to unify Orchard Road's public street space with the internal spaces of its commercial shopping centres.

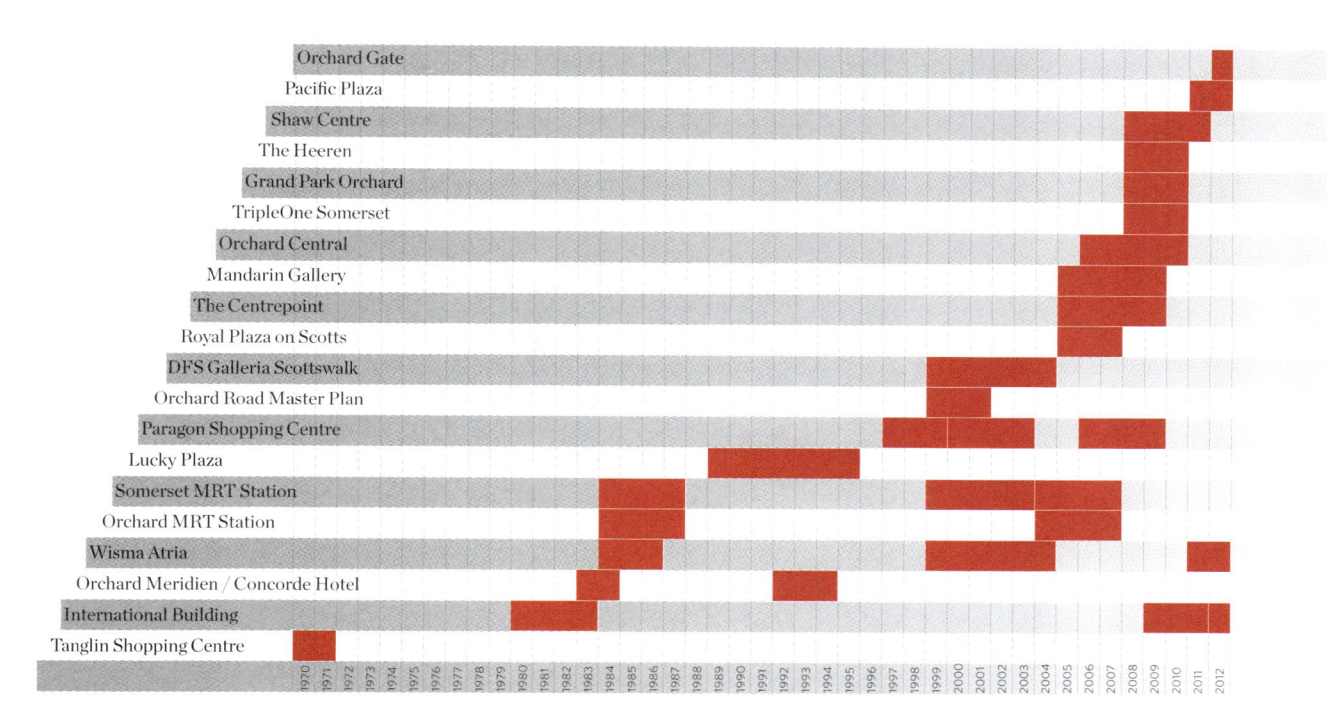

Presenting the Work

The purpose of this publication is two-fold. Firstly, it seeks to introduce Orchard Road to architectural discourse as a unique landscape of retail form – one that merges the traditionally-isolated mall with the streetscape. Secondly, it presents the sequential works of DP Architects on Orchard Road over 40 years as a continuous, ongoing project of renewal. The practice has had the opportunity to explore, test new ideas and contribute to Orchard Road's changing form in response to changing socioeconomic conditions.

Part 1, Chapters 1 and 2 discuss Orchard Road's development in relation to the history of commercial retail architecture and include a comparative study of model shopping streetscapes worldwide, such as the Champs-Élysées in Paris, Fifth Avenue in New York and Omotesandō in Tokyo.

Part 1, Chapters 3 and 4 describe the transformation of Orchard Road from the British colonial era to the 21st century by presenting a contextual history of Singapore that relates architecture and urbanism to trends in national development.

Part 2, Chapter 1 constructs a unified timeline for DP Architects' projects on Orchard Road over four decades, addressing the work as a continuum of evolving ideas.

Part 2, Chapter 2 features eight retail mall projects. This collection outlines an anthology of DP Architects' work beginning in the mid-1980s with a focus on the firm's projects completed in the first decade of the new millennium. Each project highlights a series of progressive strategies aimed at integrating a large-scale shopping centre with the public street space. The selected projects are only a sample of a larger body of work that has undoubtedly strengthened Orchard Road's presence within Singapore and contributed to its global prominence as a premier retail location.

ABOVE
DP Architects' Orchard Road projects span over 40 years. In many cases the firm has reworked the same building several times over decades.

RETAIL DESIGN SINCE THE 1960s

DP Architects, as a practice ingrained with a special understanding of regional progress and local needs, has played a critical role in developing modern Singapore's public spaces of retail. The partnership was established almost contiguously with Singapore's national independence in 1965 and for 45 years has embraced a symbiotic relationship with the evolving global city and its commercial trends. The firm's first projects, namely the People's Park Complex and the Golden Mile Complex, were built in the late 1960s and helped to introduce the nation to large-scale, mixed-use projects that were coincidentally some of its first commercial civic spaces.

Orchard Road 1971 – 2012

The firm has played a comprehensive role in the formation of Orchard Road by designing or reworking more than one million square metres of its mixed-use commercial spaces. Between 1971 and early 2012, the practice directed a series of over 30 projects that include new-build malls, hotel alterations and retrofits, in addition to serving as lead consultant in the preparation of a study for Orchard Road's master plan in 2001.

Malls in Singapore

As an equatorial nation subject to extreme heat and humidity, public activities in Singapore are largely directed indoors, and so the bulk of its urban spaces often double as spaces of shopping. Aside from DP Architects' projects on Orchard Road, the firm has worked on many of Singapore's largest and most-visited retail buildings. These include the 137,000-square-metre VivoCity, completed in collaboration with Toyo Ito Associates, Japan; and the 49-hectare, mixed-use Resorts World Sentosa, completed in collaboration with Michael Graves and Associates, USA.

A Global Presence

In the new millennium, DP Architects has expanded its portfolio of urban retail projects to cities worldwide, including those in China, India, Indonesia, South Korea and the United Arab Emirates. In 2008 the office completed The Dubai Mall – the world's largest mall at the time, and one of the largest structures ever built. The US$1.6 billion building has a gross floor area of 550,000 square metres spread over four levels and hosts 1200 shops supplemented by parking for 14,000 vehicles. In 2011 The Dubai Mall hosted more than 54 million visitors, making it the most visited building on the planet.

Operating from an Orchard Road Office

In 1967 DP Architects, then known as Design Partnership (DP), established its first office at the International Building on Orchard Road, with a staff of 20. Though the firm quickly outgrew the space and relocated in 1973, DP managed a series of additions and alterations to the International Building during the years 1980 to 1983, 2009 to 2011 and a third commencing in 2012. During the years of DP's tenancy on Orchard Road, the corridor was amidst rapid transition as sites were redeveloped for the erection of large-scale commercial structures, a shift that manifested during the 1960s and 1970s.

International Building
From 1967 to 1973, DP Architects (then known as Design Partnership) established its first office at 360 Orchard Road.

Office interior, late 1960s
Pao Ven Yuen, seated, was one of approximately 20 DP staff at the time.

The Orchard Road Shopping Corridor

Orchard Road measures 2.2 kilometres in length, stretching from Tanglin Road at its western end to Bras Basah Road in the east. The Orchard Road Planning Area covers one square kilometre of land designated primarily for commercial development.

Since the 1970s, DP Architects has completed nearly thirty projects in this region, constituting both new-build projects as well as retrofits and renovations of some 20 structures.

Projects built or renovated by DP Architects
- ■ Projects above ground
- ■ Projects below ground

1. Tanglin Shopping Centre
2. Orchard Gate
3. International Building
4. Shaw Centre
5. Pacific Plaza
6. Royal Plaza on Scotts
7. DFS Galleria Scottswalk
8. Orchard MRT Station
9. Wisma Atria
10. Lucky Plaza
11. Paragon Shopping Centre
12. Orchard Road Master Plan Study
13. Grand Park Orchard
14. Mandarin Gallery
15. The Heeren
16. TripleOne Somerset
17. Somerset MRT Station
18. Orchard Central
19. The Centrepoint
20. Orchard Meridien / Concorde Hotel

DEVELOPING A RETAIL 'LANDSCAPE'

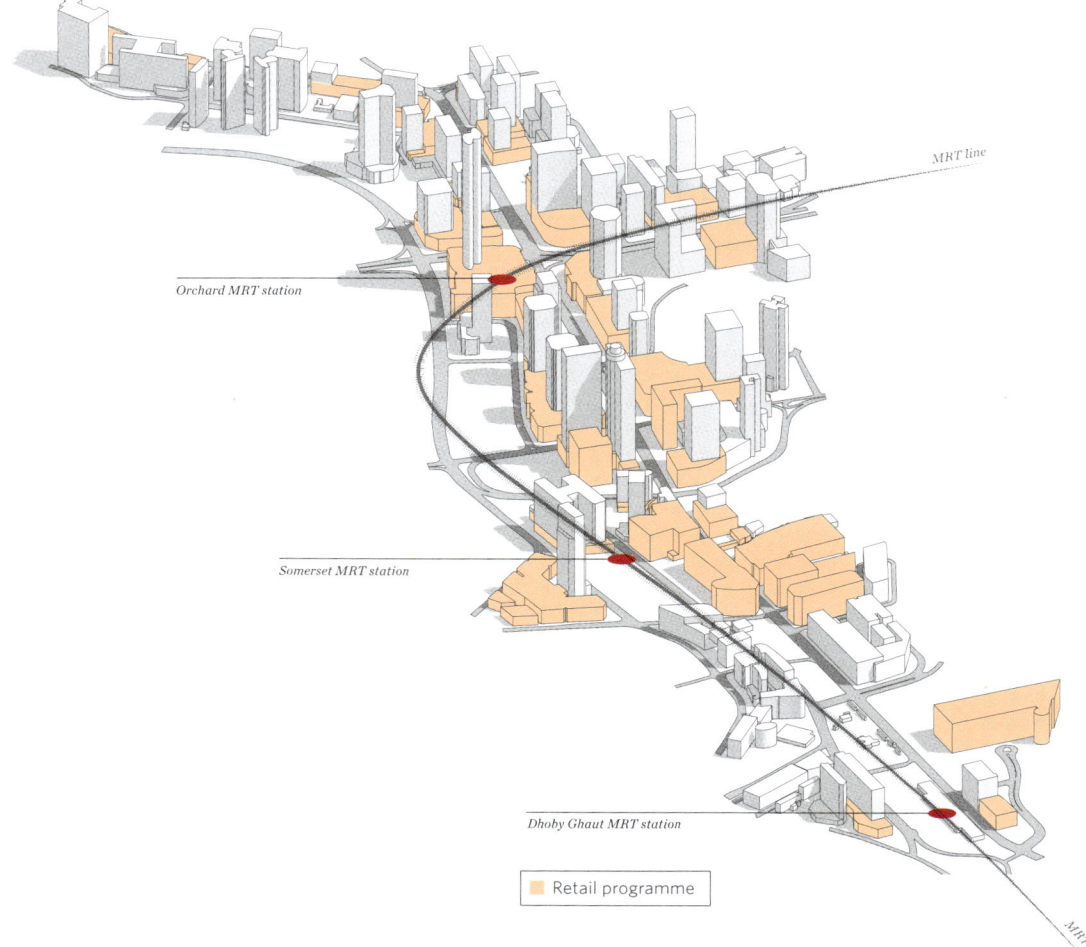

Since 2000 Orchard Road's growth has resulted in an increasingly complex and immersive network of spaces, characterised by linkages between malls on multiple storeys and below-grade – this growth, over time, has transformed the many shopping centres of Orchard Road into a nearly continuous urban form.

Such complexity was stimulated especially by the development in the late 1980s of a below-grade, national Mass Rapid Transit (MRT) system that immediately thereafter served as the region's most popular point of entry as a connection with greater Singapore for those travelling by foot. Building codes for new structures encouraged increased connectivity by requiring underground linkages to transit stations, as well as to adjacent malls; by 2010 the street's interconnectivity became so comprehensive that no substantial alteration to one mall could be made without affecting its neighbouring structures.

As a result, Orchard Road has evolved as a retail landscape identified by the following: links amongst shopping-centre podia connect nearly all structures to a unified base of retail programme; a growing number of below-grade passages programmed with commercial space, extend the shopping network beneath the roadway; exposed escalators link the sidewalks directly to upper storeys or basement-level shops; multi-layered façades support verandahs and upper-level entry decks; and, in one case, a 12th-storey roof deck directly accessible from the street functions as a public park.

ABOVE
Axonometric model of the Orchard Road Planning Area.

OPPOSITE
Orchard Road's position within Singapore's downtown and the national MRT network.

Orchard Planning Area
MRT Network

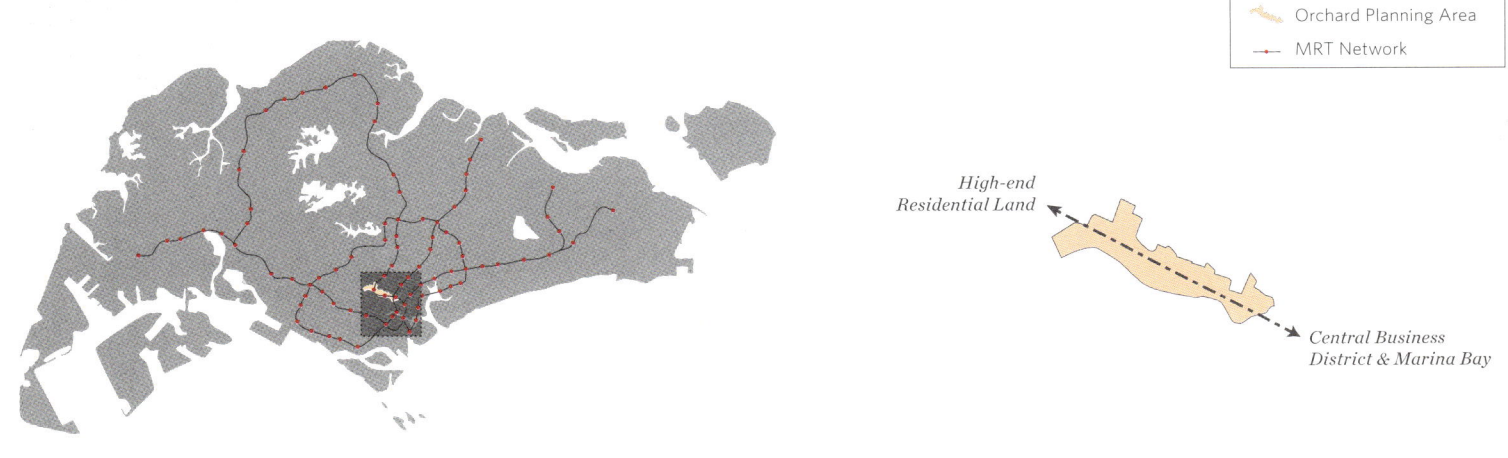

High-end Residential Land

Central Business District & Marina Bay

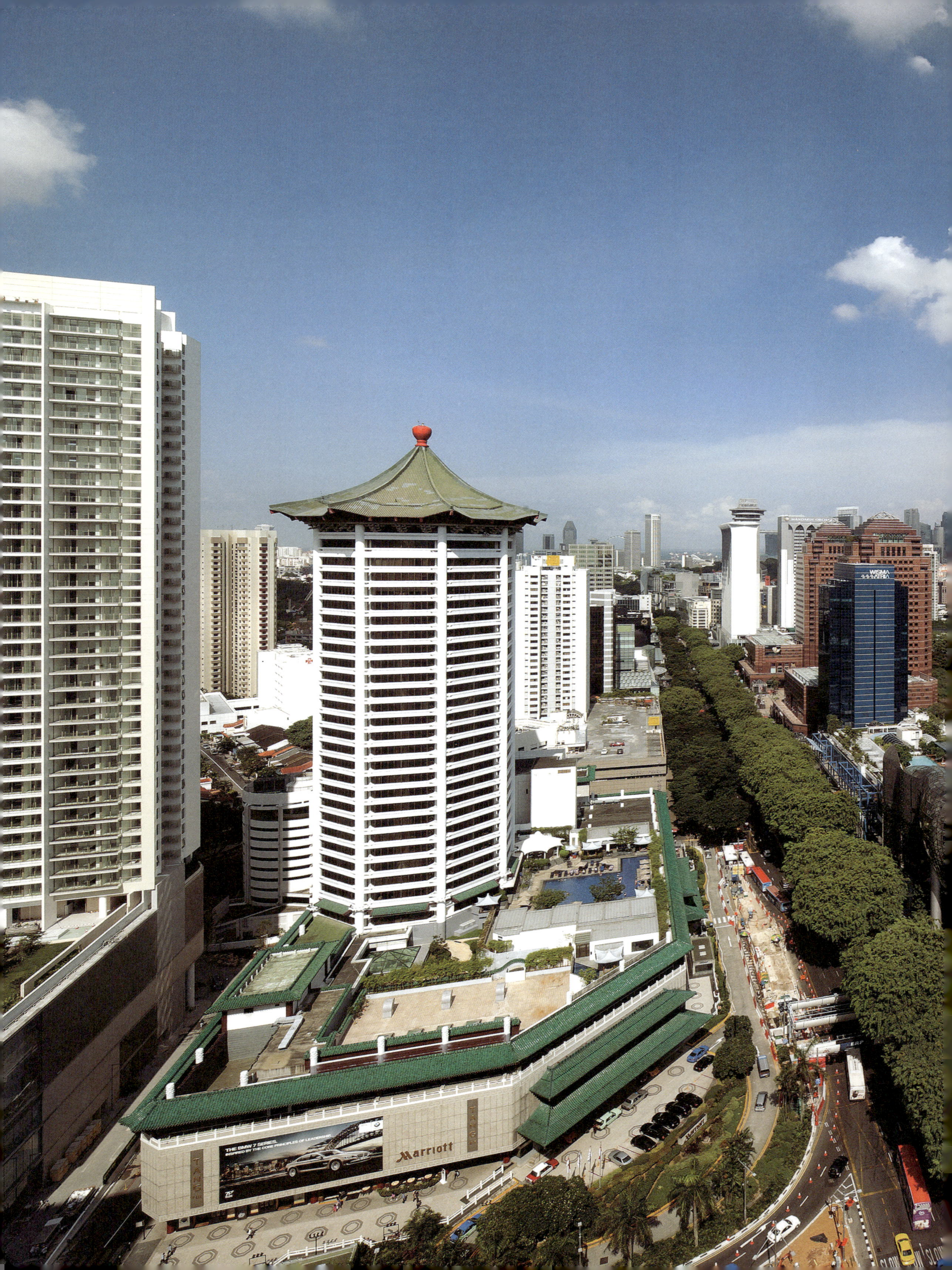
THE BMW 7 SERIES
Marriott

Part 1:
A CONTEXTUAL HISTORY

CHAPTER ONE   22   Situating Orchard Road's Malls: A History of Retail Form

CHAPTER TWO   32   A Comparison: Global Retail Streetscapes

CHAPTER THREE   46   A Contextual History of Singapore

CHAPTER FOUR   54   The Evolution of Orchard Road

Peranakan Shophouse

Situating Orchard Road's Malls:
A History of Retail Form

Any analysis of architecture's relationship with the city is, to a great extent, a social analysis. This is especially so with spaces of shopping and commerce. One can trace the evolving retail space in relation to social transformation, and pose the functionality and design of today's malls with respect to the earliest spaces of merchant trade. Changing architecture can help to describe changing urban conditions: what are the types of activities people partake in, in what types of spaces, and how do these spaces and their events affect the overall structure of a city? Articulating the evolution of retail form helps to situate the commercial patterns of Orchard Road, as they relate to architecture historically and globally.

Traditional Marketplaces

'Shopping' as we know it today emerged from a long-established history of trade and commerce. From the trade of produce to that of animals and textiles, people have always recognised the efficiencies of gathering at defined places for reasons of exchange. These 'places' began as transitory – souks, bazaars and in Asia, caravans on the Silk Road were landmarks for sellable goods and usable currency. Eventually, these became stabilised as permanent markets around which communities, towns and cities formed. In fact, several of the shopping districts within major cities today operate in close geographic proximity to markets formed centuries ago – this is the case, for instance, with the 15th-century market presently recognised as the Grand Bazaar in Istanbul, Turkey.

Permanent Structures

As the range of goods expanded along with demand and methods of production, the physical structures of markets began to change. Larger marketplaces relied on a degree of spatial flexibility, and grew beyond the confines of street networks, forming within public plazas, piazzas and squares, or on the outskirts of cities. The earliest enclosed shopping malls include the Palais-Royal in Paris and the Oxford Covered Market in England, both which pre-date 1800; an 1814 description of the Palais' spaces of business, pleasure and fashion reads as follows: 'The whole of the garden is surrounded by uniform buildings, presenting a covered way on the ground floor, lighted by one hundred and eighty arcades, and each containing a little shop'.[1] The 'arcades' of this former ecclesiastic palace have since become veritable symbols for contemporary buildings of shopping worldwide; both the walkways fronting Orchard Road's 19th-century shophouses and the continuous four-metre covered corridor fronting the street's 21st-century malls are evidence of this enduring feature.

OPPOSITE
Shophouses in Singapore were commonly built in the Peranakan-style, adopted from other Southeast Asian regions as a result of an influx of Malay and Chinese immigrants to the colony's thriving port. The shophouse's covered entryway, a protector from sun and rain, was encouraged under the Singapore's British colonial building codes.

Street Arcade

Canopies of Glass and Iron

A parallel development in shopping space began its course in the early 19th century, first in Paris, then transplanted throughout Europe and Asia. As architects and engineers made use of advancements in building technologies to canopy narrow streets of Paris with wrought iron and glass, the resulting top-lit passages formed well-ventilated, sheltered public spaces shared by several storefronts and flooded with natural light. With these 'Parisian arcades', street-shopping became a pedestrian-only, all-weather activity. This building typology was exemplified in 1850's and 1860's Europe by Les Halles in Paris, the Galeries Royales Saint-Hubert in Brussels and Galleria Vittorio Emanuele II in Milan.

It is critical to introduce the Parisian arcades within the context of Europe's Industrial Revolution and the many developments which were transforming cities during this period. Advancements in technology not only permitted the construction of the arcades, but also that of the railroads, which brought people to cities. These trajectories are inseparable from new methods of manufacturing that fuelled a wider range of available goods corresponding with luxury commodities trades and increased demands for larger store spaces. The writings of philosopher Walter Benjamin underlined the relationships between technology, architecture and the social sphere at this time; he cited from *Illustrated Guide to Paris*: 'These arcades, a new contrivance of industrial luxury, are glass covered, marble-floored passages, which obtain their light from above, there are arrayed the most elegant shops, so that such an arcade is a city, indeed a world, in miniature'.[2] Benjamin identified the arcades as amongst the first modern retail spaces, hosts to the displays of the newest fashions and products that drew a mix of visitors from all walks of life, not simply to buy and sell, but to browse shop windows and 'people-watch'. These emerging spaces for shopping within the existing urban fabric became agents of cultural production that transformed the ways in which people experienced the city.

ABOVE
Galleria Vittorio Emanuele II, a double arcade at the heart of Milan, Italy. Built between 1865 and 1877.

OPPOSITE TOP
A progression of retail architectural forms in section.
OPPOSITE BOTTOM
The construction of canopies over existing European streets resulted in naturally-lit, ventilated and sheltered public spaces.

Evolution of Form

The layout and sectional characteristics of large-scale retail malls built in the 20th and 21st centuries can be placed within a longstanding design history, linked to the earliest shopping structures. Urban malls built in recent decades are combined with a number of programmes, as integrated mixed-use shopping or lifestyle centres.

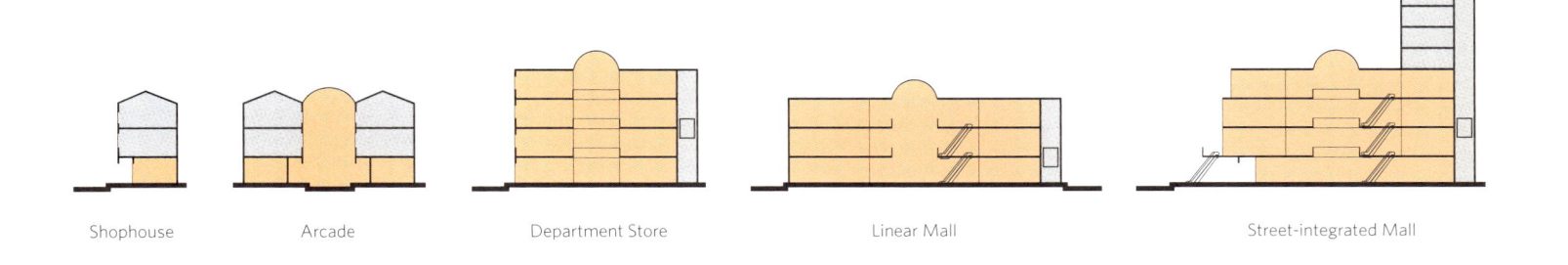

Shophouse   Arcade   Department Store   Linear Mall   Street-integrated Mall

Department Stores – Multi-level Shopping

Increased consumer spending and ever-expanding spatial requirements for product stock in the second half of the 20th century led to large-scale 'department stores' containing retail spaces spread over multiple storeys. These buildings offered numerous product options at varying price levels, and became destinations for greater numbers of people representing an even wider class spectrum. Within department stores emerged new business practices that increased the efficiency of shopping – chain stores, fixed-price goods, sales returns and wholesale marketing – which in turn continued to alter the spatial requirements and layout of buildings.[3]

As department stores materialised in Paris, the architecture was primarily of two types: glass and metal, which marked the early industrial style of the 1860s, or the decorative masonry of the Paris luxury style in the 1880s, evidencing a shift to the Second Empire neoclassicism built ubiquitously throughout the capital city.[4] Models such as Le Bon Marché introduced extensive, top-lit passages derived from the arcades and ornate, double-loaded interior corridors that simulated urban high-streets and facilitated the circulation of crowds and the display of goods for browsing. Le Bon Marché was a store of unprecedented size, with cast-iron columns and glass skylight-roofing engineered by Gustave Eiffel; it spanned an entire city block, covered 53,000 square metres that included non-revenue leisure spaces and hosted an internal depot for the distribution of goods from an off-site location.[5] Building commercial space at this scale was a practice soon adopted in America, and by 1902 Macy's in Herald Square, New York City, boasted 9 storeys of retail with 33 elevators and 4 escalators.[6]

ABOVE
Le Bon Marché department store, Paris, mid-19th century. Top-lit, double-loaded interior corridors facilitated the circulation of crowds and the display of goods over multiple storeys.

Malls – Urban-scale Shopping

A new ideal for retail architecture took its course in post-war America, as the affordability of the automobile heralded the widespread development of suburbia. Decentralised populations lead to weakening relationships with traditional town or city centres, beckoning new solutions for planning commercial retail space. The writings and built work of Austrian-American architect Victor David Gruen, forged the influential 'American Mall' that would over time reconfigure town layouts worldwide.[7] The Northland Mall (Detroit, Michigan) was completed in 1954, followed by Southdale Mall (Edina, Minnesota) in 1956; these first suburban, commercial mega-structures housed nearly 100,000 square metres in covered programme.

The 'shopping centre' simulated and repositioned the 'town centre' for the American suburb, speculatively and physically; it hosted internal streets, nodes of circulation and squares as a 'city within a city' implanted on large plots of land. Mall planning strung boutique stores along internal corridors that terminated with 'anchor tenants' – large, popular chain stores that helped secure the success of the mall. Parking became a vital spatial requirement, and this translated to sprawling vehicular lots centred on the mall.

In their existing roles, malls were characterised by inward-looking forms that fostered a level of autonomy from the outside world. Shared interior circulation spaces were naturally top-lit as in arcades and department stores, while opaque façades of concrete or brickwork inhibited visual relationships with geographic surroundings. Financial speculation termed this design method as 'pressure-cooker' space with the potential to increase commercial profits by disengaging visitors from the outside world: characteristics of place were less important to architectural design than were the qualities of being self-contained, and so malls offered a range of amenities with the capacity to fulfil nearly all the daily functions of human life. More recently 'lifestyle malls' or 'experiential malls' are infused with robust supplemental leisure and entertainment spaces, measuring up to 500,000 square metres in total area.

Flagship Stores – Designing Retail Identity

The terms 'flagship' and 'fashion' are synonymous, representative of sale models, product lines and interior design strategies that influence popular culture and media. Above all, retail flagships are investments made by corporations to establish presence within the most exclusive urban settings and, to do so, great sums of money are expended in the pursuit of creating notable landmarks. It is common that collaboration with brand-name architects and designers is sought for such endeavours. Flagship store design has become a meaningful project type to architectural discourse especially in the last decade with the completion of several high-budget projects initiated by experimental clients seeking to mould company identities. The exploratory nature of flagship design has produced a collection of innovations in material uses, fabrication methods and spatial layouts.

Whether flagships are stand-alone buildings – this is the predominant case along Tokyo's Omotesandō – is dictated by the building typology specific to regional urban composition. It is common for Orchard Road's shopping centres to incorporate multiple flagship stores within a single structure, where the design of the individual shop is focused on its storefront (Paragon Shopping Centre, for instance, showcases Gucci, Salvatore Ferragamo, Prada, Tod's and Miu Miu within a single façade). Designing malls of this type requires negotiations between two scales: large frameworks that demand a unique architectural presence, and boutique shops inserted within such a framework.

> The international trends in mall design proved especially suitable for Singapore, where a harsh equatorial climate encouraged the consolidation of stores accessed from interior common spaces, to mitigate outdoor travel on foot.

Malls in Asia Today

Cities throughout Asia including Hong Kong, Jakarta, Bangkok and Kuala Lumpur depend on the mall as a generative urban element – anchors of the economy, tourism and social customs. It is a building type that continues to grow in prominence and size, with 14 of the world's 20 largest malls located in China, the Philippines, Malaysia and Indonesia.[8] The ways in which these forms are situated in and relate to cities varies – in the sprawling city of Jakarta, these tend to remain isolated and dependent on vehicular access, whereas in Kuala Lumpur, Bangkok and Hong Kong malls are commonly amassed in groups along pedestrian-heavy streets.

Situating Orchard Road

The Orchard Road region has been intimately bound to the operations of Singapore ever since the island's colonisation under British rule: a study of Orchard Road's changing infrastructure is in many ways a study of Singapore's evolving economic and social conditions.

Orchard Road's malls were erected in the 1970s and 1980s according to international trends in mall design – top-lit, atrium-centred with primary and secondary corridors, and three to five storeys in height with little relationship to the street. The international trends in mall design proved especially suitable for Singapore, where a harsh equatorial climate encouraged the consolidation of stores accessed from interior common spaces, to mitigate outdoor travel on foot. As no efficient public transportation systems were implemented in Singapore until the late 1980s and early 1990s, mall design depended on vehicular car park structures or lots catering to drivers, despite Orchard Road's urban condition.

Underground transportation networks have since shaped Orchard Road's ongoing transition at the national scale with arterial development around MRT stations and bus lines, transforming Orchard Road at the heart of this network into a pedestrian-heavy destination with more visitors than any other location in the country. This change has in recent years demanded increased flexibility and connectivity of the malls and the streetscape at large, evidenced in the comprehensive physical alterations and planning methods that have re-worked the existing mall structures. Therefore, while Orchard Road's malls are inextricably linked to the longstanding history of retail form, specific developments have diverged from this history, in a way that demands a unique discussion within architectural discourse in Asian retail and city form – one which considers the design of malls as a blending with the design of the greater streetscape.

ABOVE
The mall, like Paragon on Orchard Road shown here, originated according to the demands of car-centric cities.

Atrium-centred Mall

FUNCTIONS OF RETAIL ARCHITECTURE

Commercial retail space is a fundamental component of nearly every city. Regional and national economies, especially those in Asia, rely on the trade of commercial goods as they have for centuries; even in the age of the internet and escalating efficiencies related to online purchases, flagship stores and malls remain venues for a majority of retail sales. The physical architecture of contemporary commercial retail shops has two primary functions:

Retail Architecture as a Means of Branding

Retail stores embody the physical face of products and their companies, and in the ultra-competitive marketplace of urban downtowns where retailers compete for presence amongst great diversity and where rates for commercial spaces rank amongst the most expensive in the world, a store's ability to succeed relies heavily upon the appeal of its design.

This can also be described more generally. The detailed glass architecture of Apple Corporation has become synonymous with its highly-designed electronic products, while the flagship stores of clothing companies, such as Abercrombie & Fitch, Nautica and Versace reflect generic, personality-specific spaces: a rustic lodge, a yacht club and a high-fashion runway, respectively; the architecture helps to provide identity and stimulate a positive nostalgia for ideal places associated with particular lifestyles. Still others rely upon fundamental visual expressions in colour, form or high-tech media to appeal to potential customers.

Retail Architecture as an Urban Element

Since the establishment of the earliest markets in the Middle Ages, venues for commerce have served as dynamic public spaces. Since the bulk production of wholesale goods was made possible by innovations in manufacturing and transportation in the 18th century, a progressively diverse set of commodities has attracted visitors to stores for purposes other than purchasing – namely, for purposes of 'window-shopping' and other forms of leisure. As a result, over the past generation department stores and shopping malls have grown to accommodate an array of supporting amenities, such as food courts and movie theatres and, at larger scales, integrated hotels, resorts, residential and corporate-commercial complexes.

Retail spaces are democratic; when shops accumulate along with supplementing recreational structures they draw vast numbers of people who flock to spend substantial amounts of time and, often, money. The long-term viability of retailers is indebted to successful spatial-planning relationships between shops and other civic spaces within the city.

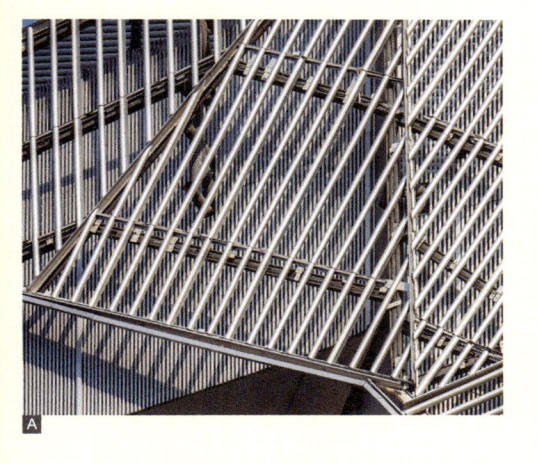

Architectural Branding

The materiality and detailing of Orchard Road's malls establish urban presence and aid commercial success.

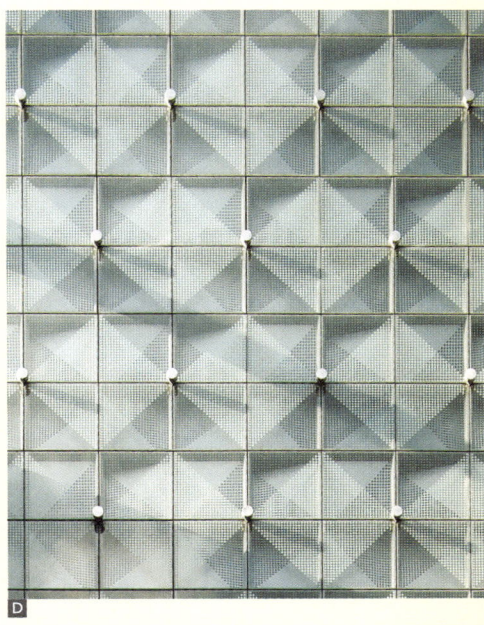

A & B Orchard Central
C Grand Park Orchard
D Paragon Shopping Centre
E The Heeren
F Mandarin Gallery

Orchard Road

A Comparison:
Global Retail Streetscapes

Pedestrian streetscapes establish many of the most vivid popular representations we have of cities. Places experienced on foot, where one is actively engaged in observing and experiencing the city and its architecture, are foundational for the building of collective urban memory. Designing a streetscape entails a conscious understanding of part-to-whole relationships that bring to light the more immediate experiences of the pedestrian, all of which help to activate the street and its users; the hierarchy amongst street, façade and landscape; the architectural qualities of materiality and detailing; and articulation and building profile.

The 'form' of a street is rarely the product of a single construction project, but a layered record of a city's organic growth over time, inseparable from regional history. By analysing a street in relation to this history, one can begin to answer questions regarding the way the city and its architecture function: How have buildings crystallised in relation to the street? And, in turn, how have architectural forms affected the nature of the streetscape and the city as a whole? Specialised planning codes and regional land development strategies enforce guidelines for building setbacks, sidewalk planning and the spatial relationships between buildings. Some celebrated streetscapes, such as the Strøget in Copenhagen or the Avenue des Champs-Élysées in Paris, are the result of comprehensive planning overhauls. Others have developed in a more spontaneous and piecemeal fashion, such as Via dei Giubbonari in Rome, or the Via Giribaldi in Genoa (formerly Strada Nuova), which remain threaded within networks of narrow, winding medieval streets.

Each of three essays in this chapter will outline the form of a prominent retail streetscape as an effect of its historical, contextual conditions within a global city: the Champs-Élysées in Paris, Fifth Avenue in New York City and Omotesandō in Tokyo, chosen as representative of the grand boulevard model, the densely urban high-rise model and the stand-alone flagship model, respectively. By comparing in detail the development narratives of these varying streetscape forms, underlying consistencies and differences can be exposed, so that the architecture of Orchard Road can be more acutely referenced to its own regional history.

Street Space – People versus Automobiles

The density of cities has always required that the street be a space of inhabitation. Specifically, as immigrant workers flooded Singapore during the initial stages of the country's growth, crowded housing conditions forced people to occupy the streets as shared public places – the emergence of the shophouse, as the common building type, makes evident this point.

Pedestrian street space has often been overlooked in city planning, a discipline that throughout the 20th century became predicated on accommodating the automobile rather than the movement of pedestrians

OPPOSITE
Orchard Road, 2000s. Widened sidewalks established a promenade lining both sides of the street, meanwhile reconstruction rendered retail outlets more accessible.

within urban cores. As with Le Corbusier's Charter of Athens, an impactful post-war urban planning manifesto that divided land use between spaces of vehicular circulation and open green spaces for human use, neglected to see the urban street as a space for the human experience.

As vehicular use reached a saturation point and its negative effects on the health of cities became evident, planning codes guiding the development of cities around the world began pursuing a reversal of these patterns. In an effort to retain the once-unchallenged global commercial presence of the Champs-Élysées, for example, an early 1990's refurbishment cleared parking areas and expanded the street's sidewalks to reclaim the public sphere that has for decades suffered from increased provisions for automobiles. Orchard Road, expanded in the 1950s to accommodate six automobile lanes, was transformed into a one-way street in 1974 and widened in 1984 with a focus on pedestrian promenades; furthermore, an underground network of cross-street passages was implemented with the later construction of the Mass Transit System as a means of divorcing pedestrian space from that of the vehicular roadway.[1]

Pedestrian Streets = Shopping Streets

It is no coincidence that the most popular streetscapes in cities around the world are also centres of commercial shopping. The criteria of accessibility, walkability and public offerings determine which streets become attractive for use by people and, as they have evolved, shopping streets have become the most populated pedestrian destinations in cities.

Unlike parks, streets have the tendency to simultaneously offer a range of permanent sheltered amenities; leisure spaces in the form of plazas, squares and pocket gardens; and an immediate supporting infrastructure of commercial offices, residences, hotels and public transportation systems. Shopping streets are planned or emerge with a particular focus on human movement and activity – people traverse them often and know them well. These streets are exploratory, experiential and embedded with highly visible landmarks, rendering them especially legible as symbolic urban spaces within the city fabric.

ABOVE
Emerald Hill of Orchard Road is a collection of Peranakan-style shophouses restored in the 1980s. It adds a historical layer to Orchard Road's contemporary retail streetscape.

OPPOSITE TOP
Plan and section, Orchard Road.
OPPOSITE BOTTOM
Map of Orchard Road and surroundings, Singapore.

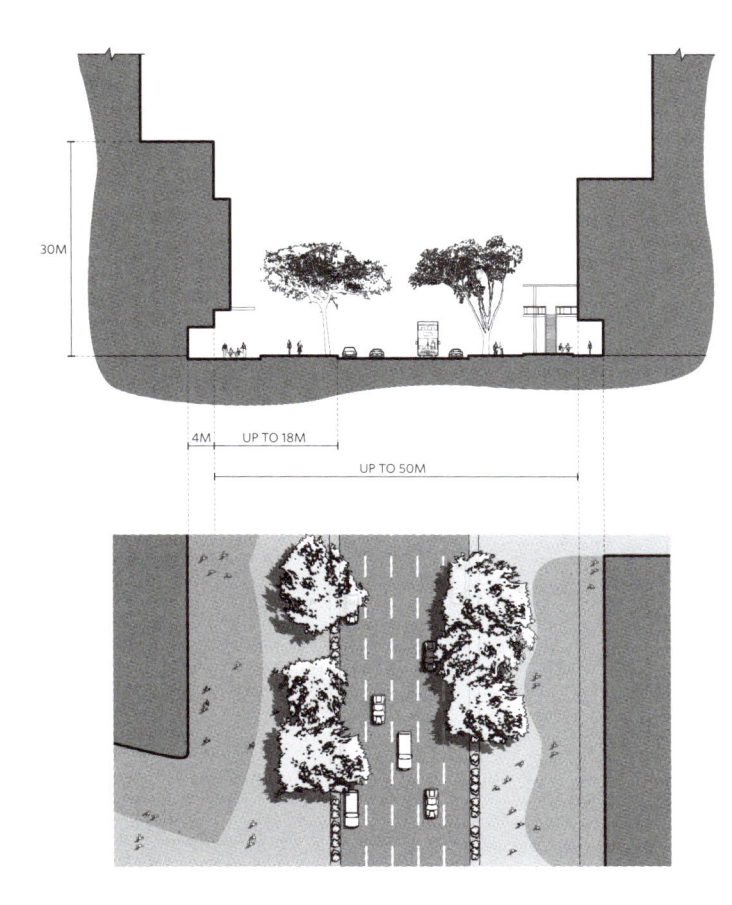

Orchard Road: Plan and Section

Orchard Road's streetscape can be identified as having a dense commercial heart flanked by transition zones to the west and east. Mall frontages extend to well over 100 metres in length along the street's non-uniform grid. These collectively establish a layer of shopping podia three to six storeys in height behind which are mixed-use commercial towers that house programme primarily for hotels and office spaces – the value of land and the type of programme permitted on each lot are influenced greatly by their relation to one of the three MRT stations.

The roadway varies between 30 metres and 50 metres in width, and the promenade commonly has 10 metres of clearance, extended by urban verandah spaces and a 4-metre covered walk along the base of buildings. An allée of Angsana trees rising to nearly 30 metres in height performs as a buffer between the wide sidewalks and vehicular traffic, and creates a thick natural canopy that shades the promenade from the harsh Singaporean sun. Plazas break the linearity of both the frontages and promenade.

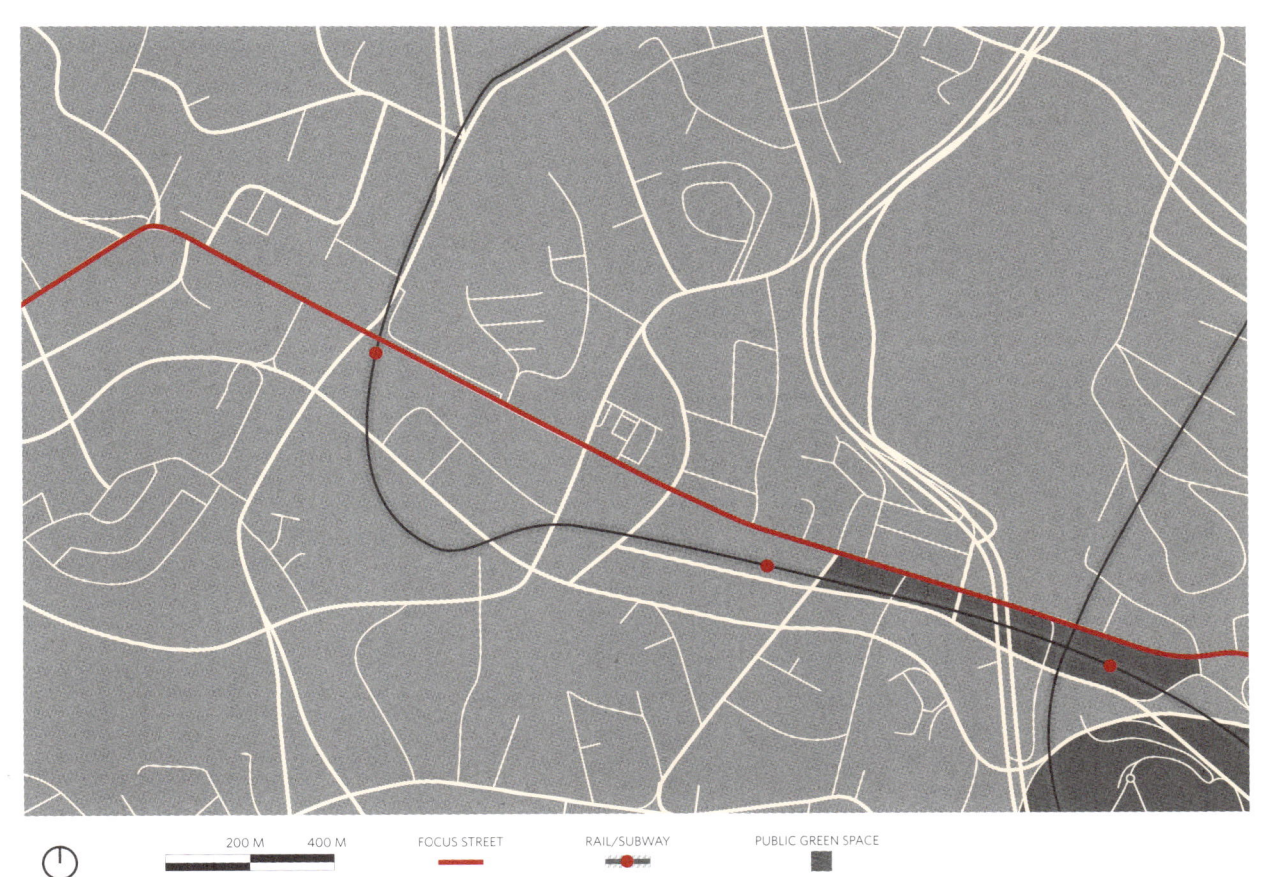

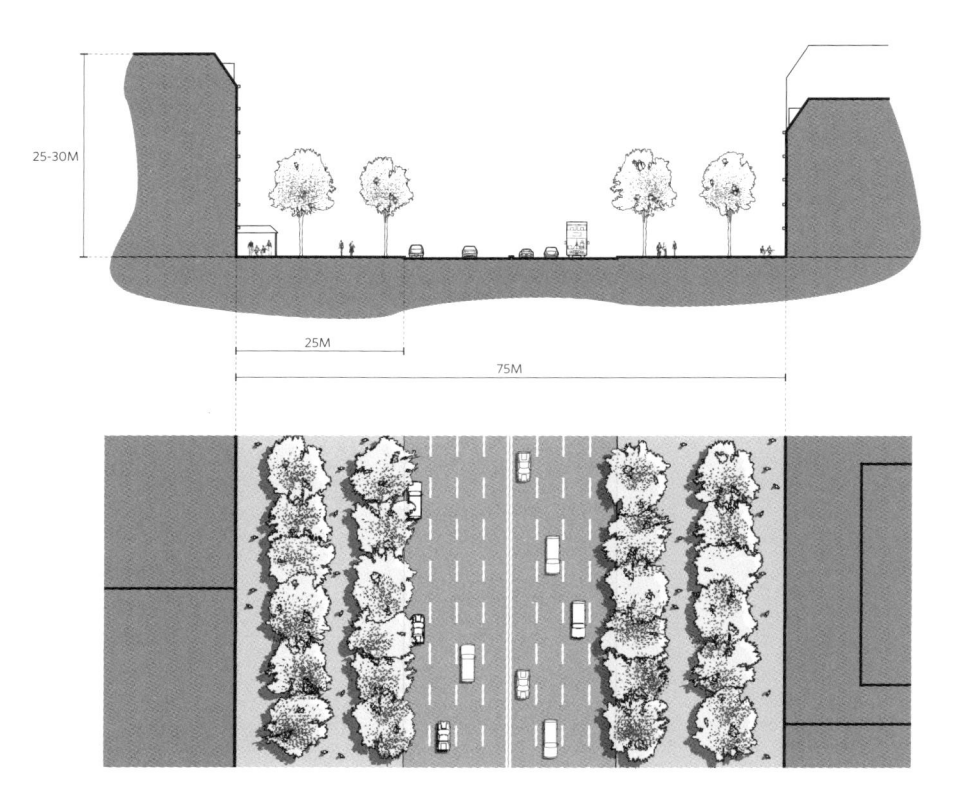

Champs-Élysées, Paris

The Avenue des Champs-Élysées in Paris has been a paradigm for streetscape planning and architecture since the mid-19th century. When it was expanded and straightened during Baron Haussmann's reconstruction of Paris commissioned by Napoleon III from 1852–1870, the Champs-Élysées' elaborateness as a civic promenade was unmatched in Europe or elsewhere at the time. The Avenue immediately became the acknowledged symbol of the modernised French capital – both a source of authority for the Second-Empire imperial regime and a source of strengthened French national identity. The new boulevard system created vast spaces amongst a formerly intricate network of medieval streets and had a profound effect on Parisian urban life.

The Champs-Élysées was first established in 1667 by landscape architect Lenôtre as an approach to the west front of the Tuileries Palace.[2] Its present form is a result of a subsequent, comprehensive expansion that erased whole regions of dense residential neighborhoods. By cutting away the former small-scale streets, an efficient travel route was established directly into Paris' core that brought transformative connectivity to the city. Two kilometres in length, the Champs-Élysées extended from the Louvre north-west through the Tuileries Gardens and the Place de la Concorde to the Arc de Triomphe – Place de l'Etoile and today its visual line-of-sight culminates at the Grande Arche de la Défense, completed in 1989.

The boulevard was characterised by its 70-metre width; its vistas that terminated at grand monuments; its neoclassical building frontages; and its tree-lined pedestrian promenades with shops and cafes. The axial perspective of the street towards the Arc de Triomphe with its dual linear arrangements of trees, became one of Europe's most recognisable urban images. Collectively all these features formed the 'model boulevard' by which streetscapes around the world were measured.

Not only did the Champs-Élysées maintain an aesthetic dominance, clearly demarcating the heart of urban Paris, but its location and programming also made it a social, political and economic capital. The promenade was a centre of the French société at its prime in the late-19th and early-20th century, host to such cultural monuments as the Beaux-Arts-style Grand Palais and the Auguste Perret-designed Théâtre des Champs-Élysées, and also the spine along which numerous Parisian salons emerged. Such gathering spaces were well-attended by Europe's elite for purposes of intellectual, social

ABOVE
Typical plan and section, the Champs-Élysées.

OPPOSITE
Map of the Champs-Élysées and surroundings, Paris, France.

Not only did the
Champs-Élysées maintain an
aesthetic dominance, clearly
demarcating the heart of urban
Paris, but its location and
programming also made it
a social, political and
economic capital.

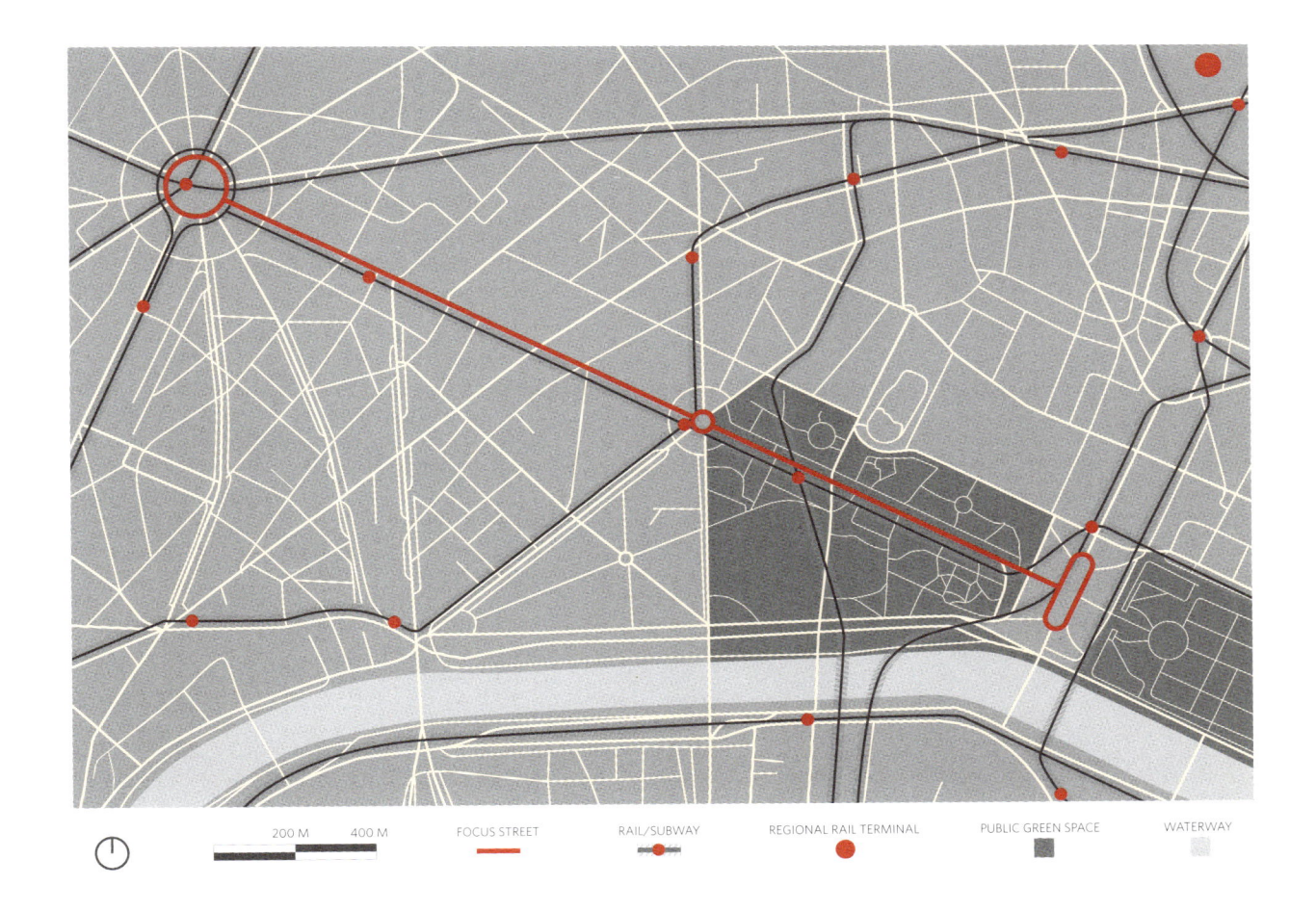

200 M   400 M   FOCUS STREET   RAIL/SUBWAY   REGIONAL RAIL TERMINAL   PUBLIC GREEN SPACE   WATERWAY

Champs-Élysées

and philosophical discourse. Notable hotels, such as the Hôtel Claridge memorialised Empire-style architecture. Meanwhile, residential apartments were built into many of the commercial buildings at the upper levels.[3]

The Champs-Élysées served as an important public thoroughfare, where the act of 'strolling' became popular within its bordering French gardens, and it was along this boulevard that such leisure walks extended into the streets and consequently evolved into 'promenading' – the exploration of the city. The 'urban flâneur' was a title bestowed upon the emergent, mid-19th-century citizen who wandered the streets for purposes of urban observation. The early implementation of gas-lighting along the Champs-Élysées extended such activities into the night, greatly influencing the social foundations of Paris.

During the Second Empire, Parisian department stores became the leading symbols of fashion and luxury goods; Paris was at the forefront of commercial architecture, with grand, multi-floor metal structures unified by a central staircase.[4] By the mid-20th century, the Champs-Élysées displayed a mix of formal neoclassicism, modernist commercial buildings and upscale apartments. To streamline the Avenue's commercial development, in 1860 the merchants of the Champs-Élysées formed the associated Syndicat d'Initiative et de Défense des Champs-Élysées. Today, the Champs-Élysées Committee pursues a continued cultural and aesthetic heritage as a basis of urban Paris. Its foremost mission is 'to adapt into daily practice the Most Beautiful Avenue in the World to the natural evolution of society in order to conserve a harmonious domination and its world class reputation'.[5] The street has over time remained a centre for high-street retailers, and in 2011 was recorded as the most expensive retail street in Europe, with annual rents averaging over US$10,000 per square metre.[6] Rental increases have led to a transition during the first decade of the 2000s towards larger retail conglomerates, a rather dramatic change as smaller businesses were forced to shut their doors.

Flanking either side of the 10-lane Champs-Élysées is a 20-metre wide promenade, an event space characterised by outdoor cafés, large shops and the uniform, neoclassical façades of commercial and residential buildings; this dynamic arrangement can be considered the primary set of elements on which Orchard Road is modelled. An allée of horse-chestnut trees frames the sidewalks, as well as the linear view from the Louvre to the Arc de Triomphe. At its elevated position and 50-metre height, this monument contrasts with the standard building frontages, which stand six to eight storeys in height.

ABOVE
The Champs-Élysées' 20-metre-wide pedestrian promenade is fitted with outdoor cafés and lined with neoclassical façades six to eight stories in height. An allée of horse-chestnut trees frames the linear views from the Louvre to the Arc de Triomphe.

OPPOSITE
Fifth Avenue is characterised by its uniform grid and high-rise towers. Street-level tenants are a combination of department stores and high-end retail flagships.

Fifth Avenue, New York

New York City's streetscape is definitively identified by its ubiquitous grid, an urban planning scheme overlaid onto Manhattan Island according to the Commissioners' Plan of 1811. The grid's common block length of 60 metres was determined in consideration of pedestrian movement and ease of navigation; the limited dimensions of the standard block, as well as the whole of Manhattan Island were driving parameters for the avenue's second-most important identifier: the skyscraper. The resulting form of each avenue is a strong linear axis bounded by the vertical profiles of towers broken rhythmically at each cross-street.

Fifth Avenue was first developed 30 metres in width along a 3-kilometre stretch, and immediately emerged as a backbone for commercial development, the site of numerous national architectural monuments. The early installation of gas lamps along Fifth Avenue in 1847 activated the sidewalk with day-and-night use as a dynamic social core. Commercial development emerged downtown amongst the residential mansions owned by the city's earliest wealthy classes, and grew outward from Madison Square – at the time a major transportation node as the home to New York Central Line rail station. Signature upper-class landmarks, such as the Waldorf Hotel at 34th Street, erected in 1893, heralded some of the world's largest examples of department store retailers including the block-length adjacent B. Altman and Company in 1906, Saks in 1924 and Woolworth's in 1935. Today, Fifth Avenue's shopping district originates in Greenwich Village and culminates at the southeastern edge of Central Park, well-defined by bookend urban landmarks: the Washington Square Arch to the south; and at the north end, the plaza hosting a mix of historic and contemporary architectural icons, including Apple's retail flagship store and the Plaza Hotel. Saint Patrick's Cathedral, the Empire State Building and

Fifth Avenue

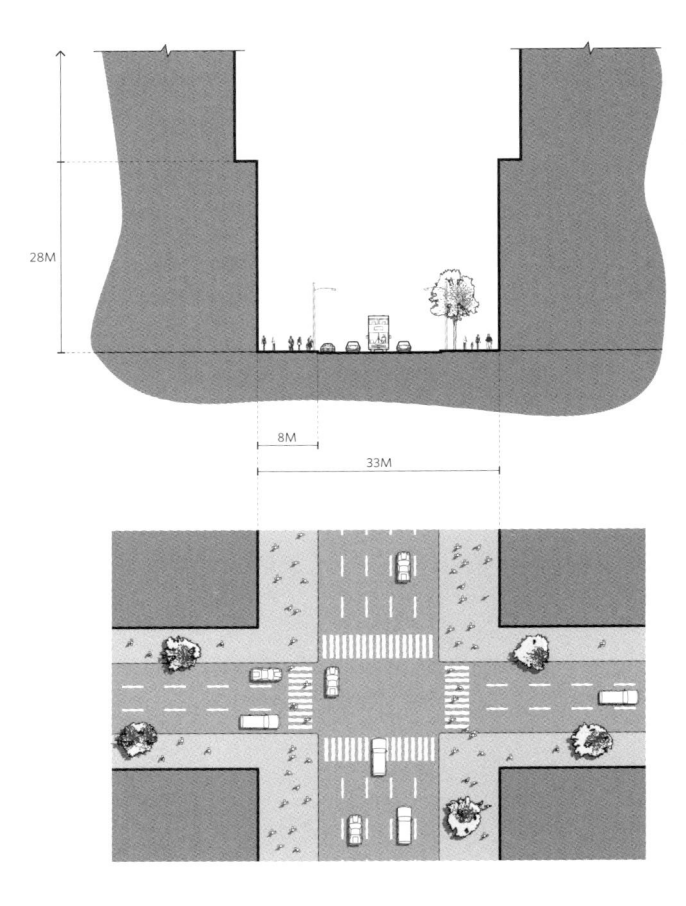

the New York Public Library break at intervals from the otherwise monotonous, densely-packed mix of curtain wall and face-brick towers erected over the last century, thereby opening up views to the sky and surrounding city, with larger public spaces at the level of the sidewalk.

The architecture that emerged along Fifth Avenue during the 19th century was primarily Beaux Arts and Art Deco, fashioned by architects such as McKim, Mead & White. Following its construction, the S H Kress & Co. department store is described as follows, 'A seven-storey marble structure designed for every shopping comfort, its Art Deco elegance was graced by airborne Mayan gods on the sales floor and Mayan-style hieroglyphs of the gloves and padlocks'.[7]

A century of specialised zoning laws have guided Fifth Avenue's development, though not all have been established in the spirit of pedestrianising the avenue: much of the street south of Central Park was widened in 1908 to public anger as sidewalks were slimmed to accommodate increased vehicular traffic.[8] The Zoning Resolution of 1916 established height and setback controls, as well as land-use guidelines, preventing the construction of high-rise towers from depriving the streets of natural light. Fifth Avenue's designation as a Special Shopping District in the 1970s protected its famed concentration of retail from the encroachment of banks and showrooms that threatened to drive out retailers; the regulation awarded bonus residential floors to new office towers planned with ground-storey retail with through-block public atria.[9] The first building erected under these Special Fifth Avenue Zoning District codes was the 51-storey, glass-curtain-walled Olympic Tower completed in 1976, its programme divided into residential apartments atop 19 storeys of office space and a public retail arcade at street level.[10]

To this day, development along Fifth Avenue is guided by special zoning which states the mission: 'In order to preserve, protect and enhance the character of the Fifth Avenue Sub-district as the showcase of New York and national retail shopping'.[11] Standard building programme is divided into a tripartite relationship shared by ground-level retailers below commercial office spaces and residential apartments. Street-level tenants remain a mix of department stores and high-end retail flagships.

ABOVE
Typical plan and section, Fifth Avenue.

OPPOSITE
Map of Fifth Avenue and surroundings, New York City, USA.

Fifth Avenue was first developed 30 metres in width along a 3-kilometre stretch, and immediately emerged as a backbone for commercial development, the site of numerous national architectural monuments.

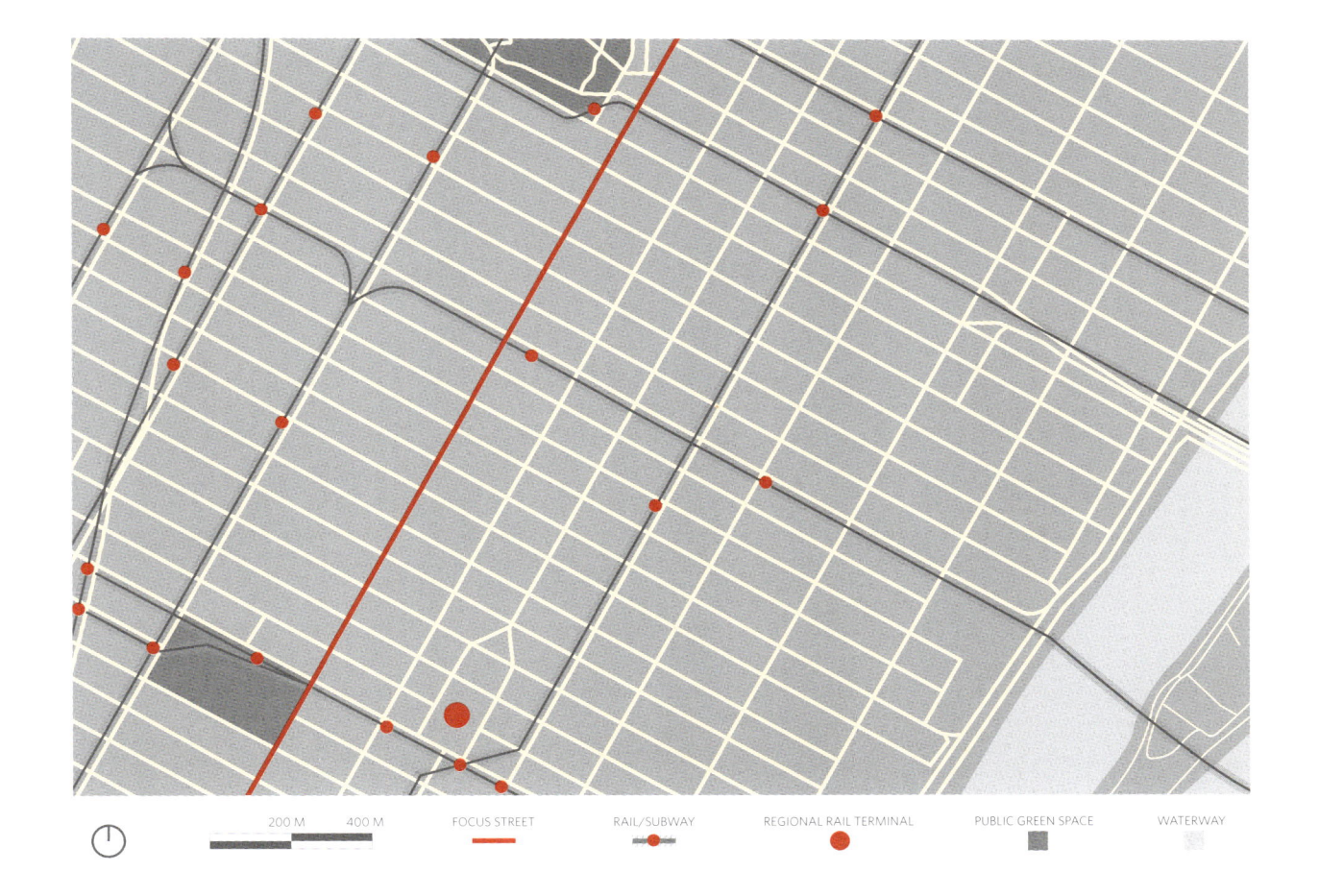

| 200 M   400 M | FOCUS STREET | RAIL/SUBWAY | REGIONAL RAIL TERMINAL | PUBLIC GREEN SPACE | WATERWAY |

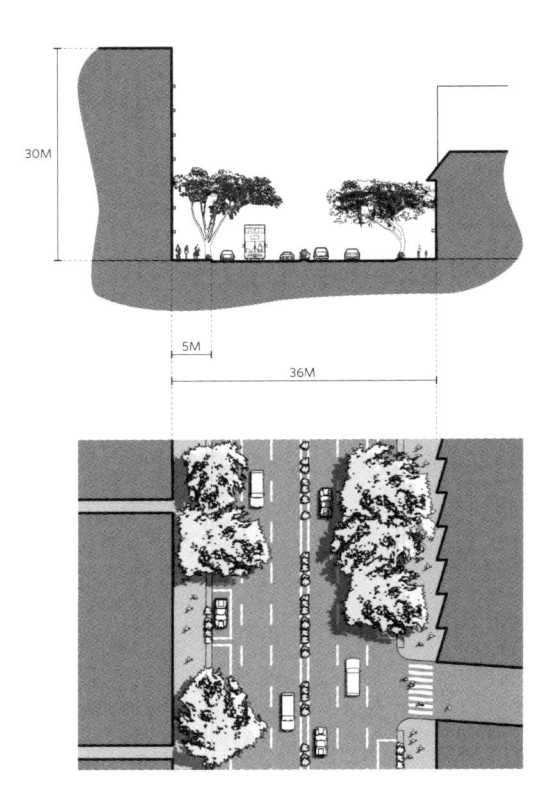

Omotesandō, Tokyo

Tokyo, Japan is a global commercial capital. While the Japanese nation is home to a wide collection of streets and shopping regions that might be deemed the nation's paradigm, none of these examples represents such a significant social history as influential for its commercial architecture as Omotesandō. As one of the world's most concentrated collections of flagships that exist as autonomous buildings along a pedestrian street, Omotesandō is Japan's foremost fashion boulevard and an international stage for high-end retail architecture landmarks.

Tokyo has a history of development dating back as early as the 12th century. Originally entitled Edo, the city was renamed Tokyo when it became the Japanese imperial capital in 1868. Despite the city's extensive history, evidence of its early building structure has all but vanished as a result of its suffering from multiple cases of widespread destruction in the 20th century – first in the wake of the devastating 1923 earthquake and once again as a target of World War II bombings in 1942 and early 1945. Omotesandō and the majority of the city's urban fabric as it exists today is reflective of comprehensive post-war reconstruction campaigns and the economic success of recent decades.

Commercialism in Japan is a primarily 20th-century phenomenon. Japanese culture and policy remained isolated from global influence until Japan extended itself to global relations by means of a late-19th-century transition to capitalism and industrialisation. Large-scale shopping spaces did pre-date international trade in the form of Japanese-vernacular shōtengai of varying scales; shōtengai were comparable to the bazaars of the west, and today exist mainly as covered, pedestrian-only arcades for local trade. As a modern interpretation of shopping space, Tokyo-based Mitsukoshi, Ltd. constructed some of the first department stores as an evolution of the Japanese dry goods storage. The company was established as a 17th-century distributor of textiles; in 1904, Mitsukoshi's Tokyo shop was given a second storey and, by 1914, central heating, a roof garden and elevators.[12] The western-influenced form became the basis for modern department store architecture throughout Japan.

Omotesandō served as an important urban transportation link, and correspondingly became a busy thoroughfare that catered to commercial development. It is situated within the larger commercial Shibuya ward of Tokyo, and acts as a transportation connector between Harajuku rail station, Omotesandō rail station and Aoyama-Dori

---

ABOVE
Typical plan and section, Omotesandō.

OPPOSITE
Map of Omotesandō and surroundings, Tokyo, Japan.

– another major commercial street. Omotesandō was originally designated as the frontal approach to the Meiji Shrine in 1912 and its name is translated as 'way to the shrine', a landmark that served as the corridor's terminus.

The region became an important nexus of Japanese and western culture for its adjacency to Yoyogi Park, a housing site for American soldiers during the Occupation and, in 1964, the accommodation centre for foreign athletes during the Tokyo Summer Olympic Games – both of these events were transformative for commercialism and urbanism in Japan. With construction of the Olympic village came an expansion of road widths for greater connectivity and an increased number of shops to serve foreigners. Stores that marketed to middle and upper-class Japanese and Americans contributed to something of a social restructuring: the young Japanese who flocked to this region spawned a culture of youth, fashion and art.[13] This was supported by a widespread residential fabric that grew in tandem with commercial development following the 1923 earthquake. Two major housing complexes built along Omotesandō were the Dojunkai Aoyama in 1923 and Central Apartments built in 1958, occupied by fashion designers, models and photographers.

All these elements established the composition of Omotesandō as a centre for fashion, and the region presents a showcase of landmark flagship stores designed by noted international architects, including Dior by SANAA, Louis Vuitton by Aoki, Prada by Herzog & de Meuron, Tod's by Toyo Ito and Gyre by MVRDV. The Ando-designed Omotesandō Hills mall built in 2005 adds to this collection of buildings that became the characteristic forms for the streetscape – a two-way boulevard some 30 metres wide, flanked by five-metre pedestrian walks and landscaped with a continuous, linear allée of broad-leaved, wide-canopied Zelkova trees.

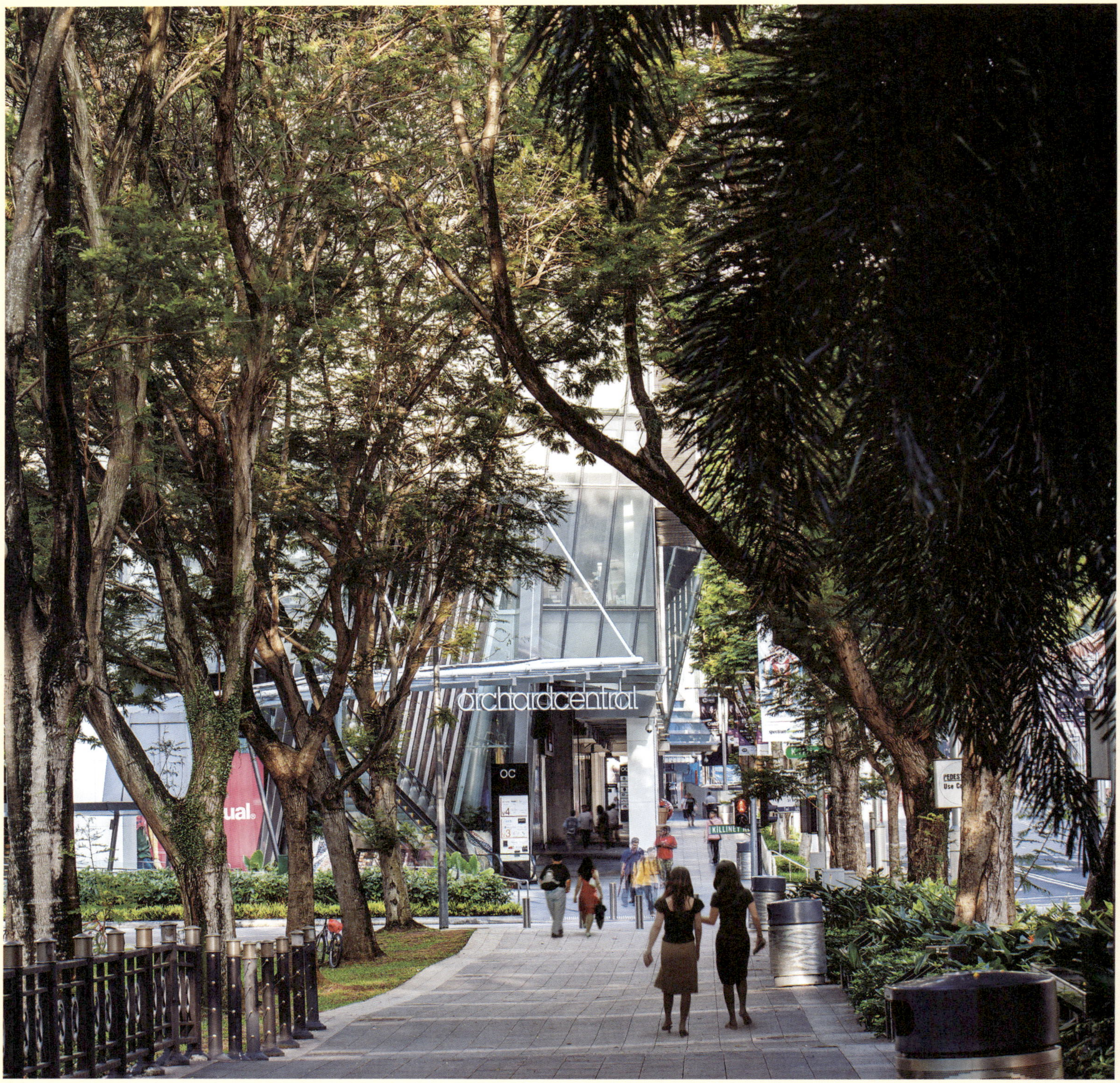
orchardcentral

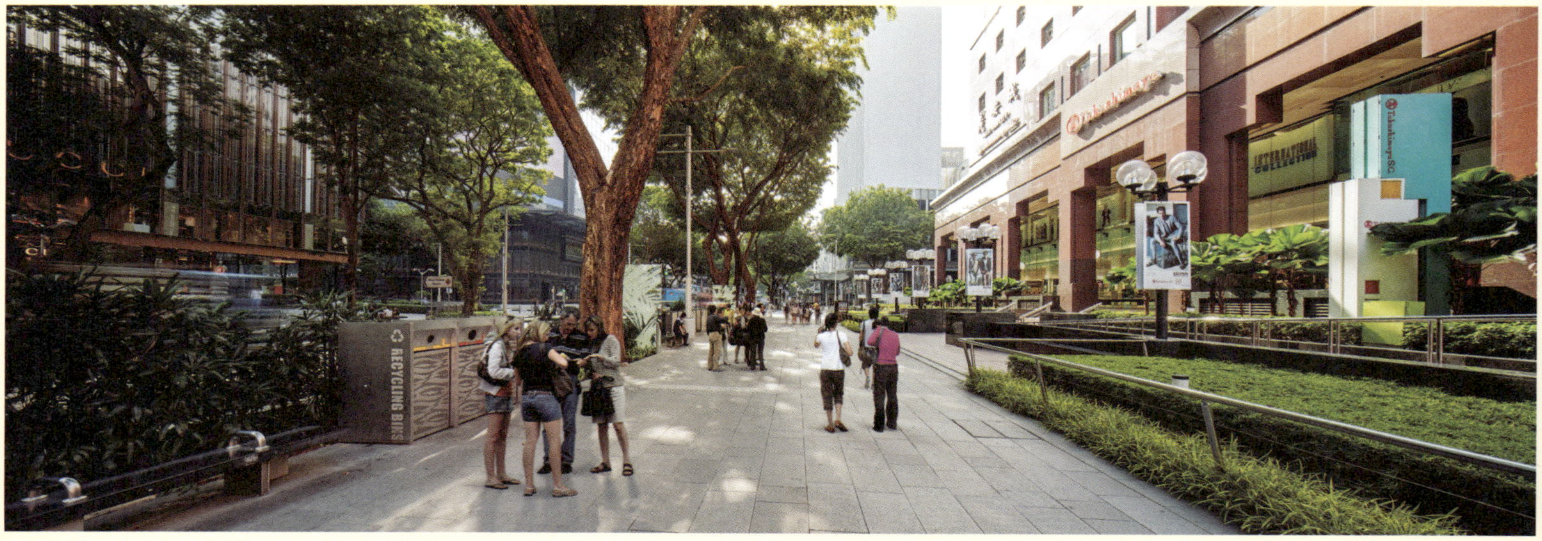

KEY INGREDIENTS

Buildings and streets are micro-elements that tie into the larger field of the city in specific ways. The form of a streetscape can be characterised by its spatial patterns: the length of its blocks; the width of its sidewalks; the number and size of public plazas, parks and shops along its length; the height of its buildings; the ways in which buildings integrate with the sidewalks; the use of landscape; and the shape and direction of the street itself. By comparing these details across many examples, one can extract a common rhetoric for the universal variables that contribute to the success of a pedestrian street.

Engaging Buildings. As the urban theorist Jane Jacobs wrote: 'Think of a city and what comes to mind? Its streets. If a city's streets look interesting, the city looks interesting; if they look dull, the city looks dull'.[14] While surface aesthetics – articulated patterning and active building profiles – are necessary for establishing visual interest, engagement extends beyond surface to the cross-sectional sequencing of a building's spaces. Readings of architecture in plan and section can describe the way buildings are programmed and accessed, and how interior spaces integrate with the activities of the street. The growing complexities of Orchard Road's composition, both in the geometries of its façades and the interconnectivity of its buildings above and below ground, capture the attention of the visitor in new ways.

Boundaries. Certain identifying features provide visitors with a sense of finite place and spatial orientation. Visible boundaries – façades, monuments and landmarks – 'contain' the streetscape within definitive edges and distinguish it as an individual fragment of the city – an important prerequisite for generating well-visited public spaces. For point of contrast, lack of such a boundary has given rise to failure in cases, such as the Place de la Concorde on the eastern portion of Champs-Élysées in Paris. The Place de la Concorde was first constructed in the mid-18th century as a transition zone between the private Tuileries Palace gardens and the public parks along the Champs-Élysées, but the rather undefined nature of the space was problematic; as described by art historian Howard Saalman: 'the Place was literally not a "place", its outline intentionally undefined, its edges fluid'.[15] As a result, the Place de la Concorde failed to become a centre of urban activity, and was converted into a vehicular traffic circle. Just one kilometre to the east, however, the denser segment of the Champs-Élysées, bounded by neoclassical façades and a dense collection of shops, has succeeded as one of the world's most-visited pedestrian spaces.

Landscape. Aside from the obvious effects of softening the built elements of cities with local plantings, landscape elements have the architectonic capacity of administering spatial hierarchy: greenery sets façades in dialogue with the sidewalk and mediates between the scales of man and building. Trees, in addition to their purpose of generating shade, form linear allées with the effect of creating defined enclosures that isolate the sidewalk from the vehicular street. Such linear arrangements can also frame key symbolic views, such as the dual stretches of horse-chestnut trees that line the Champs-Élysées to frame the Arc de Triomphe – one of the most-recognised urban perspectives in the world.

Place-making and Historical Texture. A level of historical variety is important for communicating the narrative of the city – monuments register with the collective memory and often break from a monotony of form and style. In the instance of Fifth Avenue, the comparatively low-rise Saint Patrick's Cathedral and New York Public Library building stand in stark contrast to the rhythm of high-rise glass towers, with frontal plazas that are important pockets of civic space. Meanwhile on Orchard Road, conservation efforts led to the restoration of Emerald Hill's Peranakan-style shophouses with ground-floor restaurants and narrow arcades that distinguish them from the otherwise consistent scale of the contemporary shopping podia.

OPPOSITE
Orchard Road's pedestrian sidewalk has undergone numerous expansions and transformations to add landscaped buffers, adequate lighting and well-shaded pocket plazas.

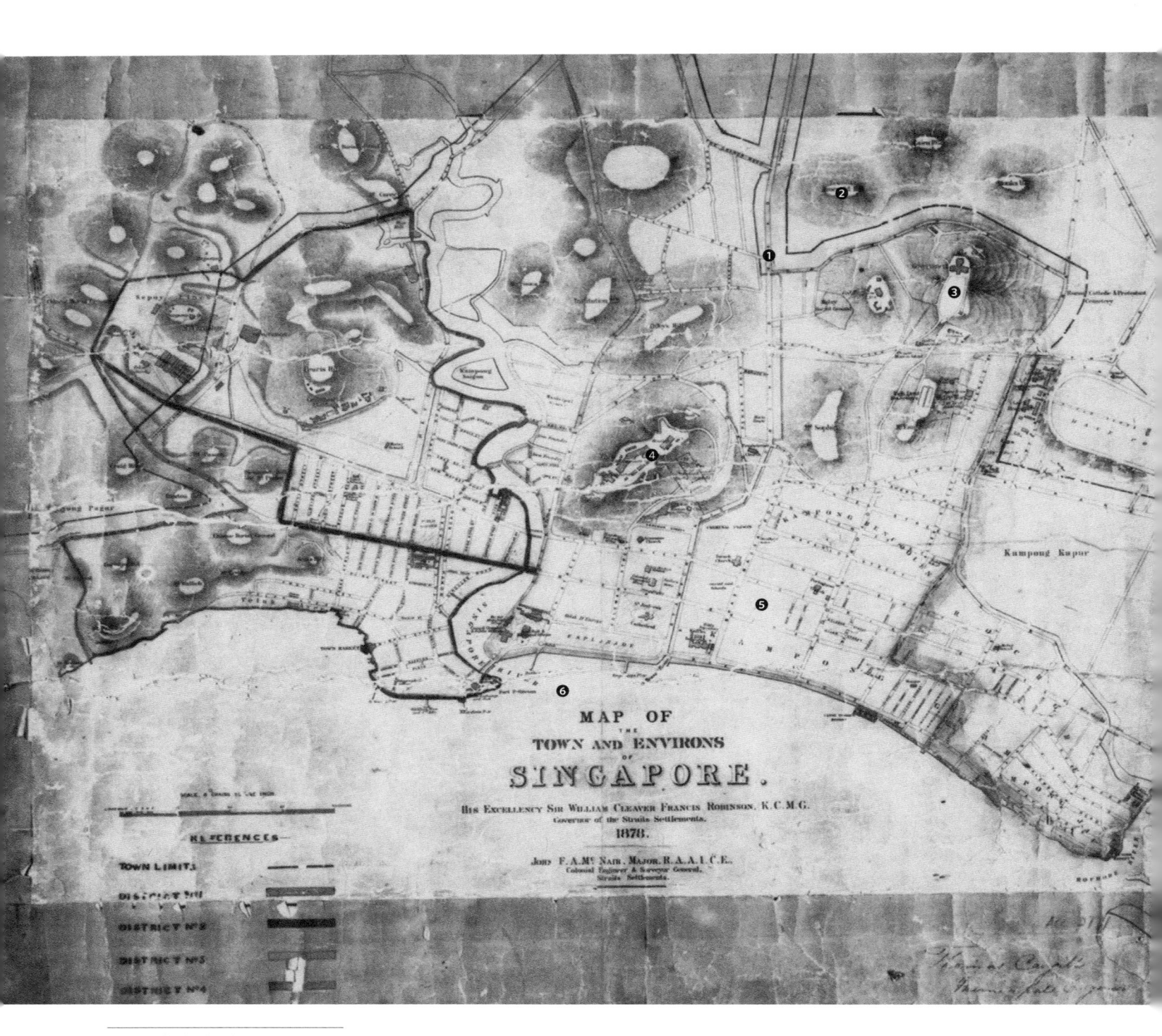

Present-day landmarks
1. Orchard Road
2. Emerald Hill
3. Istana
4. Fort Canning Park
5. Central Business District
6. Marina Bay

A Contextual History of Singapore

Architecture has always performed as a material medium of representation, serving as evidence by which a nation's layered history can be traced. As a nation that developed at the intersection of many people and cultures, Singapore is embedded with a diverse legacy of reflective architectural identities that can be read at several scales; from elements of a building, to the city's widespread urban planning strategies.

The spatial arrangement of Singapore is a result of the economic, social and political changes that have defined it for a period extending well beyond its own history as a city-state. Many residents of Singapore are older than the state itself, yet for a young nation it has been subject to a chain of land-use planning strategies applied by successive governing bodies that have transformed the island's landscape and, in doing so, redirected social and cultural progress.

Between 1965 and 2011 Singapore's population more than doubled, growing from less than two million at the time of independence, to five million today. Likewise, the nation's urban condition evolved during this period, into a complex physical and social landscape, particularly driven by the confluence of its geographic dimensions as a small island and its economic significance as a shipping port: scarce land and material resources have forced reliance upon foreign trade and, more recently, tourism – to generate revenue. Meanwhile, high land values and a dependence on efficient land-use strategies have played critical roles in the nation's evolving patterns of architecture and urbanism. It is within this greater context that Orchard Road has acquired its present function as a commercial centre vital to the national economy.

Colonial Beginnings

Though a succession of settlements are known to have existed on the island since at least the 14th-century Sang Nila Utama kingdom of Singapura, Singapore was officially established in 1819 as a trading post by British diplomats seeking to profit from the flourishing trade of Dutch-controlled South East Asia. At its founding, statesman Stamford Raffles negotiated with Malayan leaders for land rights and initiated a plan to transform a series of fishing villages into a colony of the expanding British Empire. Singapore became first a trading post with the British East India Company, and later an established territory under British imperial governance by means of the 1826 Straits Settlements.

A liberal free-port policy aided the colony's rapid

OPPOSITE
Map of the Town and Environs of Singapore, 1878.

development into a regional capital of exchange and a magnet for Chinese, Malayan and Indian immigrants. Despite immediate economic success, the sudden population influx presented overcrowding and harmful living conditions in the form of burgeoning squatter settlements. To confront this issue, in 1822 Raffles devised an organising master plan for Singapore, overlaying city streets as a grid that stemmed outwards from the port.[1] The plan was not only a tool for physical infrastructure, but addressed reform comprehensively, going so far as to establish rent control in an effort to distill an unhealthy population density that had reached upwards of 2500 persons per hectare.[2]

A Growing Architectural and Cultural Diversity

Raffles' first 'cantonment' plan adapted the traditional grid to either side of the Singapore River and was in-built with dividing lines that segregated ethnicities in favour of British colonisers. The Chinese, for instance, were allotted a portion of land south of the port, while space for Arabs and the Indonesian Bugis was fixed to the north, in the vicinity of today's Kampong Glam neighbourhood. The type of middle ground between the port and the larger estates of the wealthy Europeans – the type of land inclusive of the eventual Orchard Road corridor – proved well-suited for commercial development.

Rapid growth, subject to these zoning measures, led to the formation of ethnic communities rooted in various architectural styles and building methods transplanted from overseas.[3] Disparate forms of Asian and British-vernacular architecture emerged in concentrated developments, such as the Chinese Peranakan shophouses – two and three-storey structures built in rows that combined ground-accessible shops or workplaces with residences above. Raffles' earliest planning strategies in 1822 incorporated building regulations that supported shophouse development with ordinances that required, for instance, shade and protection from rain by means of covered walkways with common dimensions.[4] These forms became ubiquitous, and were erected along the Orchard Road corridor during its initial commercial development as a Chinese-populated midpoint between the port and the wealthy European plantations to the north; while the shophouses type generally made way for modern commercial structures, shophouse rows along Emerald Hill were restored in 1984.[5]

Towards Independence

Continuous population growth, increasing wealth and urban development halted when the British surrendered Singapore following the Japanese invasion in 1942 during World War II. Singapore was reclaimed by Britain after the war in 1945, but was absorbed by the global economic decline that arrested progress for well over a decade. During this period the British decreased their level of imperial control, and governing power shifted to the hands of the people. Self-government was granted in 1959 with the first general election won by the People's Action Party, and Singapore became a nation-state in 1965 after two years as an independent arm of Malaysia. The population rose from 560,000 in 1931 to 941,000 in 1947, and to roughly 1.9 million by 1965, primarily of Chinese ethnicity.[6]

Urban Renewal and Nation-Building

With political autonomy, Singapore's newly formed governing body recognised the urgent need for internal infrastructural development. Years of economic and political struggle had transformed the city core into a region fraught with dilapidated properties – slums and tenements had become clear evidence of widespread poverty and overcrowding. The nation's urban fabric required an injection of new public facilities to spur regional redevelopment. Thus began a continued effort by the government for comprehensive control of land use, and the next 50 years of development were subjected to government-driven building and regeneration programmes that often engaged private enterprises or foreign architectural services.

Programmes were initiated to address long-term urban planning strategies with agendas aimed at social and economic regeneration. The Urban Redevelopment Authority (URA), renamed from Urban Renewal Department in 1974, addressed land use and set out to 'plan, facilitate, and regulate the physical development of Singapore into a tropical city of excellence';[7] the Housing Development Board (HDB) dealt with the removal of slums and the resettling of residents into state-funded

Long-Range Development Plans

housing projects that, by 1996, accommodated 86% of Singaporeans;[8] and the Singapore Tourist Promotion Board – now the Singapore Tourism Board (STB) – reinforced the nation's foreign appeal and accessibility for reasons of attracting external investment. These boards remain influential agents steering Singapore's built environment.

The URA introduced the Sale of Sites programme with ambitions of revitalising the city's Central Area; the first of these in 1967 opened up 13 urban sites for private development and, over the next 20 years, 184 hectares were cleared and sold under this initiative to develop 155 projects. Piecemeal surgical implementations, these significantly contributed to Singapore's conversion into a modern financial and commercial centre. A number of the programme's sales have influenced the form of Orchard Road, and continue to do so – in 2005, for instance, sites at the corner of Orchard Road and Killiney Road were sold for commercial development.

A United Nations survey of Singapore's land-use in the 1960s led to the crystallisation of a comprehensive Concept Plan that has guided national land development since 1971 by focusing on attracting foreign investment to stimulate growth. The programme enforced a 'Ring Concept Plan' based on polycentric rings to initiate the growth of satellite towns radially about a 'Central Planning Area'; this would string together individualised developments by means of parks and recreation spaces;[9] A corresponding transportation plan anticipated a network of expressways paired with a Mass Rapid Transit (MRT) rail infrastructure to alleviate the pressures of population growth and support decentralisation; MRT construction began in 1982 and, by the late 1980s, three stations – Somerset, Orchard and Dhoby Ghaut – were built to serve the Orchard Road corridor, positioning it as a central catchment within the national system.

ABOVE
Orchard Road, 1950s. Orchard Road had become Singapore's motor vehicle distribution centre with numerous showrooms and garages.

ORCHARD ROAD
facts and figures

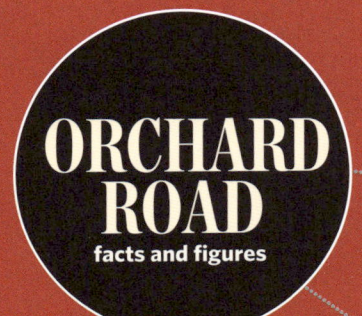

over 30 shopping centres

20% of Singapore's total private retail stock

800,000 square metres of retail, dining and entertainment programmes

19 hotels

3 mass rapid transit stations

7,000,000 annual visitors

shopping along **2.2** kilometres

5000 outlets

inclusive of **2000** brands

Strategic development plans have been amended and revised on a 10-year basis to address changing physical and economic conditions. By 1998 zoning revisions were made to accommodate larger populations in support of a national decentralisation policy encouraging town-centred growth in 55 'regional planning areas', of which the Orchard Road Planning Area is designated as a primary commercial and residential belt; today the Orchard Road Planning Area covers approximately 100 hectares of land.

A 2001 Concept Plan outlined a 50-year development proposal based upon an estimated population of 5.5 million, and is also in-built with speculative land-use patterns for commercial retail space.[10] The Concept Plan since 1971 has been the root cause of the Orchard Road Planning Area's progressive development as the nation's retail core and, as of 2010, home to over 20 per cent of the nation's total stock of private retail space.[11]

Tourism, the Economy and Orchard Road

Singapore's initial urban-planning strategies were in-built to address the means of attracting foreign interests. The Singapore Tourist Promotion Board (STPB – this became STB when renamed the Singapore Tourism Board in 1997) was first established by the government in 1964 to promote Singapore as a tourist destination and to coordinate the efforts of travel with adequate provisions of accommodations, entertainment venues and sightseeing landmarks. By the early 1970s, tourism task forces targeted select destinations to absorb revenue from foreign exchange, and Orchard Road was singled out as the nation's primary shopping district (other tourism projects included the Jurong Bird Park, and the recreational development of Blakang Mati, now Sentosa island). In 1995, the Ministry of Trade and Industry launched Tourism 21, an outline for transforming Singapore into a regional tourism capital that would attract 10 million visitors and US$11 billion in annual revenue by 2000; with Orchard Road performing as the 'Mall of Singapore'.[12]

In the organisation's first year, 1964, the STPB estimated 91,000 visitors to Singapore; this number had grown to 13.2 million in 2011. Orchard Road has been critical to the national economy and the tourism sector for the past 10 years, attracting more than half of total tourist visitors. In 2005 the STB announced plans for US$1.2 billion in private and public sector investment to rejuvenate Orchard Road and contribute to a targeted doubling of Singapore's visitor arrivals to 17 million, and tripling of its tourism receipts to US$24 billion, by 2015.[13]

Heritage and Conservation

Ever since its period as a British imperial port, Singapore's cultural identity has represented a mix of Chinese, Malay, Indian, Arab and other ethnicities as a population consisting completely of foreigners. Amidst such diversity, government-led building programmes following the nation's independence became a means of forming a visible, unifying architectural language. Though following a widespread removal of pre-war building stock in the process of city-building, by the 1980s it became clear that ties to the nation's built past were fading. In 1989 both the Planning Act and associated Conservation Master Plan were drawn up to protect Singapore's Asian heritage, leading to the preservation of some 5600 buildings between 1989 and 2005.[14]

For years, the city has been facing ideological confrontations over its limited land space, navigating between the increasing desire to preserve existing monuments and the efforts to construct a 21st-century metropolis. The importance of positioning historical landmarks within public spaces, both for local and foreign appreciation, is evident. As one of the most visited tourist destinations in the country, planning measures have helped to layer Orchard Road with a historic texture containing visible links to the nation's past. The efforts have protected a number of sites: the Istana, office and residence of the nation's President; Sri Temasek, original home to the Colonial Secretary of the Straits Settlements; and the MacDonald House, a neo-Georgian office building in brick, one of the nation's first large-scale buildings built following the war.

In Context – SINGAPORE'S FIRST MIXED-USE RETAIL DEVELOPMENTS

DP Architects was established as Design Partnership (DP) in 1967. The practice was involved in producing some of the first large-scale, mixed-use buildings in post-independence Singapore – these stemmed from the government 'Sale of Sites' programme and became fundamental in setting standards for the nation's modern architecture movement.

Two projects that were undoubtedly influential in this generation of transition were the People's Park Complex and the Golden Mile Complex; both downtown sites were selected for redevelopment to confront problems posed by overcrowding and poor regional housing conditions, each offering a combination of residential, commercial, entertainment and office workspace within a single building. Concurrent with larger architectural experiments unfolding throughout Asia and the West (Brutalism and Metabolism, notably), these projects aimed to perform as 'self-contained cities' with aspirations of reinventing the postwar urban lifestyle.

The functional and sectional similarities between these mixed-use, public-private projects and the more recent series of commercial projects completed by DP Architects on Orchard Road are undeniably evident, and to a degree these may indicate a continuum in the firm's civic design practices. The following two projects will be used as a basis for comparison or, at the very least, as a starting point in DP Architects' mixed-use design thinking.

People's Park Complex

In the post-independence years of the late 1960s, Singapore's Chinatown was one of the most densely populated and tradition-rich enclaves in the nation. While rent-control maintained affordable housing for the region's poor migrant workers, there were few incentives instituted to stimulate new development or improvements to existing buildings; this led to overcrowded, tenement-like living conditions.

The architects of the People's Park Complex sought to design a building that would perpetuate the region's deeply rooted Chinese community. Opened in 1973, the People's Park Complex became Singapore's first, multi-use building with shopping, residential, office and car parking facilities within a single structure. It was divided into

TOP
People's Park Complex in the 1970s.
BOTTOM
Transverse section, People's Park Complex, 1973. The retail podium is topped by office spaces and apartments.

OPPOSITE TOP
Golden Mile Complex in the 1970s.
OPPOSITE BOTTOM
Transverse section, Golden Mile Complex, 1974. The mixed-use project was programmed as a 16-storey 'vertical city'.

Golden Mile Complex

The sale was intended to catalyse urban revitalisation in the form of a 'Golden Mile' of development along Beach Road; a stretch of land roughly two kilometres from Singapore's city centre.

The Golden Mile Complex presented a revolutionary design concept as the first segment of a comprehensive urban network. The project was programmed as a 16-storey 'vertical city' that contained all the amenities needed for urban life: residential communities were situated above a commercial centre, and an upper-level 'garden in the sky' terrace offered shared outdoor space for recreation and socialising. The upper platform was designed with the potential to be extended into a kilometre-long pedestrian promenade that would link each 'Golden Mile' building. Such a pedestrian thoroughfare would lend a new strategy for urban connectivity as a network of circulation autonomous from the vehicular streets below. Internal programming on the lower floors accommodated three storeys of commercial spaces with kiosks, coffee bars, a bank, department store, supermarket, 360 shopping units and office studios, all located within a central atrium running the full length of the building.

The building's form responded to site conditions, climate, circulation, views and sun orientation. Its shallow, staggered profile provided each residential unit with the protective shading necessary for housing in tropical climates and enhanced the performance of ventilation and natural light. The architectural expression provided a spatial order amongst programmatic and structural parts. The bookend towers, for instance, emphasised vertical circulation, as well as the ability to carry horizontal wind loads.

two realms: a public retail and commercial podium for shops and businesses at ground level; and a private residential zone in the tower above. Both zones were planned around central, shared spaces. Commercial spaces within the podium were organised along a wide concourse and atrium, while residences were arranged along 'streets in the air' – wide, outdoor recreation corridors. When the building was completed in 1973 the podium's large internal atrium was the first of its kind in Asia. The space was to become 'the people's living room', a public domain open day and night where residents of the surrounding neighbourhood could socialise, eat, shop and perform all the activities of everyday life.

Established businesses in Chinatown purchased shop units in the complex, and moved from the crowded streets into the modern, sanitised and air-conditioned spaces. These served as a magnet for residents that helped transform the People's Park Complex into a focal point for the Chinese community.

1900s

The Evolution of Orchard Road

Orchard Road is perpetually in transition, bound to the tides of the economy, as much as it is continually transformed by trends in commodities and fashion. As the Urban Redevelopment Authority and the Singapore Tourism Board work in conjunction with relevant government agencies such as the National Parks Board and Land Transport Authority to rewrite guidelines for building development in anticipation of an annual supply of 17 million tourists to Singapore by 2015, and as Orchard Road landowners are driven by the competitive nature of retail to frequently renovate their malls, architects who become engaged in Orchard Road projects are faced with designing amidst a continuum of reconstruction and change. Understanding Orchard Road's history is crucial to designing successfully for its future.

The perennial impact of Orchard Road on the national economy and urban life of Singapore allows it to claim a stake as a foundational element to the composition of the city today. Orchard Road is fundamental to Singaporean tourism, and its streetscape performs as a source of national identity. As a popular commercial centre, its property values have risen steadily over the past decades, with malls and their associated office or hospitality spaces valued at nearly US$1 billion per development.[1] Orchard Road's retail rents rank amongst the highest in the world, while residential prices for the surrounding land consistently rank amongst the highest in the nation.

In its modern state, Orchard Road is characterised by its collection of large-scale mall podia, topped by high-rise commercial offices and hotels, its wide promenades lined with shade-producing Angsana trees and its interconnected network of below-grade passages and above-ground inter-mall linkages. The history of events that have influenced Orchard Road's present condition spans some 190 years, extending as far back as the colonisation of Singapore under Stamford Raffles in the early 19th century. The root cause of the region's commercial development may be attributed to its coincidental geographic position between a business centre to the south and high-end residences to the north. And amongst the most influential forces driving the form of its streetscape and malls are the climatic conditions of Singapore's equatorial location and the construction of a national Mass Rapid Transit (MRT) system beginning in the late 1980s.

OPPOSITE
Orchard Road, 1900s. By the turn of the 20th century, Orchard Road had established itself as a merchant centre for the trading of goods and services.

Orchard Road's Present Composition

The commercial heart of Orchard Road is bordered on either end by transition zones: at the western end, a shift between commercial and up-scale residential programme occurs near Tanglin Shopping Centre, where the road turns and splits; the eastern end is marked by Dhoby Ghaut MRT station, where the public Istana Park and private Istana Presidential estate produce a buffer that separates the dense activity of Orchard Road from the Bras Basah 'Museum Precinct' and, further to the east, Singapore's Marina Bay.

Vertically, mall podia contain the space of the street, while commercial and residential towers establish a strong visual enclosure above. Mall frontages extend to upwards of 100 metres in length. The plot ratio and allowable size of a commercial development – a mall and its integrated, mixed-use towers – is guided strongly by its distance to one of Orchard Road's three MRT stations.

Orchard Road runs along the centreline of a geographical valley, parallel to the Stamford Canal, a waterway that drains a catchment area of more than 600 hectares into Marina Bay. A succession of projects over the last century has addressed the canal's consistent flooding issues, and the level of the roadway has been raised over time to ease constraints on the canal.[2] Throughout the 1970s and 1980s the Ministry of National Development and Urban Redevelopment Authority covered the canal as one method of developing a wide 'pedestrian mall' on both sides of the carriageway (the only place where this occurs in Singapore). Also accounted for by expanding the roadway between 30 metres and 50 metres in width, the promenade commonly has 10 metres of clearance, extended by urban verandah spaces and a 4-metre covered walk along the base of buildings.

In the 1970s, a national 'Garden City Movement' encouraged the planting of additional Angsana trees – a species introduced to Singapore in the late 19th century that reaches a height of more than 30 metres. Today the Angsana's allée along Orchard Road performs as a buffer between the wide sidewalks and vehicular traffic, and creates a thick natural canopy that shades the promenade from the harsh Singaporean sun. Plazas break the linearity of both the frontages and promenade at Ngee Ann City and within the concentration of shophouses at Peranakan Place on Emerald Hill. Peranakan Place in particular creates a stark contrast in scale, with a rich array of colonial-era details.

An Early History of Orchard Road

The spatial history of Orchard Road can be traced to the spice trade that linked Asia with Europe following Singapore's colonisation. Guided by the master plan strategies of the British settlement, the Orchard Road region was apportioned into large estates, many of which became nutmeg plantations that in part supplied the British East India Company; Orchard Road's name stems from these agricultural beginnings, a street bordering the plantation of William Scotts.[3]

While a plant disease eventually led to the widespread devastation of crops, the area's setting within walking distance of the Padang-area trading port positioned it as valuable real estate ripe for infrastructural development, and the region yielded to residential construction; estates were further sub-divided into lots and shophouses were erected along either side of Orchard Road, as was a Presbyterian church erected at the junction of Orchard Road and Dhoby Ghaut in 1878 – this remains the street's easternmost landmark.[4] At the western end, Chinese Peranakan bungalows developed along Scotts and Tanglin Roads.

OPPOSITE TOP
Orchard Road, 1910s. Orchard Road's large-scale commercial development was initiated with the 1905 opening of the Singapore Cold Storage Company.

OPPOSITE BOTTOM
Orchard Road, 1920s.

1910s

1920s

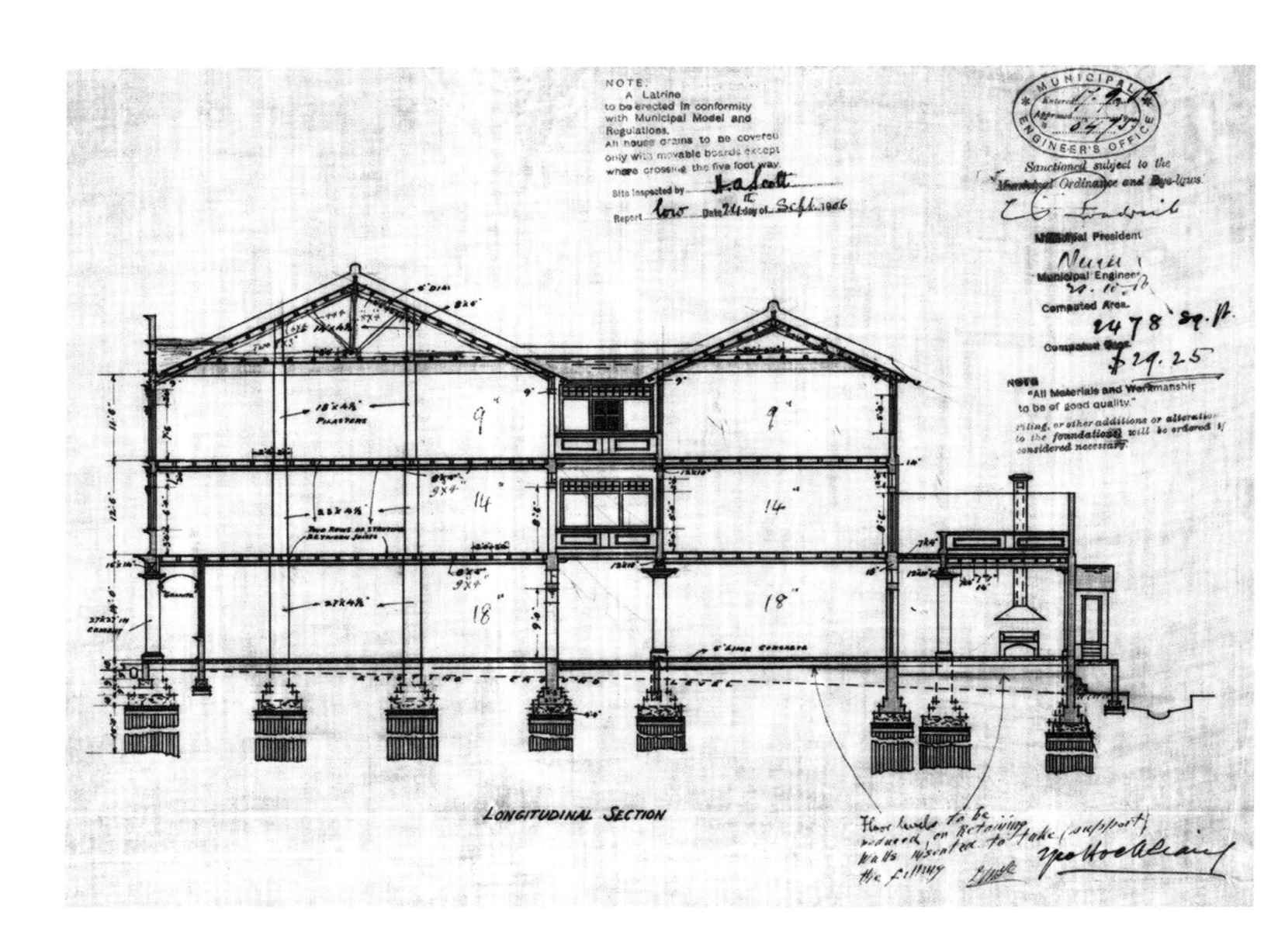

ABOVE
Section, Orchard Road shophouse. Drawing dated 1906.

OPPOSITE
Orchard Road, 1940s. As a corridor connecting the port with wealthy residential estates, outlets were built to cater to the upper classes.

1940s

Dense residential development supported a growing population throughout the middle of the 19th century, and Orchard Road became lined with Chinese, Sumatran and Jewish graveyards. Secondary streets restructured the region beginning 1900 as Cavenagh Road, Clemenceau Avenue and Emerald Hill were built in addition to a Singapore-Malayan railway that in 1903 first crossed Orchard Road by bridge at the site of Centrepoint Shopping Centre; this terminated at Tank Road Terminal near Fort Canning, and was replaced by an alternative line in 1932.[5]

Orchard Road's early development was spurred primarily by private enterprise, and its modern commercialisation was initiated with the 1905 opening of the Singapore Cold Storage Company – a retail storehouse and distribution business offering frozen meats, poultry and dairy products delivered from Queensland, Australia. Cold Storage's Orchard Road Market provided fresh produce, and the company expanded to become an outlet store in 1917.

A number of additional outlets moved to the region over the next four decades, consolidating by specialty: in the 1950s the Dhoby Ghaut region became a major motor vehicle distribution centre with numerous showrooms and garages catering to the wealthier classes.[6] Other examples of enclaves of high-ranking Europeans include the Teutonia Club built at the turn of the century on Scotts Avenue for the benefit of German expatriates; this later became the upscale Goodwood Park Hotel.

Orchard Road's national provenance made it a base for political operations. The Indonesian embassy once stood at the site of Wisma Atria, and the site of the Royal Thai Embassy currently borders that of the International Building. The embassies of Australia, India, Poland, Sweden, the United Kingdom and United States are all located in the vicinity of the Orchard Road corridor. The neo-Palladian-style Istana is also a major landmark here: sited on a 40-hectare estate, the Istana was originally home to the British Governor when completed in 1869 and became home to Singapore's President on the nation's independence.

The Infusion of Large-Scale, Mixed-Use Buildings

Singapore today is recognised internationally for the popularity of its malls and the extent to which mall activity is fundamental to national lifestyle. The establishment of the retail typology is attributable to Singapore's first up-scale department store constructed on Orchard Road in 1958 at the western intersection of Scotts Road and Orchard Road. Chinese salesman-turned-entrepreneur Tang Choon Keng established the CK Tang Shopping Centre, with a landmark Chinese green-tiled roof bearing strong resemblance to the Chinese Imperial Palace of the Forbidden City; like the Chinese-Peranakan shophouses, it continues to root Orchard Road in Chinese-influenced architecture.

With Singapore's growing need for employment during the mid-20th century, tourism was encouraged by the government to create jobs. With increasing numbers of visitors came a boom in hotel development, which included Forum Hotel, Ming Court Hotel (now Orchard Parade Hotel), Meritus Mandarin Singapore (now Mandarin Orchard Singapore), Dynasty Hotel Singapore (now Singapore Marriott Hotel) and Hilton Singapore. Today, more than 20 hotels are located in the Orchard Road Planning Area. Vertical growth was initiated by the 1949 construction of the MacDonald House office building, leading to high-rise residential buildings, such as Ngee Ann City, which combined living quarters with shopping, entertainment and office spaces.

By the 1960s Orchard Road had become the nation's centre for goods and shopping. The following is a description of Orchard Road in a 1962 Tourist Shopping Guide: 'Orchard Road has perhaps the most comprehensive selection in Singapore of Indian brass, Indonesian carvings, Malay, Thai and Indonesian silvers, and Chinese works of art, although the shops are scattered and Orchard Road is a long road to walk along in the heat of the day'.[7] The region marked by CK Tang and the subsequent Ngee Ann Building was the foremost retail centre, on which additional large-scale buildings were erected over time.

Through the 1960s and 1970s, Orchard Road became home to a succession of entertainment centres that supported retail malls: Lido Cinema, Pavilion Cinema and Orchard Theatre, which hosted the famed Jackie's Bowl. From the 1970s onward, the demand for large-scale shopping centres surged along with rising land values, driven most significantly by the construction of three Mass Rapid Transit stations in 1987.

TOURISM & SHOPPING IN SINGAPORE

In 2011

13.2 million
tourists visited Singapore

US$3.6 billion
was spent on shopping

US$17.7 billion
was spent in total

An Economic Engine

As an island with limited natural resources, Singapore's economy is heavily dependent on commercialism and tourism, and Orchard Road since the early 20th century has been a leading enterprise for these industries. From 2000-2009, for instance, Orchard Road was the nation's most visited destination for tourists, annually receiving more than 50 per cent of Singapore's visitors. The region's concentration of upscale retailers pay monthly rents that rank amongst the highest in the world.

Orchard Road's critical position as an intermediary stretch of land connecting the flourishing Singapore trading port with European estates in the island's earliest years as a British colony, primed it for success as a commercial centre. As such, the 2.2-kilometre length of Orchard Road has been subject to nearly constant structural development since its 1840's conversion from a series of nutmeg plantations. Today it remains prime real estate within Singapore's Central Region – the nation's commercial and entertainment core – that links Singapore's downtown Business District and Marina Bay with exclusive residential areas to the northwest. Over Orchard Road's 190-year history, the last decade is perhaps the most dynamic and comprehensive, with nearly every building fronting the street undergoing significant alteration.

ABOVE
Orchard Road, 1960s. Orchard Road became Singapore's retail landmark following the 1958 construction of CK Tang Shopping Centre, the nation's first up-scale department store.

1960s

The comprehensive plan intended to guide Orchard Road's evolution as a tourist destination to global renown by contributing to Singapore's growth as a 'garden city'.

The Orchard Road Master Plan

Throughout Orchard Road's development history, it has been subject to numerous government-driven overhauls at the planning level, intended to reposition it as a stronger force for the tourism industry. In 1991 the URA released the revised Concept Plan with ambitions to modernise the Orchard Road area as a vibrant commercial corridor with day and night activity. Four planning strategies were identified focusing on land use, transportation, development of key activity hubs centred on MRT stations and further development of the 'urbanscape'. Beginning in 1994 a series of adjustments included the clearing of vehicular access points to buildings along Orchard Road to expand the extent of the pedestrian promenade.

From 1999 to 2001 DP Architects served as lead consultant to an international team assembled to develop a schematic planning study for the Orchard Road Planning Area. The comprehensive plan intended to guide Orchard Road's evolution as a tourist destination to global renown by contributing to Singapore's growth as a 'garden city'. It treated the corridor as a large-scale urban garden that would accommodate the equatorial climate and facilitate greater connectivity with networks of landscaped plazas, courts, promenades and canopied walkways strengthened by additional lighting, water features and landscaping. Essential recommended alterations included extending sheltered connectivity and decreasing the number of pedestrian-vehicular intersections; more widespread goals included clarifying the limits of specific zones to create spaces of greater legibility, increasing the specialisation of malls and mitigating architectural uniformity. Many of these recommendations have become critical guides to Orchard Road's recent development.

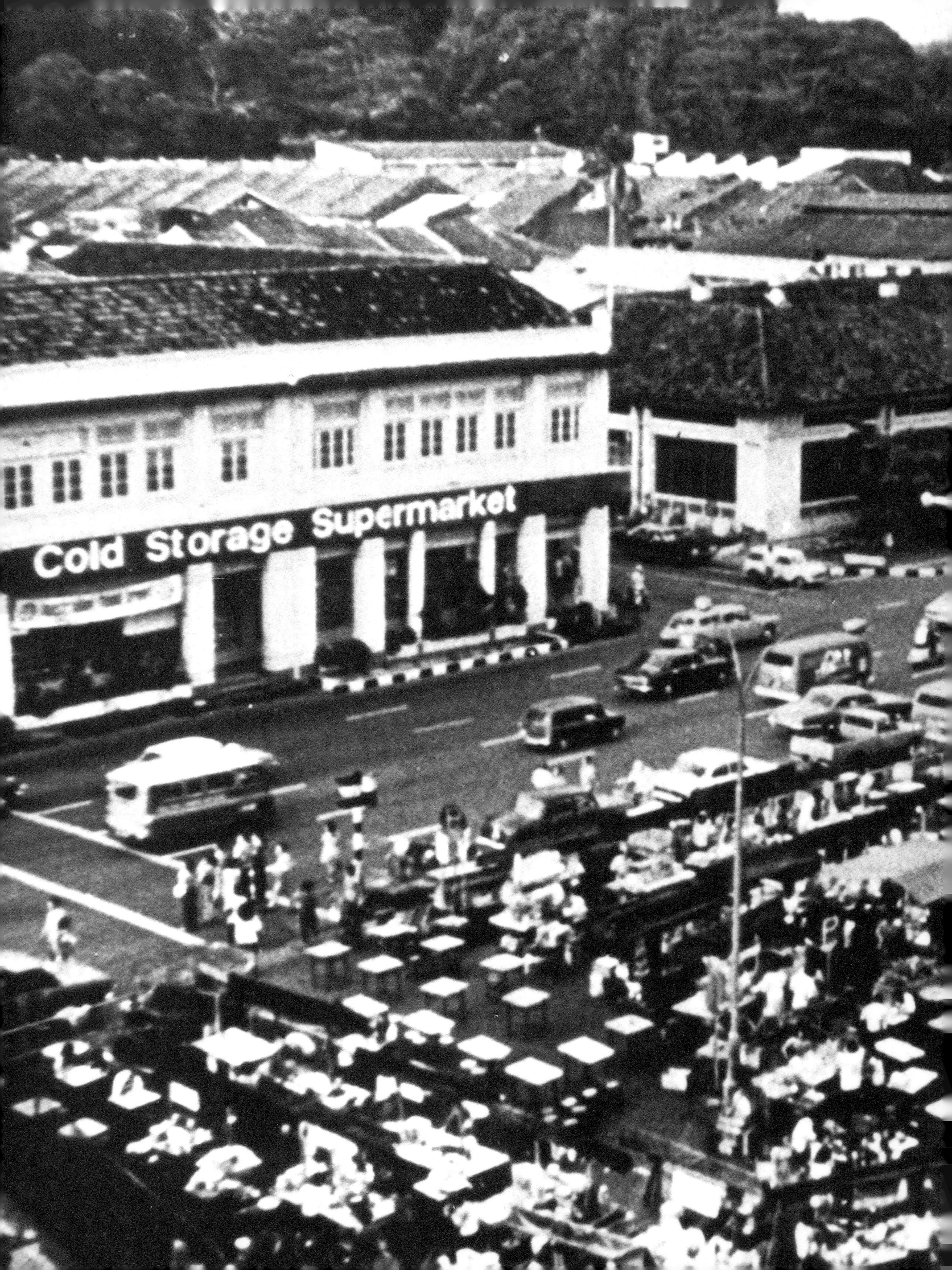
Cold Storage Supermarket

A History of Public Space

Gluttons Square was one of the first celebrated public spaces of Orchard Road. Established in the 1960s, this temporary, outdoor hawker market became famous amongst locals and tourists over the next decade, attracting immense crowds that came in search of popular local food. The lot where it was set up after hours each day, eventually became a multi-storey car park, serving the adjacent Specialists' Shopping Centre. While both of these structures were demolished to make way for Orchard Central mall, completed in 2009, the historic car park is in part commemorated as an architectural feature in the new mall's design, situated within the top two storeys of the 12-storey mall, and surrounded in a LED-animated envelope that has become a landmark structure within the core portion of Orchard Road.

Gluttons Square, 1970. Site of today's Orchard Central and The Centrepoint.

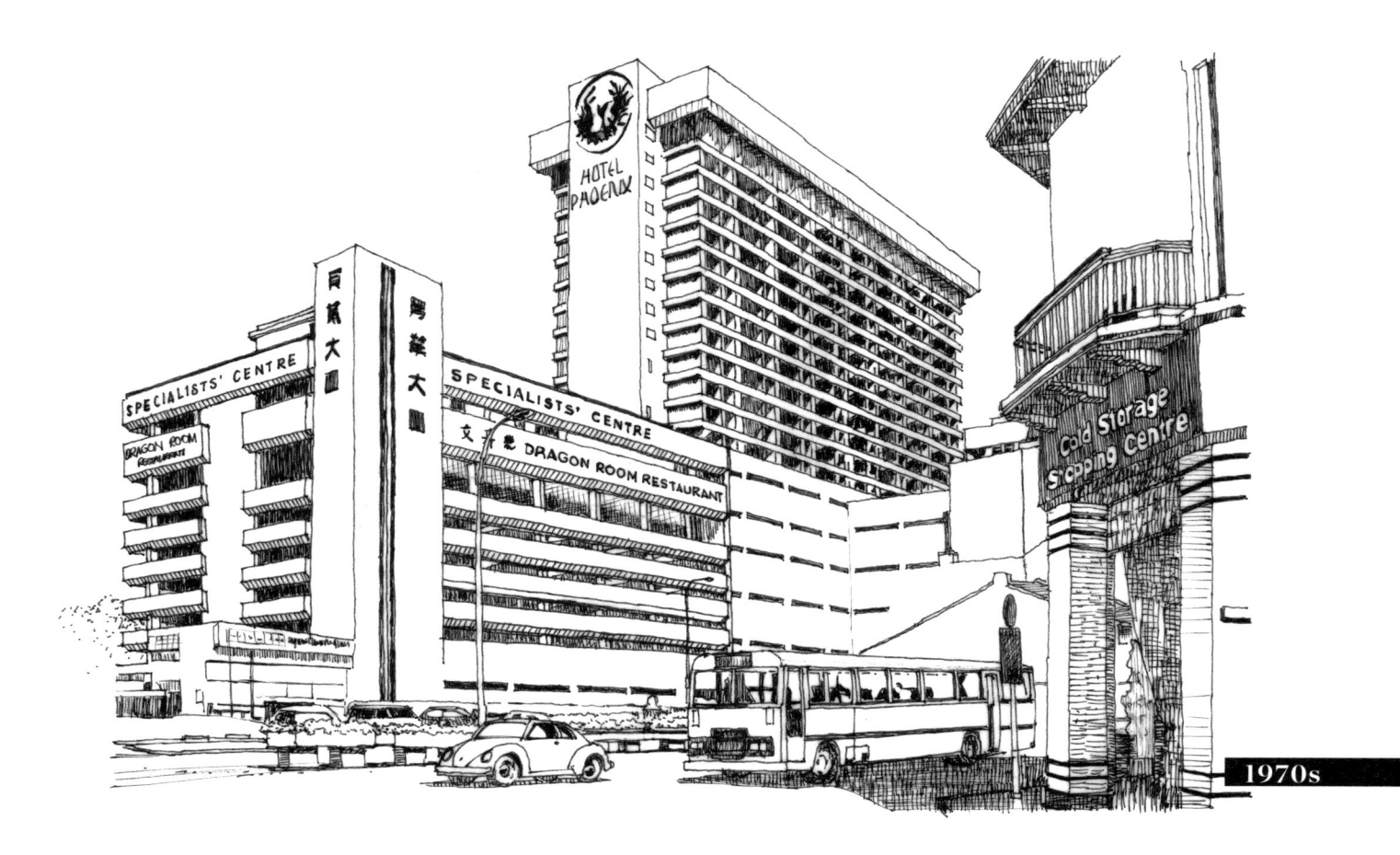

Remaining Relevant – Retail Architecture and Change

Retail is by nature a business of competitive trends – a store's relevance is contingent on its ability to remain fashionable. This pertains to architecture and the built environment just as it does to merchandise. With continually rising land value and rental costs, retail space on Orchard Road has depended upon a high rate of renovation, subjecting buildings to constant alteration. For example, CK Tang's 1958 department store was in 1982 renamed simply to 'Tang's' and transformed into a 33-storey hotel and a shopping complex before expanding its sales in 1987 to become a clothing and lifestyle retailer. Others include Paragon Shopping Centre, renovated by DP Architects in 1999, 2003 and 2009; and Wisma Atria, first designed by DP Architects in 1986 and subsequently re-worked in 2004 and again in 2012. The architectonic timeline of Orchard Road reveals changing opinions and development programmes that seek to renovate the face of the street and, at a grander level, the nature of shopping.

One of the drivers of Orchard Road's constant upkeep is the Orchard Road Business Association (ORBA), which since 1998 has acted as an arm of the STB to initiate investment capital for commercial growth; it represents the merchants of Orchard Road and comprises: landowners; owners of department stores; retailers; hoteliers and restauranteurs. ORBA organises public events for the region including the annual 'Christmas Light-Up' – a nationally attended celebration at the start of the holiday season ushered in by Singapore's President.

ABOVE
Orchard Road, 1970s. The widespread construction of high-rise towers dotted Orchard Road with hotels and commercial office spaces.

OPPOSITE
Orchard Road, 1970s. By 1974, Orchard Road became a fully one-way street, and over the next decade a number of low-rise buildings made way for large-scale shopping centres.

Retail is by nature a business of competitive trends – a store's relevance is contingent on its ability to remain fashionable.

1970s

1,000,000 +

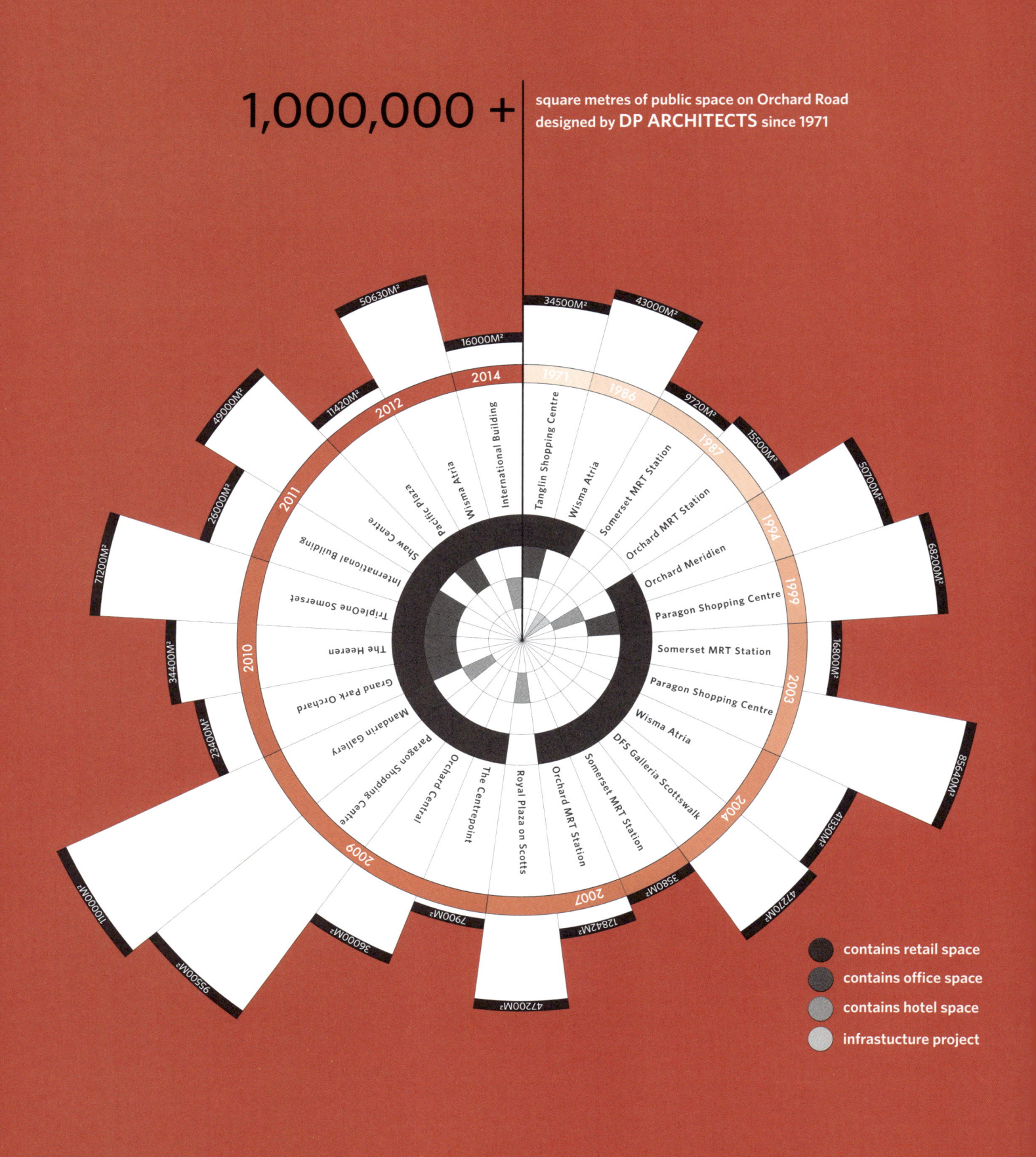

square metres of public space on Orchard Road designed by **DP ARCHITECTS** since 1971

- contains retail space
- contains office space
- contains hotel space
- infrastructure project

THE EVOLUTION OF ORCHARD ROAD   CHAPTER FOUR   69

Fifth Avenue — New York: $2150
Via Monte Napoleone — Milan: $962
Ermou Street — Athens: $283
Nanjing Road West — Shanghai: $249
Russell Street — Hong Kong: $1510
Post Street — San Francisco: $340
Avenue des Champs-Élysées — Paris: $873
Old Bond Street — London: $944
King Fahad Road — Riyadh: $447
Orchard Road — Singapore: $366
Central District — Seoul: $326
Chuo Street — Ginza, Tokyo: $610

2011 Rental Rates

Orchard Road ranked

26th

most expensive premier retail location globally.

4th

most expensive premier retail location in Asia.

Recent Development

In 2007 the Singapore Tourism Board STB began planning a US$26 million renovation to expand Orchard Road's pedestrian walkways and to create 'urban green rooms' for art exhibitions, performances or major events, such as the Chingay annual parade showcasing cultural performance groups.[8] The Urban Redevelopment Authority has also called for continued redevelopment of underground links, to benefit from increased connectivity and additional commercial retail space.

With the nation's highest residential land values assigned to sites just beyond Orchard Road's extents, the number of high-rise condominiums has steadily increased over the last decade. Condominium building was first made popular here by foreigners in the mid-20th century, and proposals for a string of new developments will continue to amplify the region's concentration of residential buildings and its complementary settled population in the immediate future.

ABOVE
2011 average retail rental rates for premier retail streets globally.
Values represent US$/square foot/year.

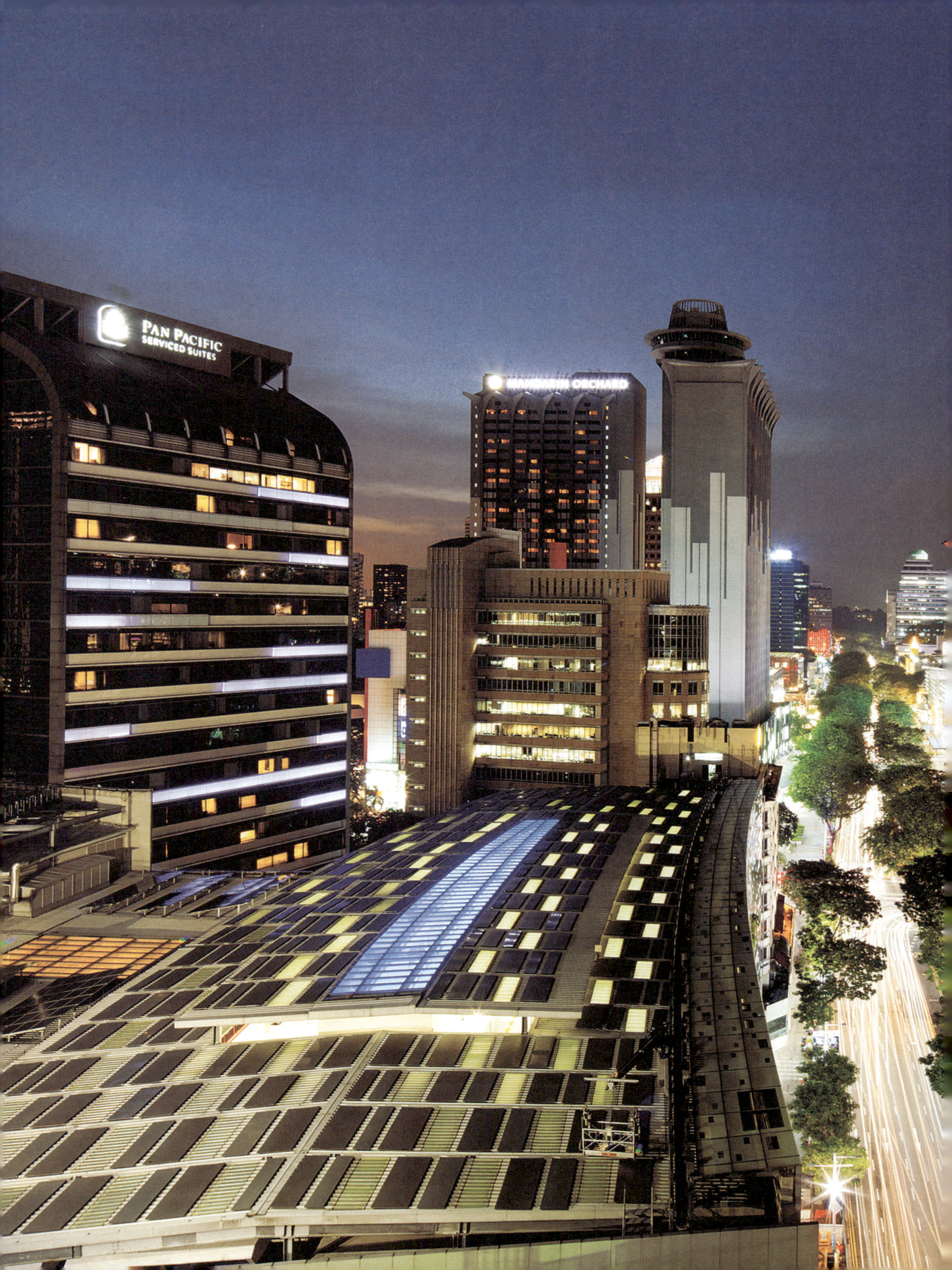
PAN PACIFIC
SERVICED SUITES
ORCHARD

Part 2:
CONTRIBUTIONS OF DP ARCHITECTS

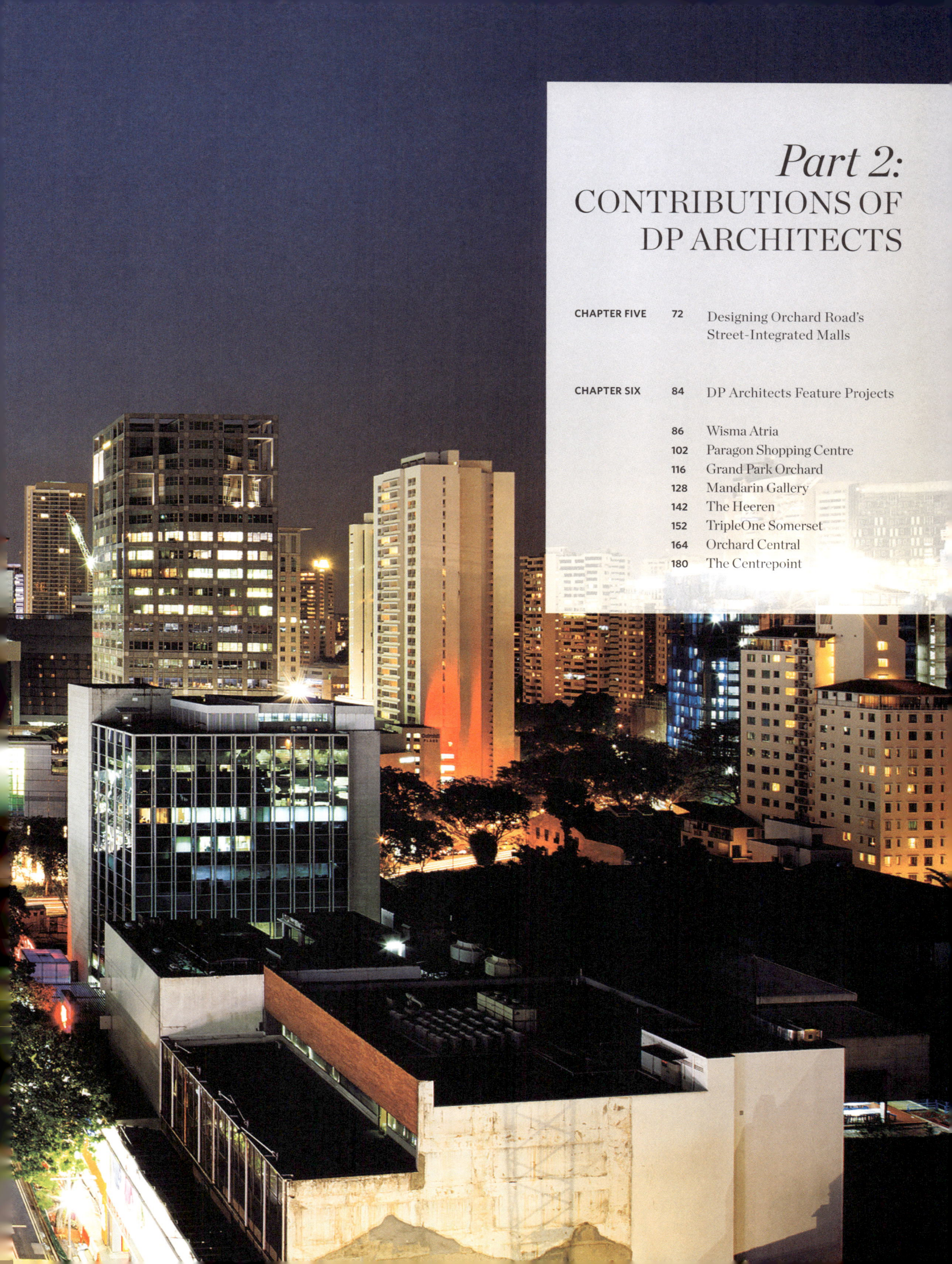

CHAPTER FIVE 72 Designing Orchard Road's Street-Integrated Malls

CHAPTER SIX 84 DP Architects Feature Projects

86 Wisma Atria
102 Paragon Shopping Centre
116 Grand Park Orchard
128 Mandarin Gallery
142 The Heeren
152 TripleOne Somerset
164 Orchard Central
180 The Centrepoint

2005

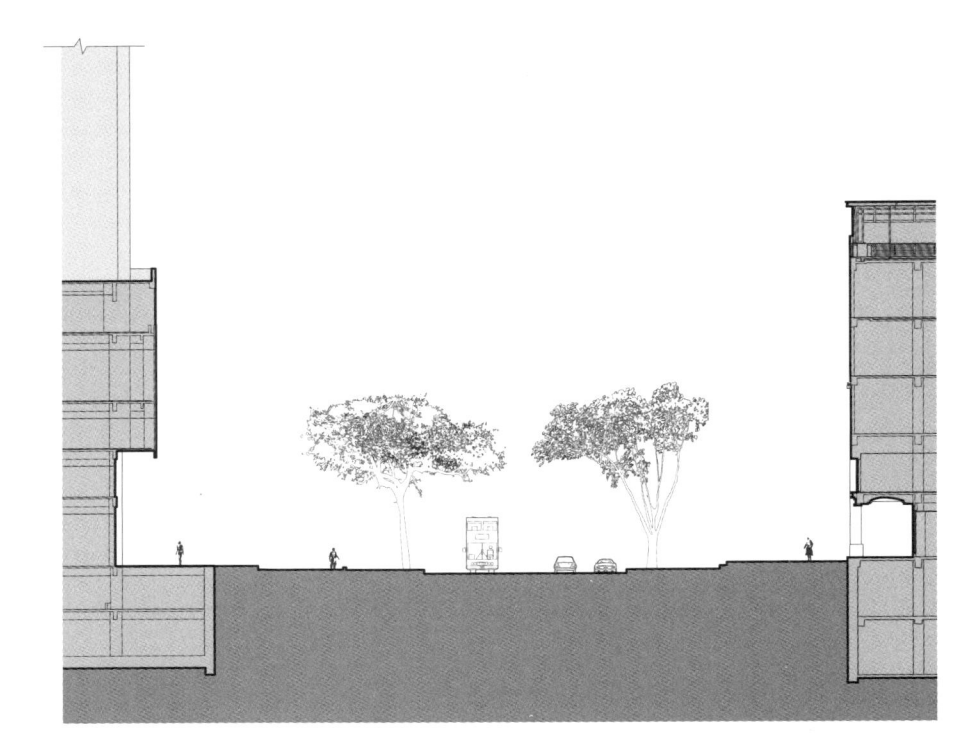

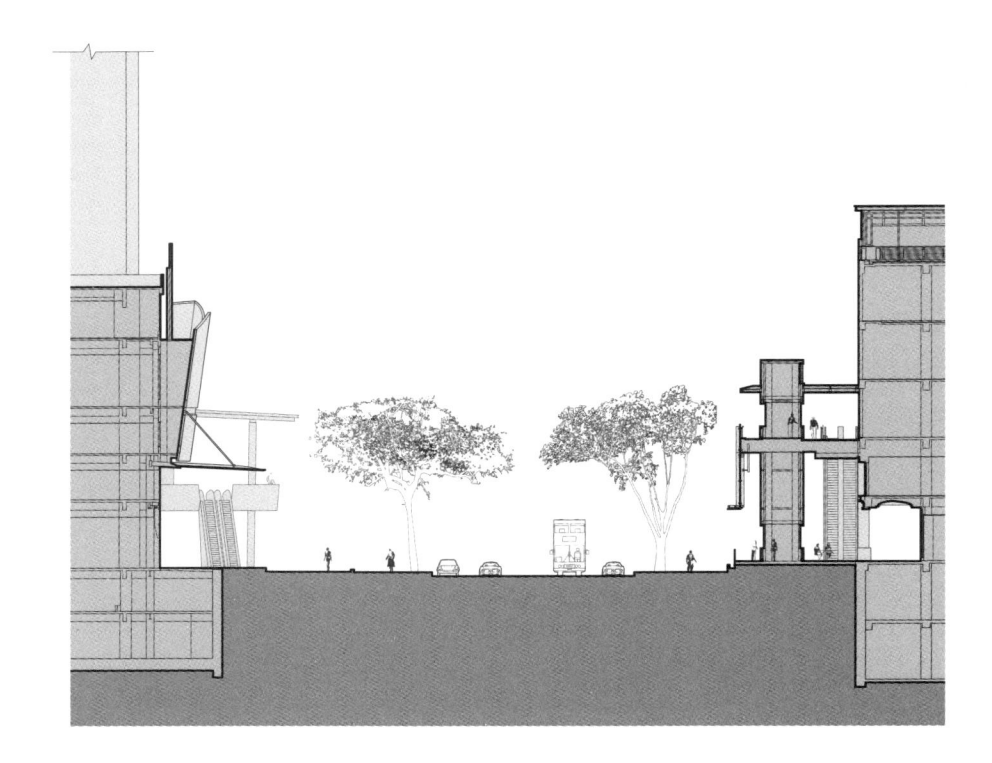

2009

Designing Orchard Road's
Street-Integrated Malls

DP Architects has re-worked over 1 million square metres of commercial space on Orchard Road over the last 45 years and, with the exception of Orchard Central, every one of these projects completed within the last two decades has been an alteration or retrofit. In some cases, DP Architects has had the opportunity to revisit the same building multiple times, over a period spanning a decade or more. Such phased work is a rare example of a comprehensive, long-term development of an urban centre by a single design firm. The work associated with DP Architects has certainly played a leading role in Orchard Road's transformation into one of Singapore's great urban spaces.

Orchard Road's prerequisite for constant change is driven primarily by economy and, as the region's rental rates continue to increase with land value, buildings must frequently be renovated to remain competitive – the uncontested value of retail programme accessible from the street has incentivised nearly every building owner to renovate in the last ten years. Because the built-up nature of Orchard Road renders complete demolition for rebuilding impractical, architects are left to contend with existing structures and so each design project becomes a combination of preservation and progression.

The most consistent trend of DP Architects' work on Orchard Road involves the functional and visual integration of podium-level retail with the space of the street. This trend has led over time to the establishment of a common mall form, best described as 'the street-integrated urban mall'.

The firm's projects generally fall into two categories. The first is an adaptation of the closed-form, top-lit, atrium-centred mall originally built between the 1960s and 1980s. The second is an infusion of retail space into the base of an existing structure originally programmed for other commercial uses, most commonly an office or hotel. Many of these projects have required inserting new programme into buildings with pre-existing, dominant architectural languages – this has introduced a number of design challenges.

By working at intervals over several decades, DP Architects has had the opportunity to engage in Orchard Road's gradual transformation in tandem with Singapore's changing social and economic conditions. Each project represents a layering of additions, alterations and reprogramming techniques that establish a strengthened dialogue with the sidewalk. By analysing the firm's design strategies with reference to the development trends of Orchard Road and changing construction technologies generally, we can begin to formulate a clearer understanding of the firm's varied works as a single set of explorations and ambitions.

OPPOSITE
A partial section through Mandarin Gallery and The Heeren.

Constructing a Retail 'Landscape'

It is difficult to speak about a single building on Orchard Road without referencing its many programmatic linkages and adjacencies. Despite a single shopping centre's ability to be viewed as a discrete object in space with clear boundaries and design style, each is highly interconnected above and below grade to a complex network of linkways. The spaces of the buildings, the street and the subterranean links bleed into one another, amounting to an immersive, three-dimensional urban topography that expands the streetscape and provides shoppers with great freedom of movement – a limitless number of potential routes by which to explore the street.

This composition allows one to liken Orchard Road to a retail 'landscape'.[1] Its nearly continuous form is made up of kilometres of interconnected commercial spaces that incorporate public transit and civic amenities. These amenities range from food and beverage kiosks to plazas and water features; indoor atria work like outdoor plazas distributed along the road and vertical connectivity by outdoor escalators multiplies this condition over many levels. Collectively, these factors embody a single, massive element of urban infrastructure, layered organically over time with outdoor escalators, exposed circulation routes, multi-level terraces and programmed garden roofs with views of the surrounding city. Few examples of such large-scale integration exist, and one might reference the multi-layered shopping district of Hong Kong as the closest precedent to Orchard Road in this aspect.

Orchard Road has a special dynamism that has to do with the flow of people and vehicles above and below ground and amongst the different spaces of the streets, building interiors, façades and roofscapes. Movement around and through this horizontally and vertically networked system activates the street and results in the promenade's rather continuous presence within the buildings.

The following characteristics of the retail landscape are primarily attributable to applied building codes and regional conditions; however, it is important to describe these in the context of DP Architects' design work to reveal the firm's significant influence on this system as a result of nearly 30 major projects.

Climate and Connectivity: Singapore's location immediately north of the equator subjects it to a climate of year-round extreme heat and humidity, a condition addressed on Orchard Road by its comprehensive network of underground links and covered passageways, strung along building perimeters to unify nearly the entire length of Orchard Road. All buildings are connected to a single circulatory system.

Underground networks, for instance, work in conjunction with the internal spaces of the malls as a complex extension to and expansion of Orchard Road's streetscape that is often programmed with retail spaces or eateries. The construction of the transformative MRT system in the 1980s sparked the networked development of below-grade linkages. Most large-scale structures built along Orchard Road prior to the MRT system were later subjected to programming overhauls that re-established entrances and ground-level layouts with reference to stations.

ABOVE
Ground-level plans of retail podia built or renovated by DP Architects.

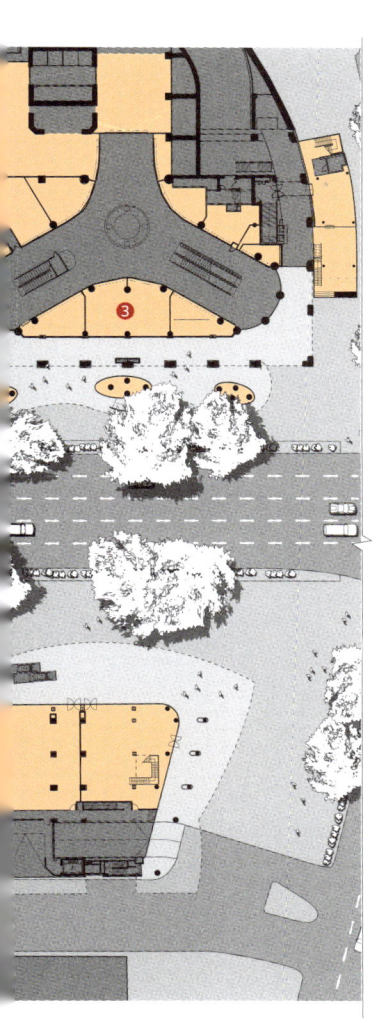

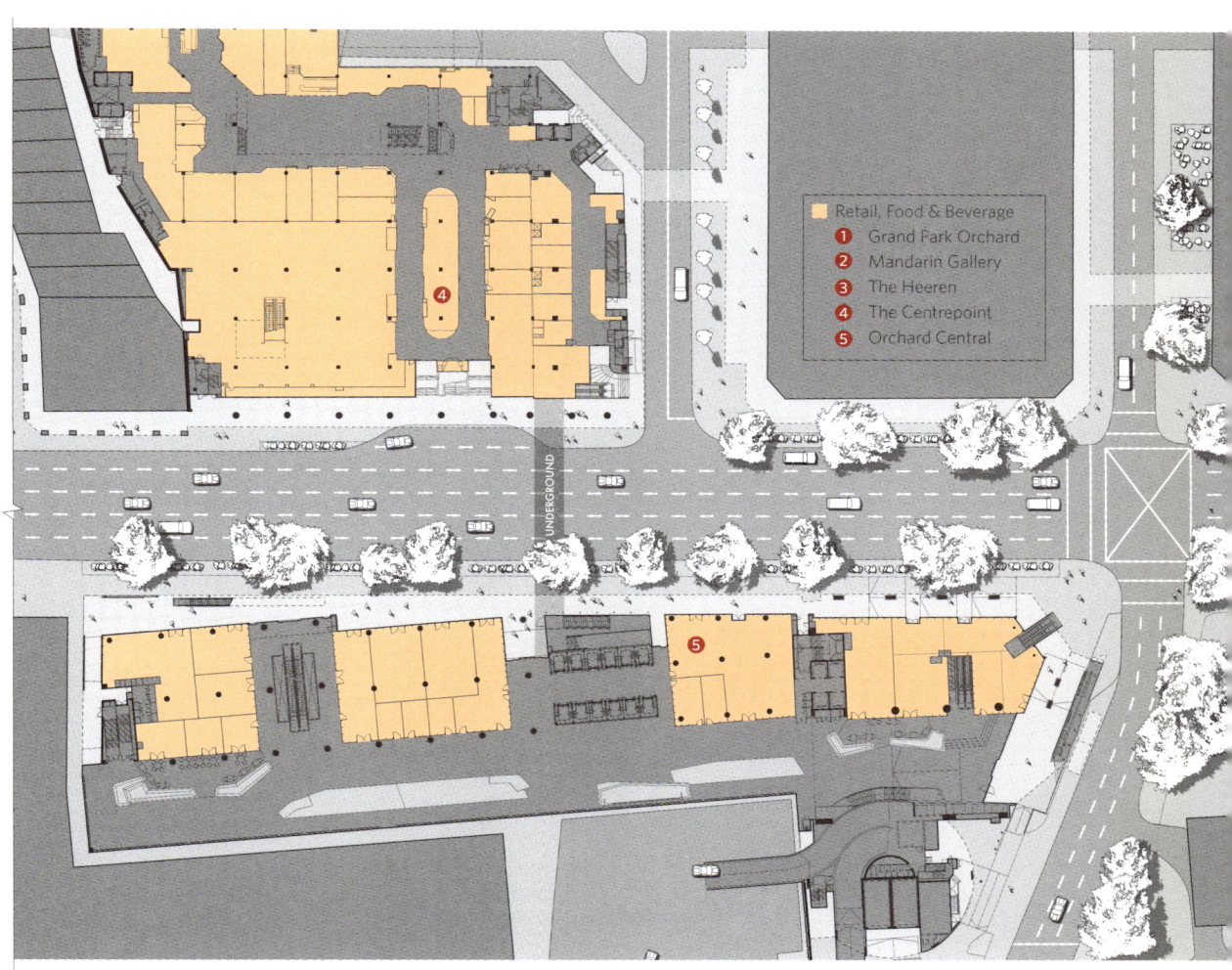

Retail, Food & Beverage
1. Grand Park Orchard
2. Mandarin Gallery
3. The Heeren
4. The Centrepoint
5. Orchard Central

Land value is especially dependent upon relationships with MRT stations and connectivity, with building heights and plot ratios subject to variable allowances based upon a site's proximity to a station.

Façades are programmed as inhabitable public spaces, amplifying building porosity by blending interior – exterior boundaries at the building perimeter. Vertical connectivity via façade circulation is established with upper-level terraces, verandahs and, in the case of Orchard Central, a 12th-storey roofscape.

Growth and Change: Shopping space requires periodic facelifts to remain fashionable and competitive amidst continued additions to the supply of retail building stock. Frequent renovation is inevitable. As a result, Orchard Road's impermanent architecture is progressively adapted to changes in social, consumer and commercial culture.

Form: The need for malls and, in many cases, individual flagship shops or anchor tenants to be visibly prominent has provided architects with a number of opportunities to explore form-making. The analogy of the landscape can be extended to describe a recent trajectory by which forms have become more geological and organic – by means of innovative building materials or construction methods. This is evidenced in the crystalline forms of Orchard Central and Wisma Atria, both by DP Architects, or the amorphous form of Ion Orchard by Benoy.

Commercial Value: Such immersive planning is fuelled by financial incentives. Integrated retail networks have activated Orchard Road as an engaging destination people come to for the very purpose of 'exploration' and, the strength of this network depends on a formulaic tenant mix. In other words, each mall benefits from increased connectivity with other malls.

REVAMPING ORCHARD ROAD'S FAÇADES

Architecture in cities is largely informed by building regulations, and the evolving set of codes specific to Orchard Road has been undeniably important to the development of its current form. Podium setback heights, for instance, and a common four-metre covered corridor, established to protect from rain and direct sunlight, are amongst the most evident codes affecting design across the streetscape.

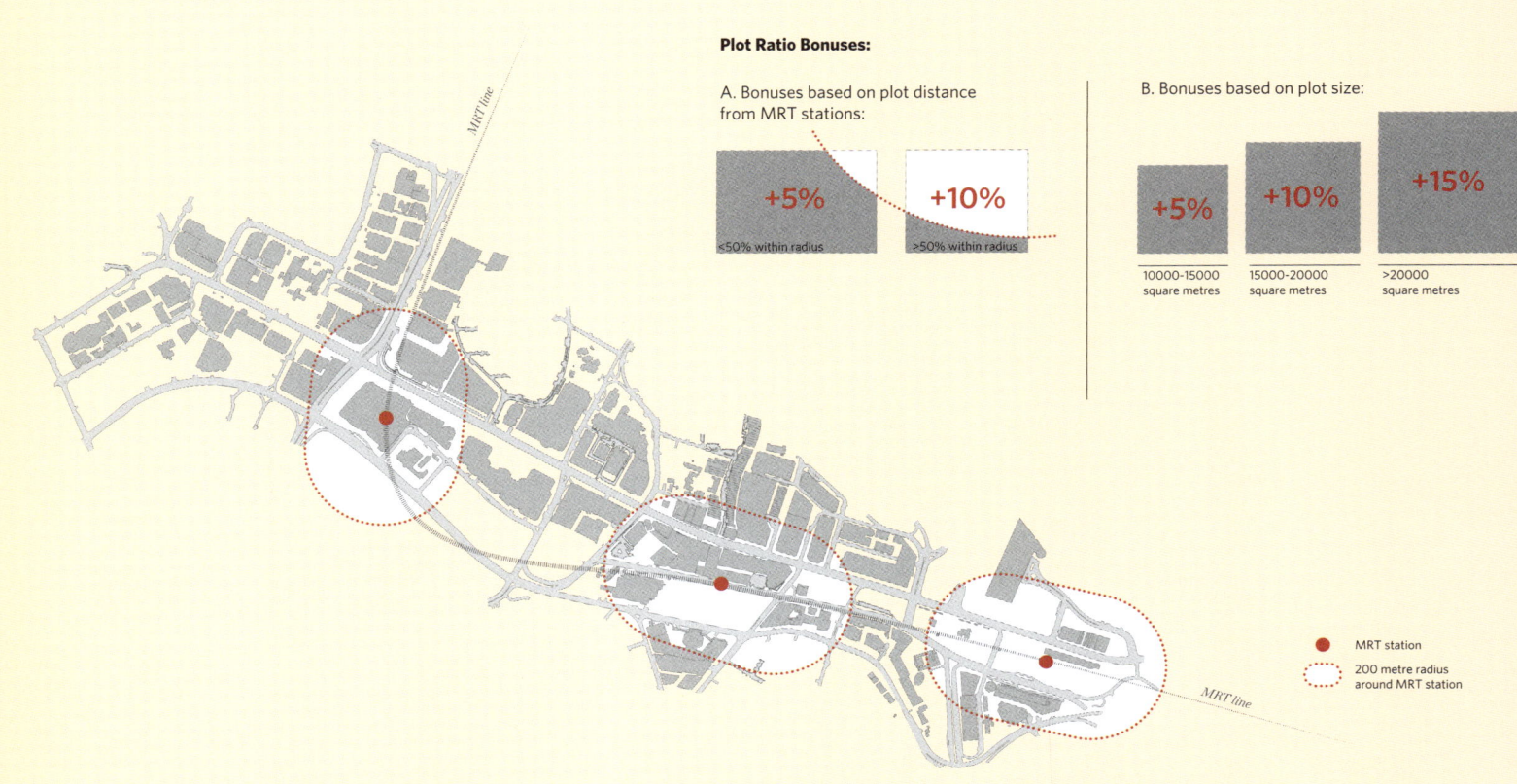

Plot Ratio Bonuses:

A. Bonuses based on plot distance from MRT stations:
- +5% <50% within radius
- +10% >50% within radius

B. Bonuses based on plot size:
- +5% 10000-15000 square metres
- +10% 15000-20000 square metres
- +15% >20000 square metres

● MRT station
⚪ 200 metre radius around MRT station

Most influential to the region's design overhauls through the last decade, the Urban Redevelopment Authority's 'Urban Design Plans and Guidelines for the Orchard Planning Area', was initiated in 2002 to encourage the articulation and increased dynamic design of the façade. By allowing up to 4-metre build-outs towards the street (this was increased to 7.5 metres in 2009), building owners are permitted additional gross floor area for rentable retail space in return for procuring a new façade with 'an interesting and cohesive architectural expression'.[2] Between 2002 and 2011, nearly every building fronting the street underwent a façade transformation in return for additional income-producing space. Bonuses are granted for façades that integrate 'urban verandahs' and programmed activity-generating spaces for food or entertainment along the sidewalk.

Designs are also shaped by requirements specialised on a per-site basis according to building tenders, and include: minimum covered walkway dimensions along the façade and within the building envelope; covered connections to adjacent buildings; space for kiosks and verandahs; and receiving underground passages that connect to MRT concourses. Guidelines are individualised to adapt each building to a site's specific patterns of human movement and circulation, according to the government's more widespread ambitions for unifying Orchard Road's many parts.[3]

ABOVE
Urban Redevelopment Authority building codes for Orchard Road Planning Area incentivise additions based on a site's distance to MRT stations.

Façade articulation codes, 2002

Urban Redevelopment Authority codes outline the extent to which shopping centres can extend into the space of the pedestrian sidewalk. Each façade design projects offers a unique response, endowing Orchard Road with a variety of architectural forms and materials.

60% OF BUILDING FRONTAGE LENGTH

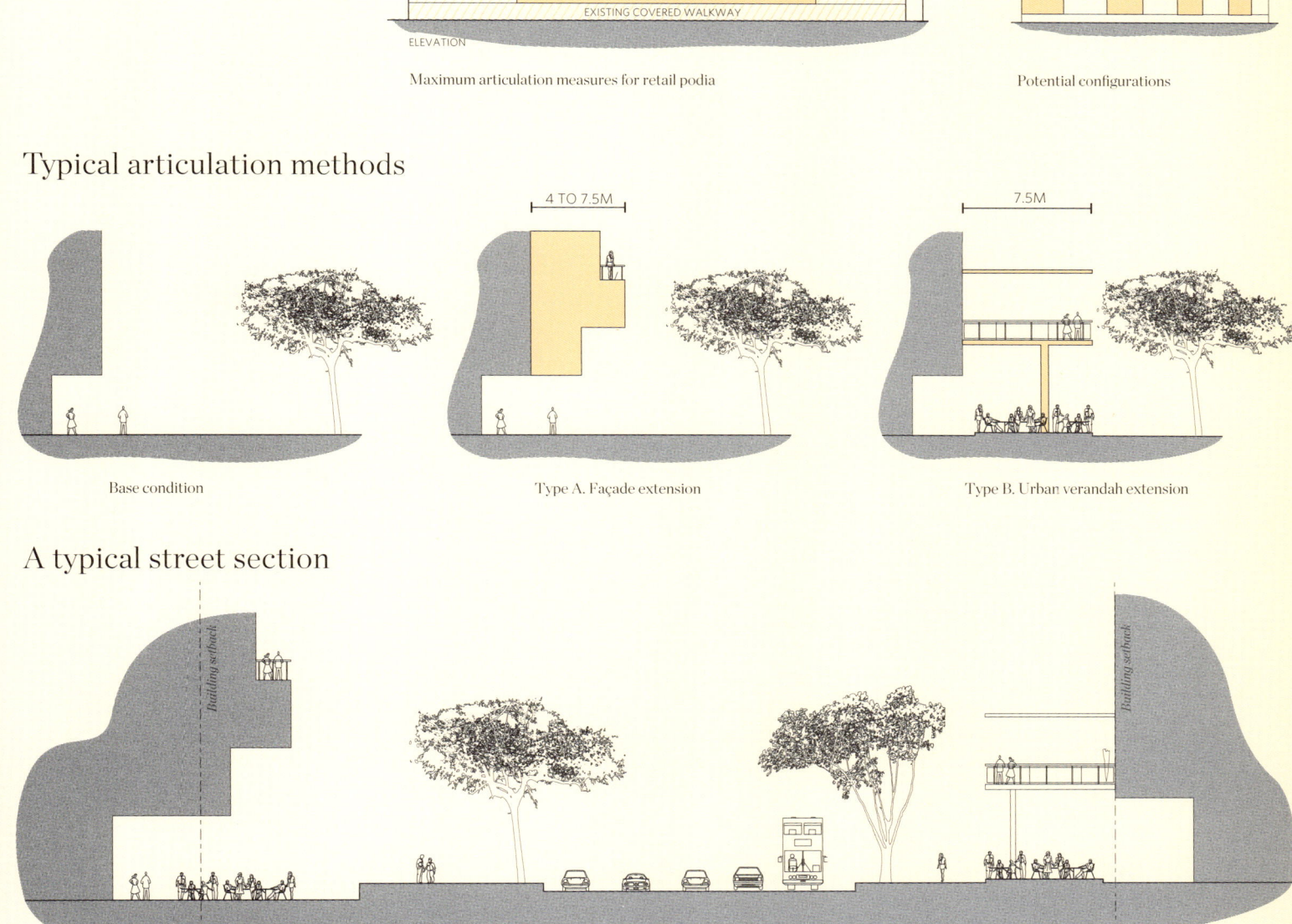

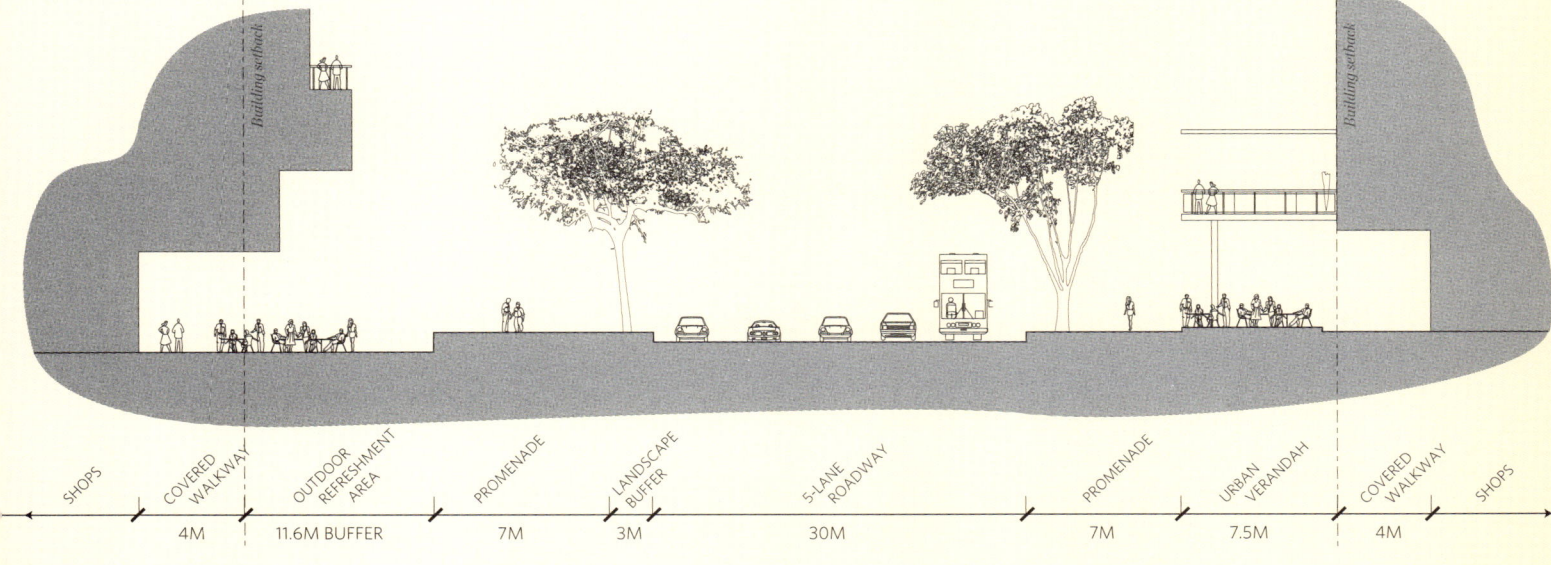

4M max.

EXISTING COVERED WALKWAY

PLAN

25% OF TOTAL PODIUM FRONTAGE

30M max.

EXISTING COVERED WALKWAY

ELEVATION

Maximum articulation measures for retail podia

Potential configurations

Typical articulation methods

Base condition

4 TO 7.5M

Type A. Façade extension

7.5M

Type B. Urban verandah extension

A typical street section

Building setback — Building setback

SHOPS	COVERED WALKWAY	OUTDOOR REFRESHMENT AREA	PROMENADE	LANDSCAPE BUFFER	5-LANE ROADWAY	PROMENADE	URBAN VERANDAH	COVERED WALKWAY	SHOPS
	4M	11.6M BUFFER	7M	3M	30M	7M	7.5M	4M	

STOREFRONT DESIGN TOOLS

By consistently applying a set of design parameters to each of its façade renovations, DP Architects has changed the face and functionality of Orchard Road. These operations have helped to reshape a building's connectivity with the street.

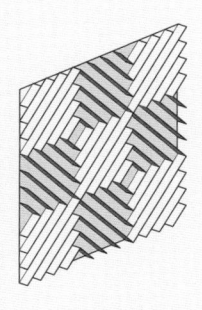

Materiality

Materiality and patterning is used as a mechanism for architectonic branding. The aggregated build-up of small-scale patterns establishes textures across surfaces: recognisable, visual graphics or motifs that lend to mall identity.

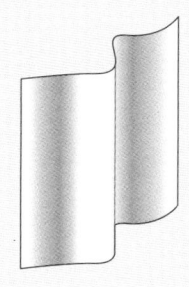

Articulation

Active profiles have a powerful effect on visual interest by engaging the eye. The Avenue des Champs-Élysées is lined with Neoclassical buildings dramatically articulated by columns, cornices and window details. In comparatively contemporary streets, such as Orchard Road, active building profiles are calibrated on a larger scale by more varied geometries, both sectionally and in elevation.

DP Architects has instituted a wide range of forms that work at two scales to break up the monotony of otherwise simple rectangular floorplates and expansive elevations. At the scale of the building, macro-forms serve to retain overall coherence: Mandarin Gallery and The Heeren, for instance, employ sweeping curvilinear canopies and undulating surfaces; The Centrepoint and Paragon Shopping Centre are divided into sequences of block forms.

Micro-detailing works on a smaller scale to induce surfaces with patterns or articulations, a technique often dependent upon materiality or lighting technologies: the double-glazed elevations of Grand Park Orchard are backed with LEDs to illuminate a frosted herringbone pattern; the metal rainscreen fronting Orchard Central's upper-level car park is also embedded with a system of dynamic LEDs.

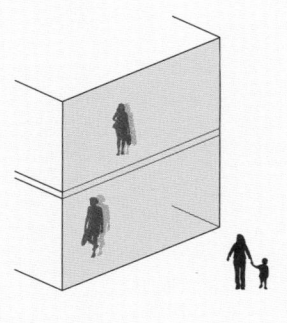

Transparency

To resituate malls in greater dialogue with the activity of the street, the frontages of existing buildings are altered to support all-glass façades. Increased transparency enhances visual connectivity amongst interior commercial spaces and spaces of the promenade. Entire podia have been transformed into multiple-storey showcase windows.

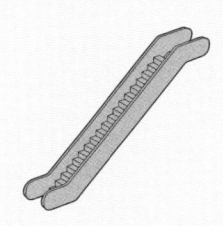

Connectivity

Escalators are installed into the frontages of malls to increase circulation and to provide direct access to upper levels and basements from the sidewalk. This connectivity increases the commercial value of otherwise secondary spaces.

DESIGNING ORCHARD ROAD'S STREET-INTEGRATED MALLS — CHAPTER ONE

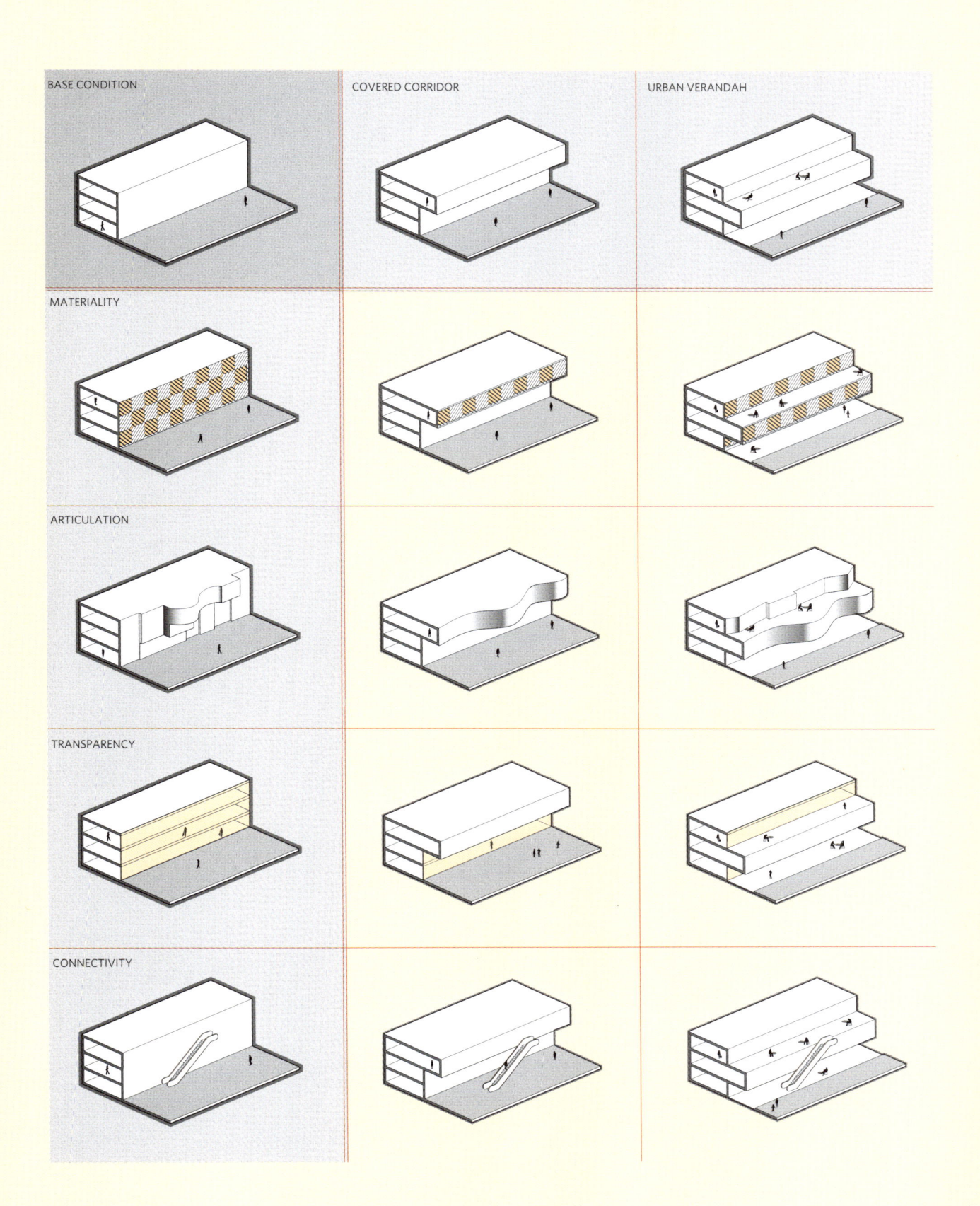

	BASE CONDITION	COVERED CORRIDOR	URBAN VERANDAH
MATERIALITY			
ARTICULATION			
TRANSPARENCY			
CONNECTIVITY			

ABOVE
Design matrix. The façade design tools are applied in a variety of different ways to transform the interface between the mall and sidewalk.

Project Genealogy – Connecting the Dots

Designing for Orchard Road over 40 years, DP Architects has had the opportunity to apply a range of functional methodologies, experiment with geometric forms and interpret building codes in a number of ways, as contextual conditions or available construction technologies evolved. While the buildings of Orchard Road are not necessarily unified architecturally, the design ideas that have been consistently applied to projects by DP Architects have to a great extent unified the road functionally. A legible DNA of strategies can be detected across the firm's many projects:

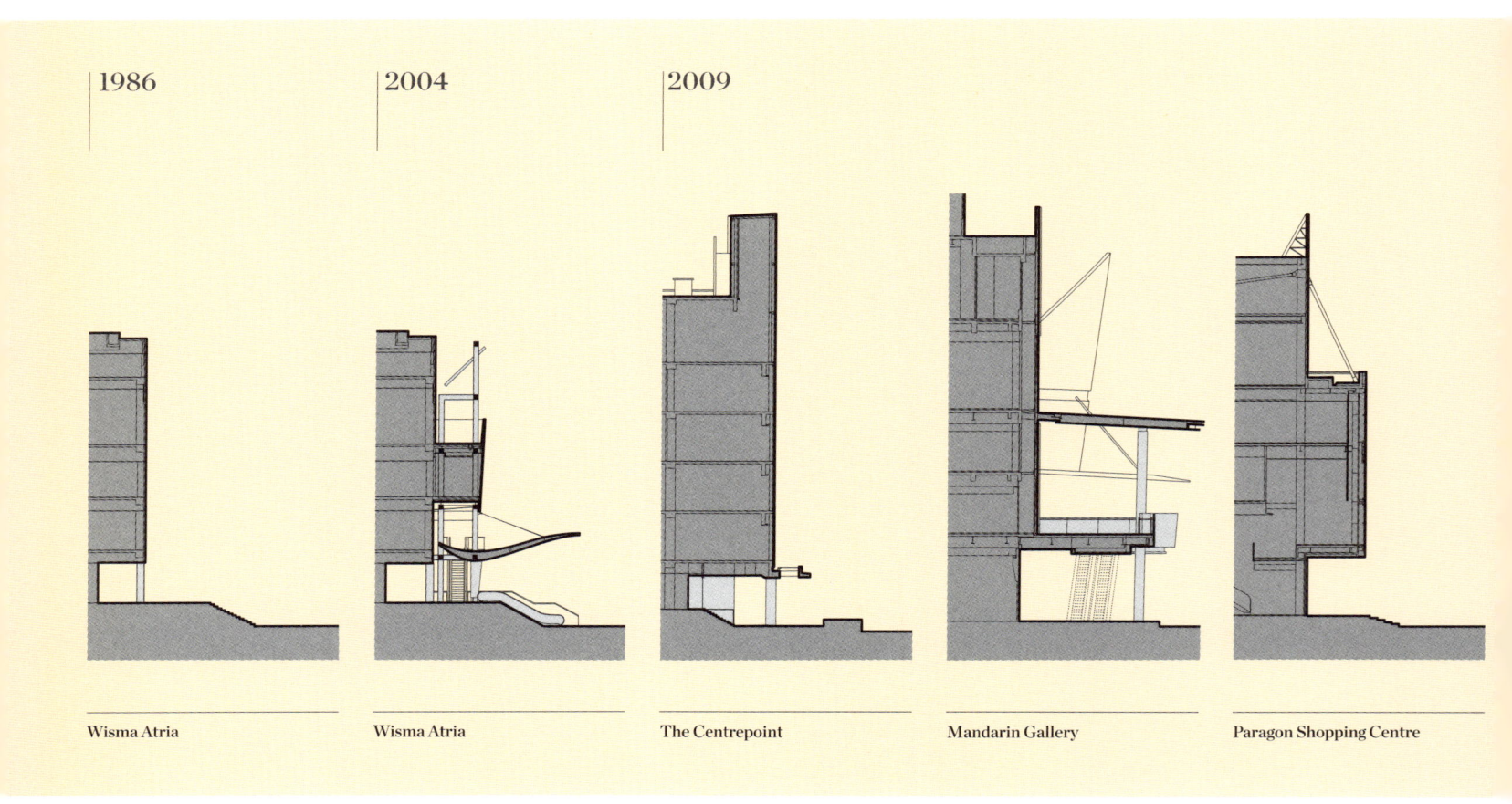

1986	2004	2009		
Wisma Atria	Wisma Atria	The Centrepoint	Mandarin Gallery	Paragon Shopping Centre

The 2004 project for Wisma Atria was canonical for Orchard Road's development. Its implementation of external escalators and fully-transparent frontages to showcase interior spaces became two design elements applied in nearly every subsequent project. Formal connections and material applications can also be made across projects, for instance, in the crystalline geometries that were first used in the design of Orchard Central and replicated in the 2012 alteration of Wisma Atria; similar comparisons can be made between the curvilinear glass forms in the façades of The Heeren and Mandarin Gallery.

All explorations to this point can be described as having culminated with Orchard Central in 2009 – one of the few new-build malls on Orchard Road in recent years, and the first high-rise mall in Singapore. Being a new construction, DP Architects was able to apply lessons learnt from previous explorations in the conception of a mall built from zero. It is no coincidence that this new mall is embedded with many characteristics of the typical section that is characteristic of Orchard Road's otherwise readapted malls.

ABOVE
A comparison of storefronts designed by DP Architects, 1986-2012.

| 2010 | | 2012 |

| Orchard Central | TripleOne Somerset | Grand Park Orchard | The Heeren | Wisma Atria |

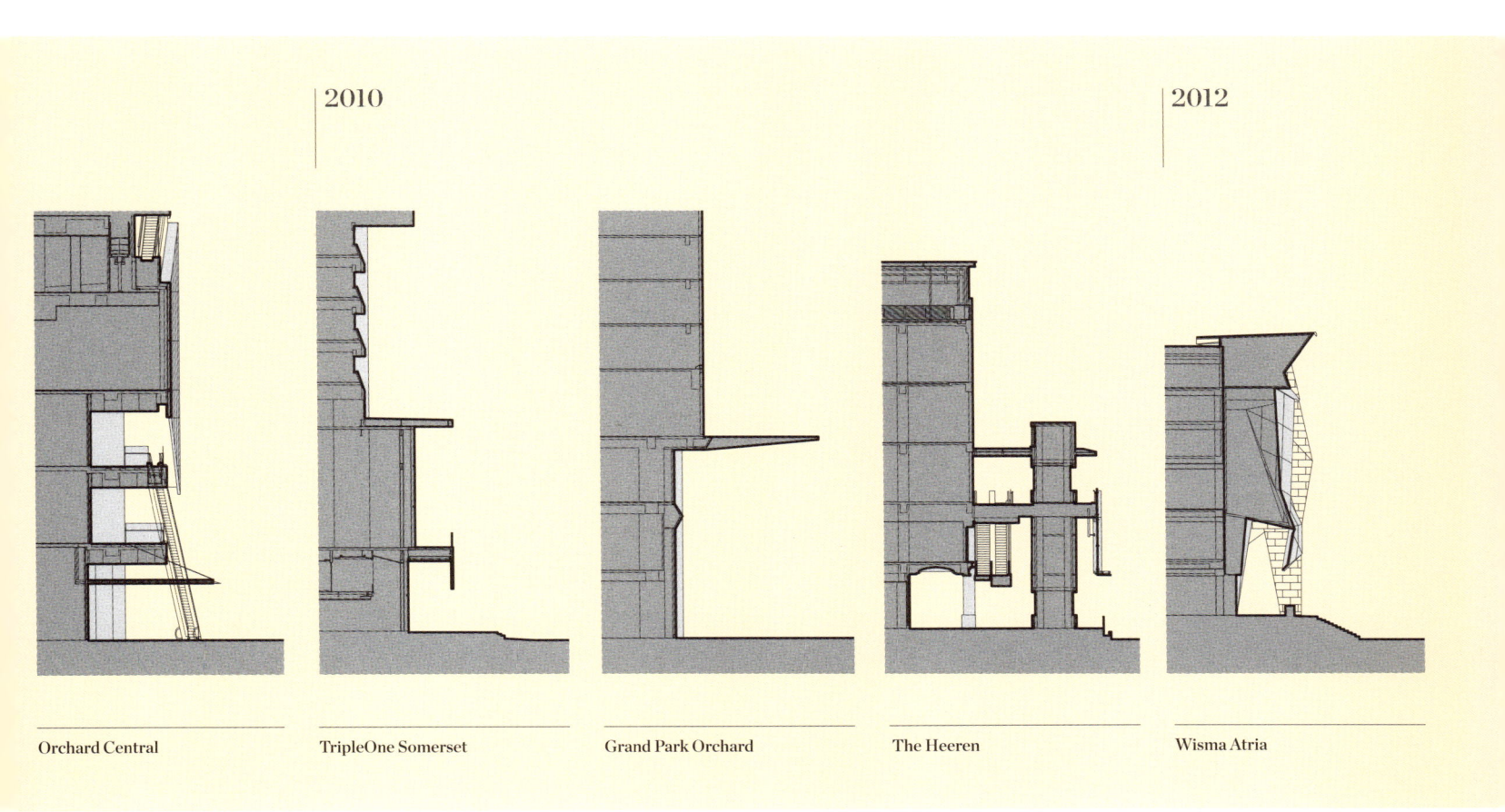

Orchard Central is a strengthening element of Orchard Road's retail 'landscape', and might prove to be the model by which future Orchard Road projects under DP Architects are designed. Its fully-inhabitable façade articulates vertical circulation; the building's design activates all 12 storeys of the mall with street connectivity, and offers a number of vantage points from open-air escalators and landings; the 12th-storey, landscaped roof deck is directly accessible from the sidewalk so layers the building with an extension of the public street space.

The street-integrated mall is an urban form that has developed in a progressive, piecemeal fashion. As Kenneth Frampton has observed in his foreword, it is a form that has not yet been fully realised, but serves, rather, as a basis for continued experimentation. It is representative of an evolving set of ideas that underlie each of DP Architects' projects, and embodies the tools the firm exercises in its effort to integrate Orchard Road's mall spaces with the space of the pedestrian streetscape.

THE TYPICAL SECTION

By analysing today's buildings in section an array of programmatic relationships are exposed that can provide us with a greater understanding of Orchard Road's functionality. Many of DP Architects' consistently-applied design moves have contributed to the making of a 'typical' mall section.

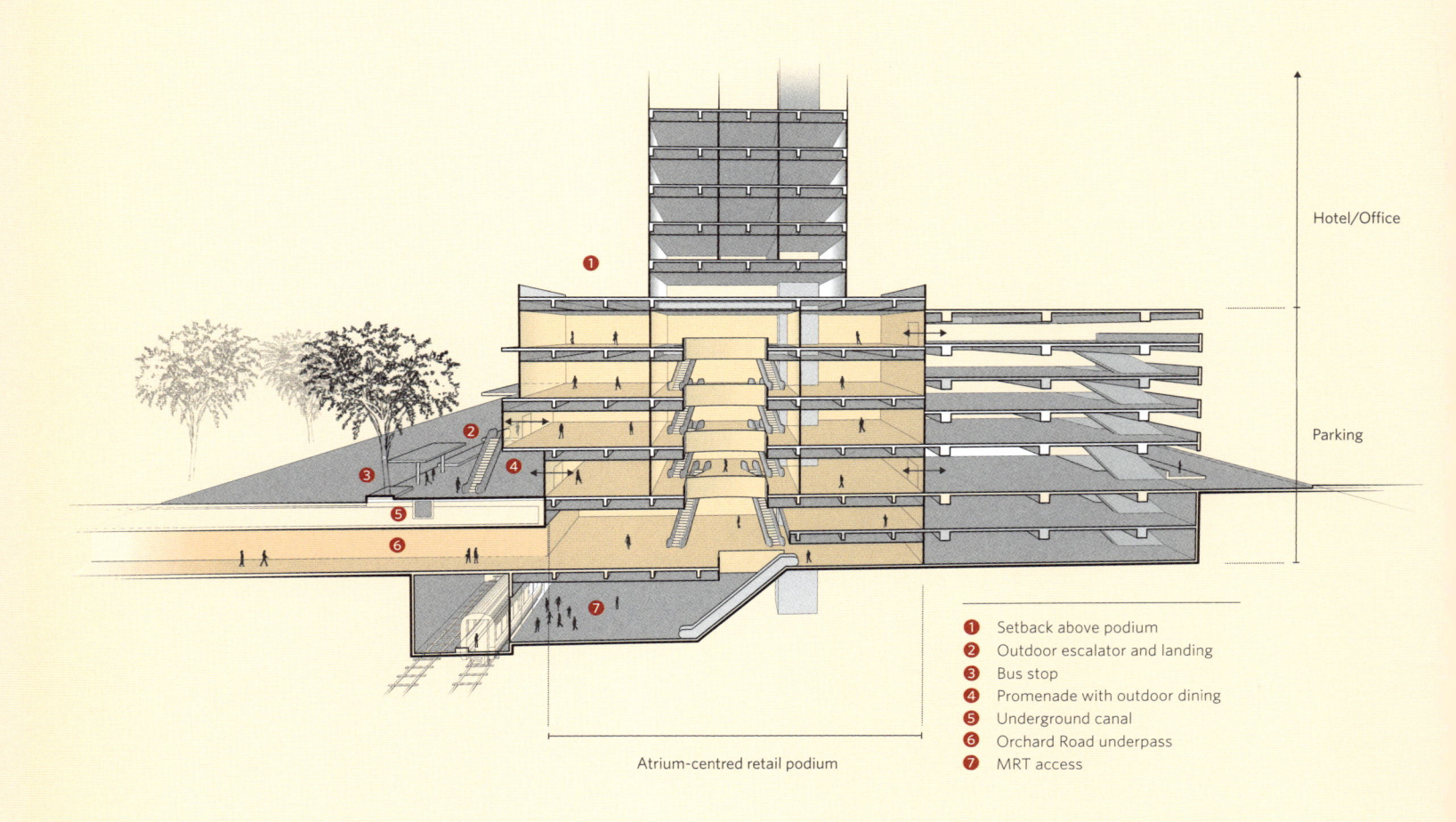

① Setback above podium
② Outdoor escalator and landing
③ Bus stop
④ Promenade with outdoor dining
⑤ Underground canal
⑥ Orchard Road underpass
⑦ MRT access

Atrium-centred retail podium

Hotel/Office
Parking

It is comprised of **mixed-use programme**: an atrium-centred mall that opens to the street, commercial office spaces or hotels, multi-storey car parks and often additional basement-level retail. The atrium tends to work as the mall's internal centre of activity.

It is served by a **below-grade mass transit system** that is the primary point of access to the structure and to the space of the street.

Additional access to amenities is offered at-grade, served by bus transit stops; and over multiple levels with entries via outdoor escalators, mall-to-mall linkages or integrated, private car parks.

Projecting upper-storeys over the promenade provide protective coverage to circulation and alfresco dining verandahs below or additional exterior spaces above in the form of terraces.

Renovations have successively overlaid **generic floorplates** and elevations with more expressive, exploratory geometries. Original floorplates are designed as simple and rectilinear with entry points on multiple sides of the building that converge within the atria.

An Ongoing Evolution

Malls in Singapore are sites of leisure and entertainment. As in many Asian countries, the recreational patterns that have emerged in 21st-century Singapore position malls as central to urban life. Malls contain spaces capable of supporting a range of activities so large that the performance of the individual building is comparable to that of a traditional city. In climates as harsh as Singapore, urban malls serve the particular role of mitigating the need for outdoor pedestrian travel.

Throughout the United States, Europe and Asia, the mall was a post-war, mid-20th-century phenomenon, initially conceived to replace the traditional shopping street and resulting in introverted forms intentionally disconnected from the urban fabric. In the case of Orchard Road, these forms have been redeveloped over recent decades as a result of public and private desires to improve the performance of the streetscape and its ability to draw visitors. The success of the individual shopping centre here is, after all, a function of the success of the street, and vice versa. Since the construction of the Mass Rapid Transit (MRT) system in the late 1980s, surging numbers of visitors to Orchard Road have compelled the Urban Redevelopment Authority to implement a series of specialised building codes.

DP Architects has consistently responded with design solutions that have dramatically influenced the nature of the street. A sequence of projects beginning with the alteration of Wisma Atria in 2004 have helped in part to reverse the disconnected nature of existing structures: transparent glass façades have converted entire building elevations into storefront windows; outdoor escalators have connected sidewalks with multiple storeys of retail above and below-grade, developing a more expedient relationship with the street; and urban verandahs, 'green rooms' and roof decks with public art have established new civic identities for buildings.

ABOVE
The implementation of external escalators has transformed the connectivity among the sidewalks and commercial spaces on multiple levels.

84 PART 2 CONTRIBUTIONS OF DP ARCHITECTS

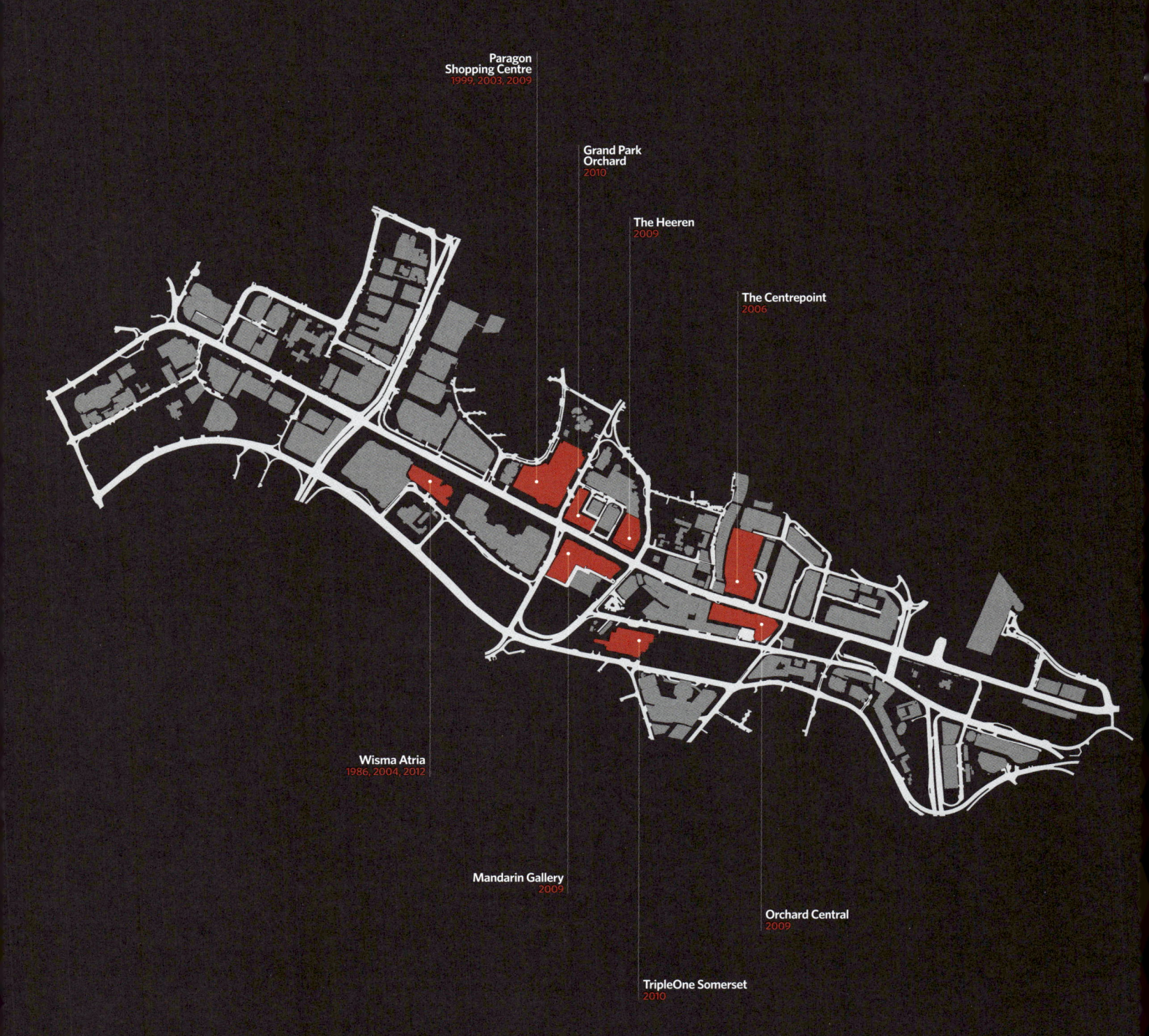

Paragon Shopping Centre
1999, 2003, 2009

Grand Park Orchard
2010

The Heeren
2009

The Centrepoint
2006

Wisma Atria
1986, 2004, 2012

Mandarin Gallery
2009

Orchard Central
2009

TripleOne Somerset
2010

DP Architects
Feature Projects

The comprehensive influence of DP Architects on Orchard Road's form demands an analysis that records this firm's work as an important part of the region's modern history. The practice has responded to local design codes, municipal demands and changing consumer patterns over 40 years, to generate the street-integrated urban mall that is unique to Orchard Road.

Wisma Atria, first built by DP Architects in 1986, was the first building to undergo a full reincarnation by which an existing closed-form commercial block was opened up to the street, and in 2004 the firm was able to revisit its initial design, making use of a set of 2002 building codes to reinvent the interface between multiple storeys of retail programme and the pedestrian promenade. The implementation of outdoor escalators leading to upper storeys completely transformed Orchard Road's customer circulation patterns, and DP Architects has since utilised this design strategy in a number of subsequent projects, to the extent that it has become a typical design characteristic for the region's malls.

The following eight projects are explored case by case, referencing site-specific history and urban conditions to outline design concepts and resulting architectural forms. Each project is highlighted by a series of material and programmatic strategies aimed at unifying a large-scale shopping centre with the public street space by engaging the pedestrian. The selected anthology focuses on the firm's projects completed within the first decade of the new millennium and represents a larger body of work that has positioned Orchard Road as a premier retail streetscape.

OPPOSITE
A key map of Orchard Road highlighting eight projects featured in this chapter.

WISMA ATRIA
VICTORINOX
SWISS ARMY
LAUNCH OF
SUMMER COLLECTION
ALL WATCHES
WISMA ATRIA

Feature Projects
Wisma Atria

Year Completed : 1986, 2004, 2012
Project Type : New build (1986); addition and alteration (2004, 2012)
Area : 40,000 square metres (1986); 41,300 square metres (2004, 2012)

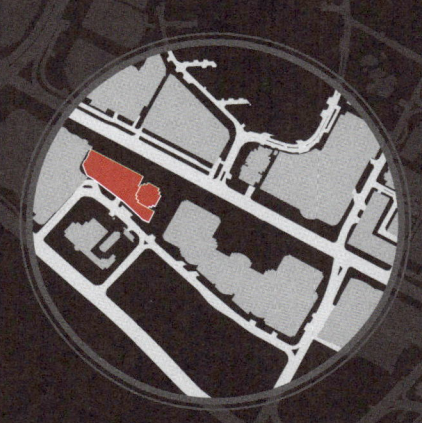

The 2004 transformation of Wisma Atria can be considered the transition project for DP Architects towards Orchard Road's extroverted urban mall type. A façade expansion created new visual and functional links between the interior retail space and exterior promenade; the use of glass increased transparency and external escalators connected upper retail storeys directly to the street by means of an external escalator – design moves that comprehensively resituated a 1980's retail mall as a street-integrated shopping centre. First designed by DP Architects in 1986 with additions and alterations in 2004, Wisma Atria is undergoing a third incarnation by DP Architects planned to open in 2012. The mall's architectural progression, like many retail developments on Orchard Road, continues to take place within the contours of the building's original structure.

Once land reserved for a Chinese cemetery, this site was sold and developed in the 1950s, becoming home to Ngee Ann City – one of Orchard Road's first large-scale commercial centres – in addition to the adjacent Indonesian Embassy, opened in 1967; the embassy site was later redeveloped in 1986, designed by DP Architects as a 22-storey office tower with a 5-storey retail podium.

OPPOSITE
The 2004 makeover of Wisma Atria.

The architecture of Wisma Atria in 1986 aligned with contemporaneous global design patterns for retail buildings of its scale. An introverted, atrium-centred 'box form' mall, its blue-tile cladding became emblematic for the centre. Built prior to the adjacent Orchard Mass Rapid Transit (MRT) station, the building has since become highly connected, linked underground both to the MRT station to the west and Ngee Ann City Shopping Centre to the east.

Wisma Atria's 2004 facelift made it the first retail centre in the region to have undergone a reversal of its closed form. Its blue-tile cladding was largely replaced with glass, while a unifying backdrop blue grid was implemented to retain the mall's representative colouring. A blue, four-metre deep frame expanded the façade toward the promenade as permitted by 2002 local ordinances instituted to encourage architectural dynamism. The new storefront dismantled the older building's shell by juxtaposing glass-enclosed spaces with empty squares of the grid, and blurring the line between the interior commercial space and the public space of the sidewalk. The three-dimensional grid operated as a moment of transition.

This frame reworked sidewalk circulation and the surrounding urban context by encouraging pedestrians to reposition their routes with reference to the grid. Focal points within the grid – landings or entrances – created new axes of circulation, and an external escalator connected multiple levels of retail with the sidewalk, functionally transforming these upper storeys into street-accessible space. In all these ways, the addition to Wisma Atria developed a striking new relationship with the street.

TOP
The façade before and after its 2004 renovation.
BOTTOM RIGHT
Façade design concept sketches.

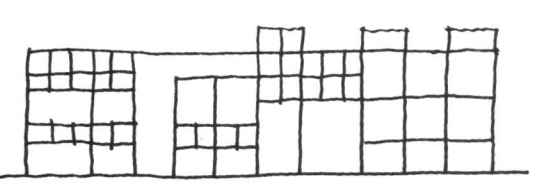

Grid Study — superimpose on Facade organisational grid for signs, escalators......

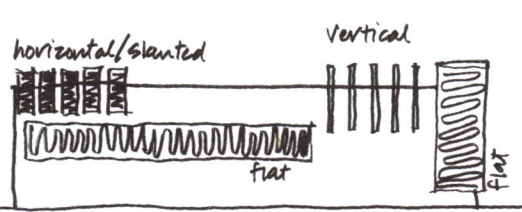

control/organise the advertisement areas ... and the facade will not be destroyed by tenants

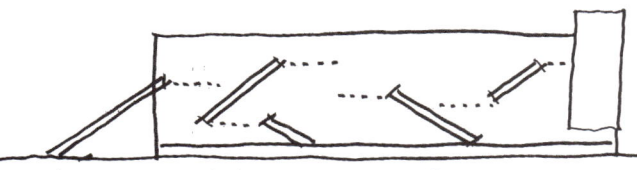

External escalators — study of access Direct access from Ground Floor to all levels.

Where is the Building sign most visible?

> The three-dimensional grid dismantled the older building's shell and blurred the line between the interior commercial space and public space of the street. It operated as a moment of transition.

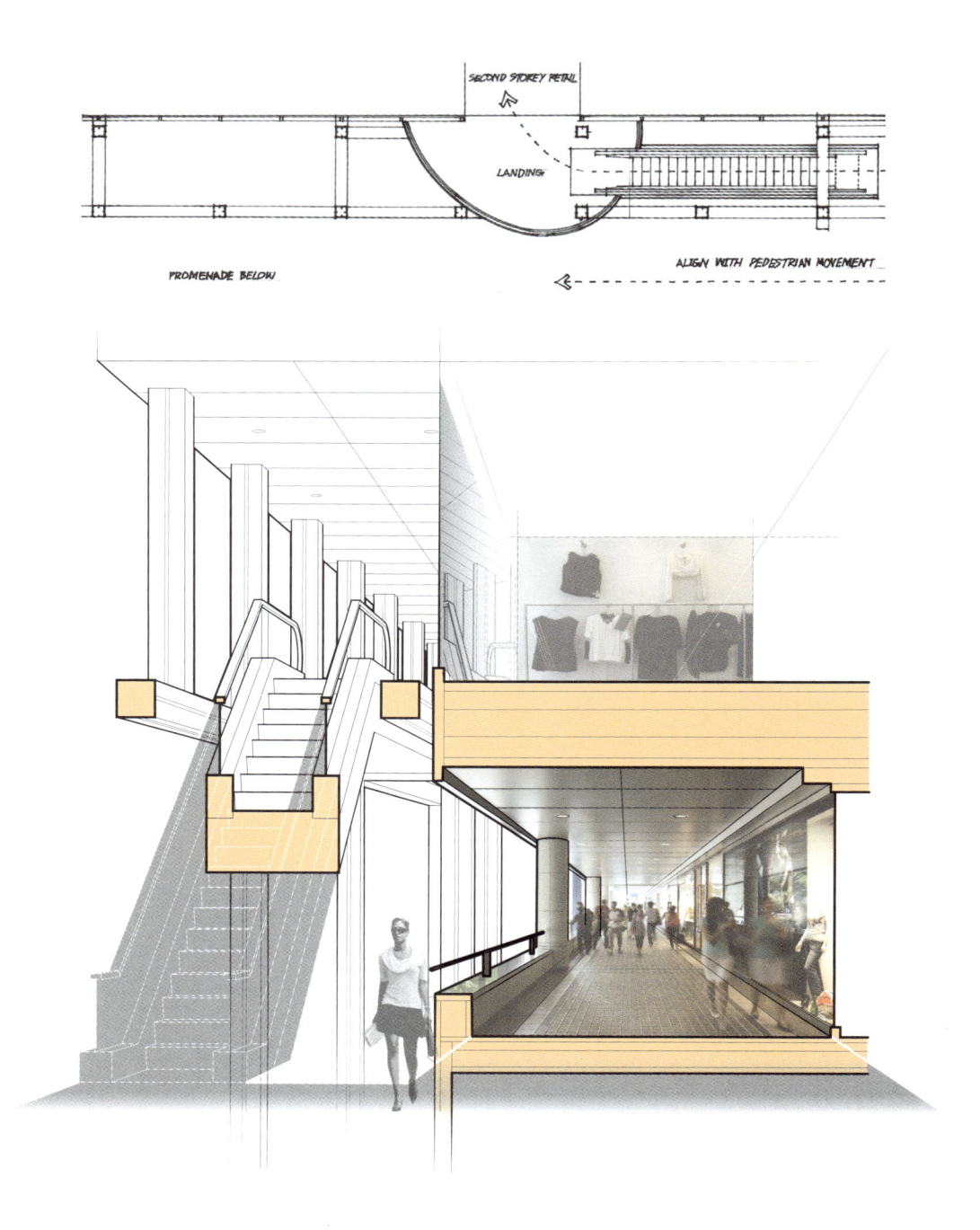

ABOVE
The external escalator allowed multiple storeys of retail to be accessed directly from the street.

OPPOSITE TOP
The storefront and entrances were designed to open up to the street.

OPPOSITE BOTTOM
An escalator with access to an upper-level food court.

FEATURE PROJECTS — WISMA ATRIA   CHAPTER TWO

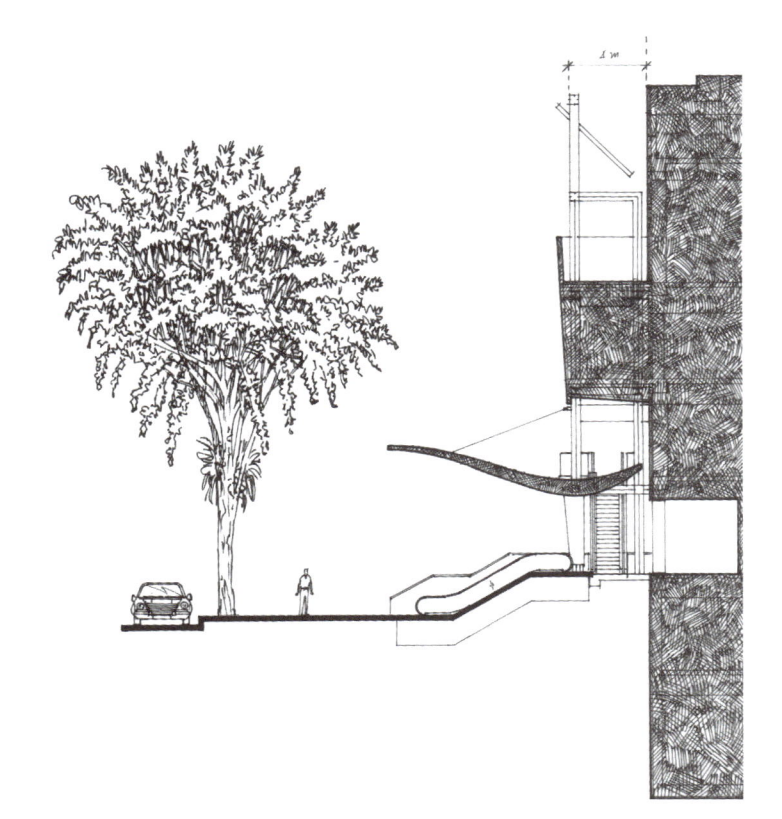

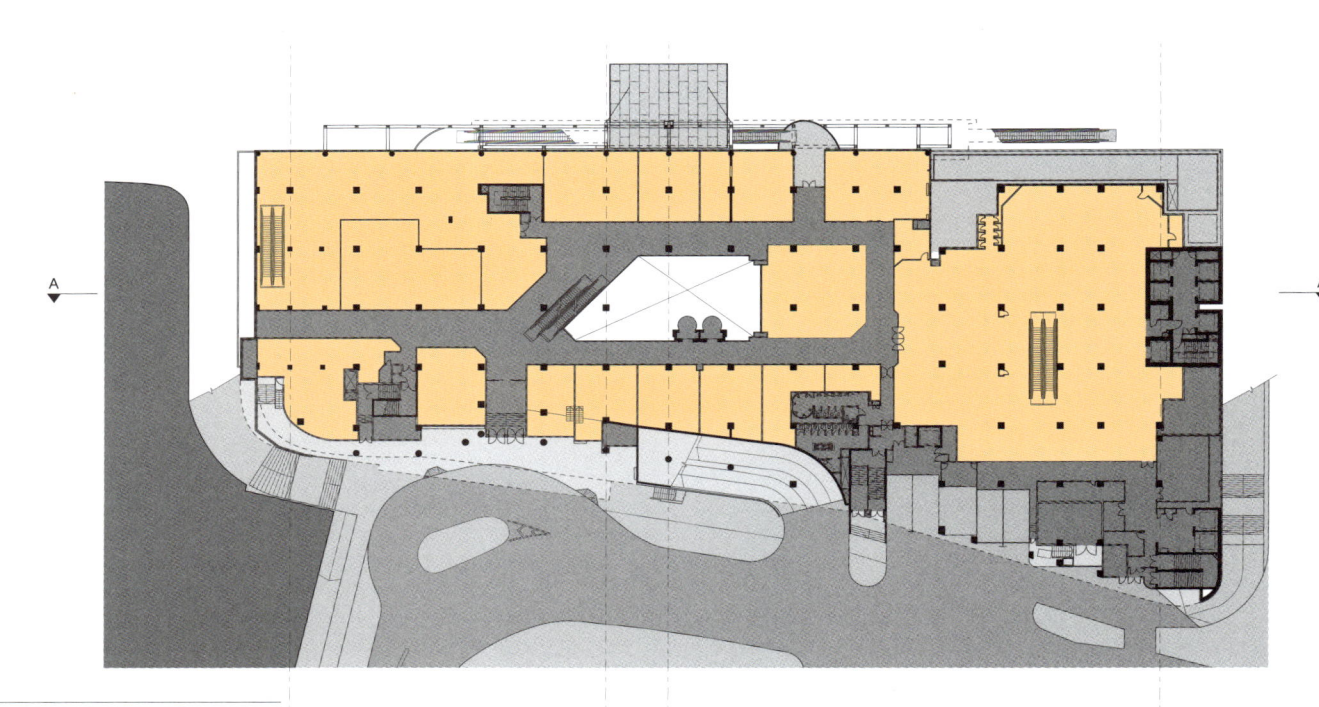

Level 3 and site plan, 2004

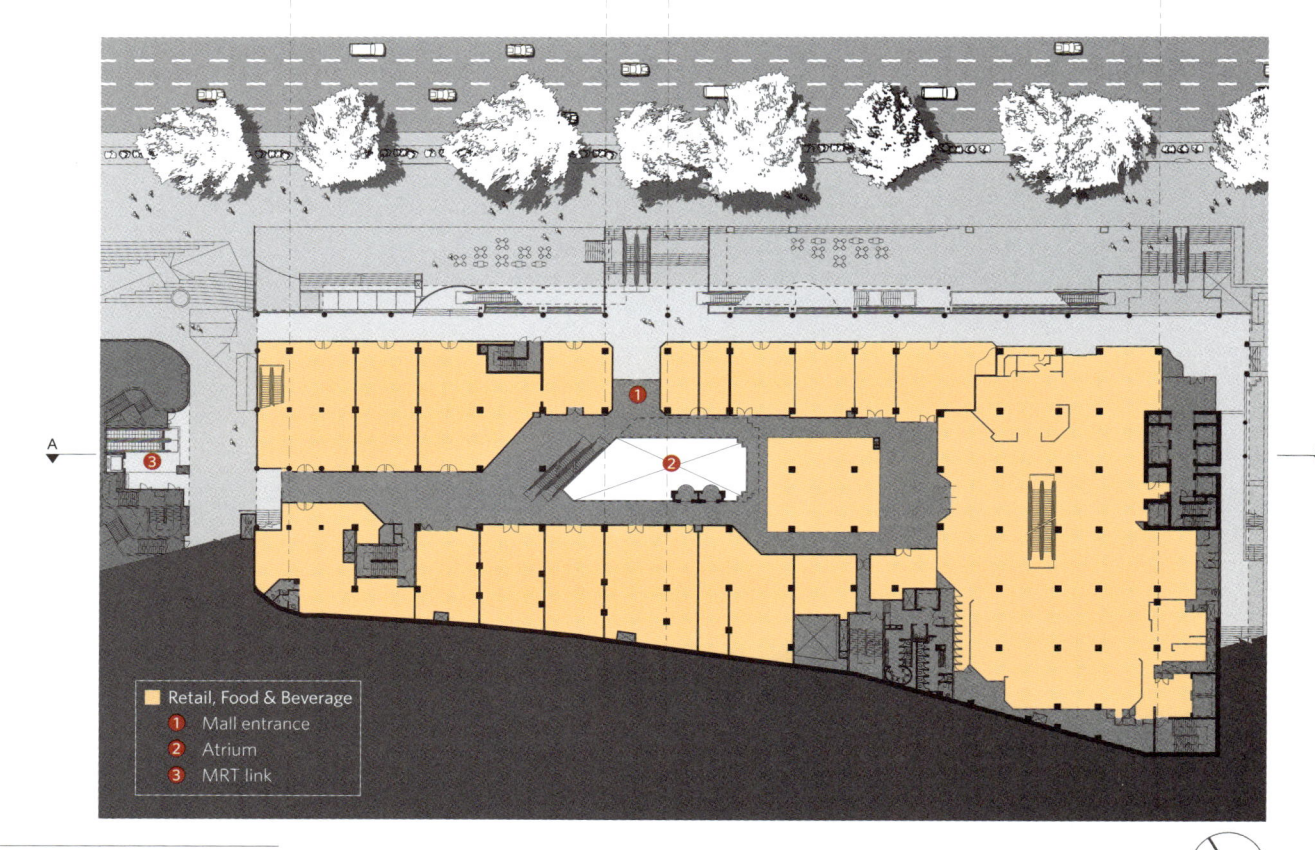

Retail, Food & Beverage
1. Mall entrance
2. Atrium
3. MRT link

Ground level and site plan, 2004

FEATURE PROJECTS – WISMA ATRIA   CHAPTER TWO   93

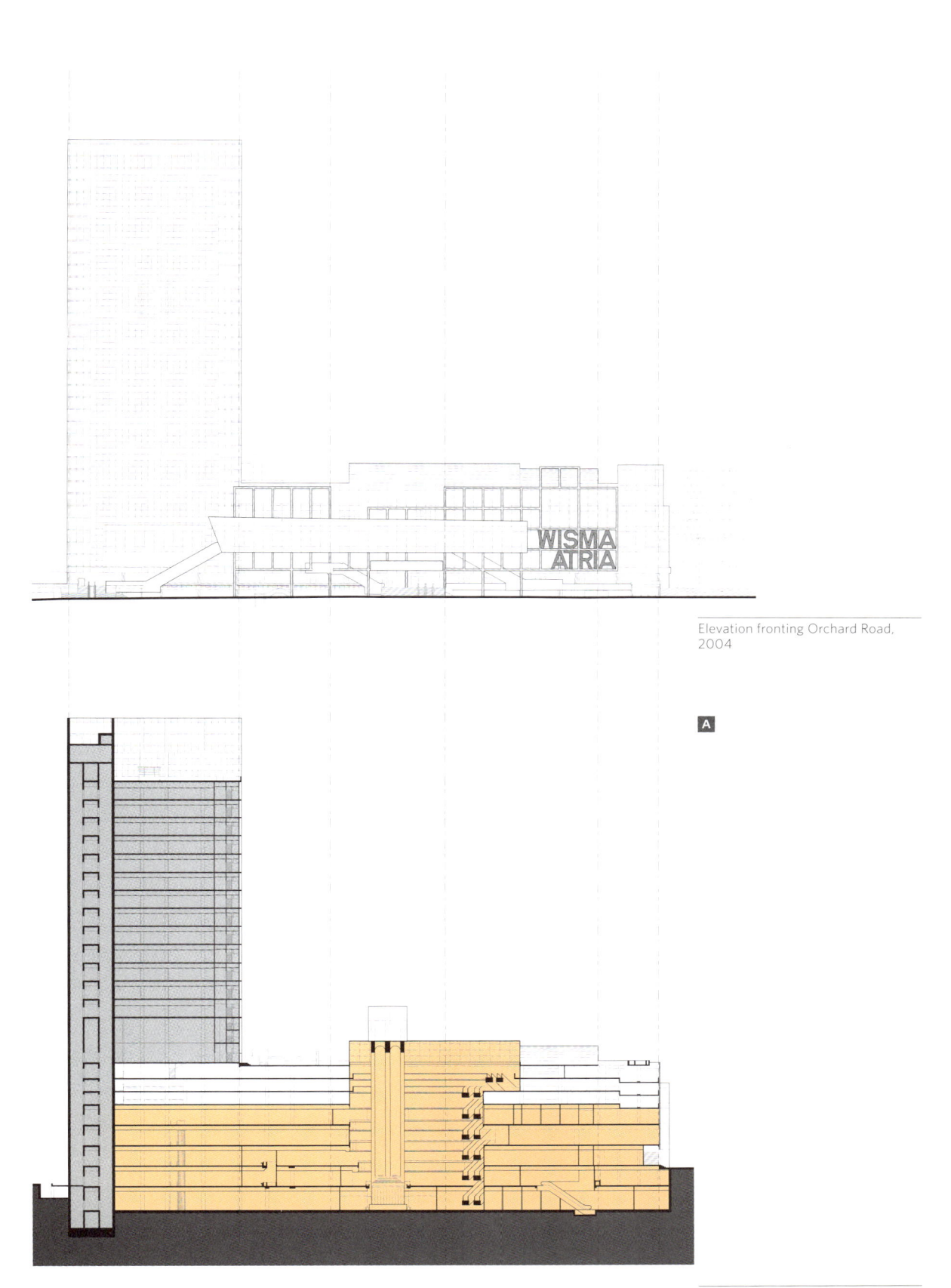

Elevation fronting Orchard Road, 2004

Longitudinal section through atrium, 2004

Wisma Atria's 2004 facelift made it the first retail centre in the region to have undergone a reversal of its closed form. A blue, four-metre deep frame expanded the façade toward the promenade.

Exploded axonometric, façade
1. Escalators
2. Enclosed retail programme
3. 4-metre frame
4. Transparent curtain wall

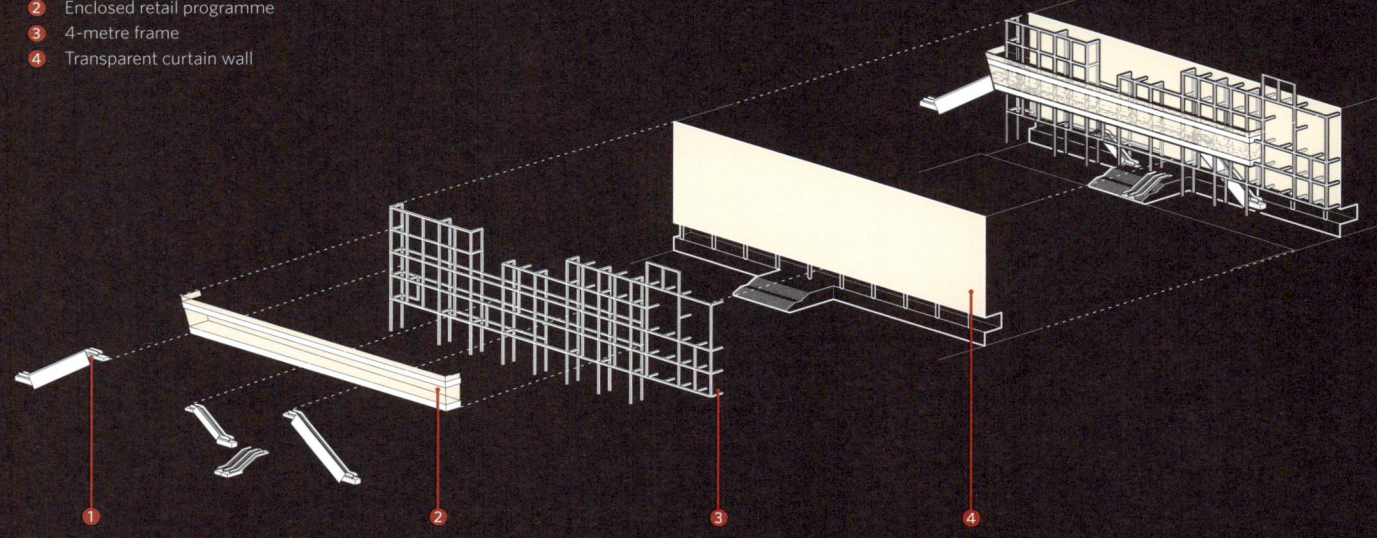

WISMA ATRIA
- Addition and alteration, 2004

1. **Outdoor dining** programmed at ground level.

2. **Escalators** connect upper-level retail and Food & Beverage programme with the pedestrian flows of the promenade, thereby increasing the value of these commercial spaces.

3. **A 4-metre façade extension** enhances connectivity among pedestrian space and interior retail.

4. **An ordered grid** showcases retail advertisements.

5. **A glass curtainwall** opens up the existing closed-shell mall to permit visibility to interior spaces, reworking the façade as a multi-storey storefront.

The 2004 renovation of Wisma Atria included a façade expansion to establish new visual and functional links between interior retail spaces and the Orchard Road promenade. A four-metre deep frame operated as a transition point, replacing the existing closed-form mall with a façade of transparent glazing and multiple outdoor escalators.

2012 Wisma Atria Makeover

The 2012 transformation of Wisma Atria is designed to further augment street visibility and respond to patterns of human movement through the site. A high-visibility, faceted glass wrapping performs as a dynamic envelope, articulated to extend 7.5 metres from the original structure. It projects an additional 3 metres beyond the former blue frame, the first project on Orchard Road to take advantage of a 2009 code amendment permitting increased articulation to encourage street engagement.

The new façade is a crystalline form built over the existing 4-metre frame, and gestures towards the MRT station and anchor tenant for maximum visibility. Its materiality is a dialogue between triangulated, faceted glass storefronts and a matte-aluminium finish for the cladding of structure and mechanical systems. A backdrop façade on the mall's upper levels is clad in blue horizontal strips of hollow channel, a continued reference to the mall's earliest form, articulated to establish a stronger presence for this composition.

Wisma Atria's plan also underwent significant alterations to engage the site's high-frequency circulation afforded by the adjacent MRT station: the main entrance was realigned on-centre with interior circulation; sunken basement-level programming was closed to establish a uniform podium as a refined seam linking promenade space with the mall, flexible enough to double as a multi-purpose event area; and new ramps were designed to channel pedestrians arriving from the MRT station and flanking malls directly into Wisma Atria's retail spaces.

ABOVE & OPPOSITE
Wisma Atria's existing façade structure is re-clad in faceted glass and matte-aluminium panelling.

OPPOSITE TOP
Concept sketch. The crystalline form gestures towards the MRT station and emphasises the anchor tenant.

FEATURE PROJECTS – WISMA ATRIA   CHAPTER TWO   97

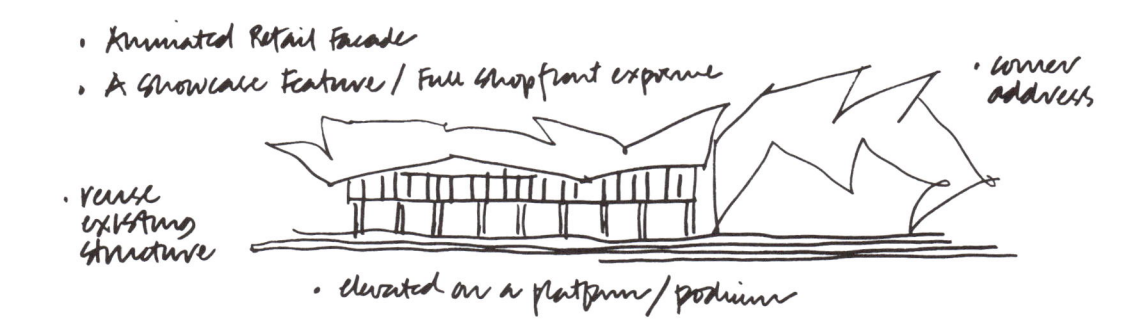

- Animated Retail Facade
- A Showcase Feature / Full shopfront exposure
- corner address
- reuse existing structure
- elevated on a platform / podium

1986 (A)   **2004 (A)**   **2012 (A)**   **2012 (B)**

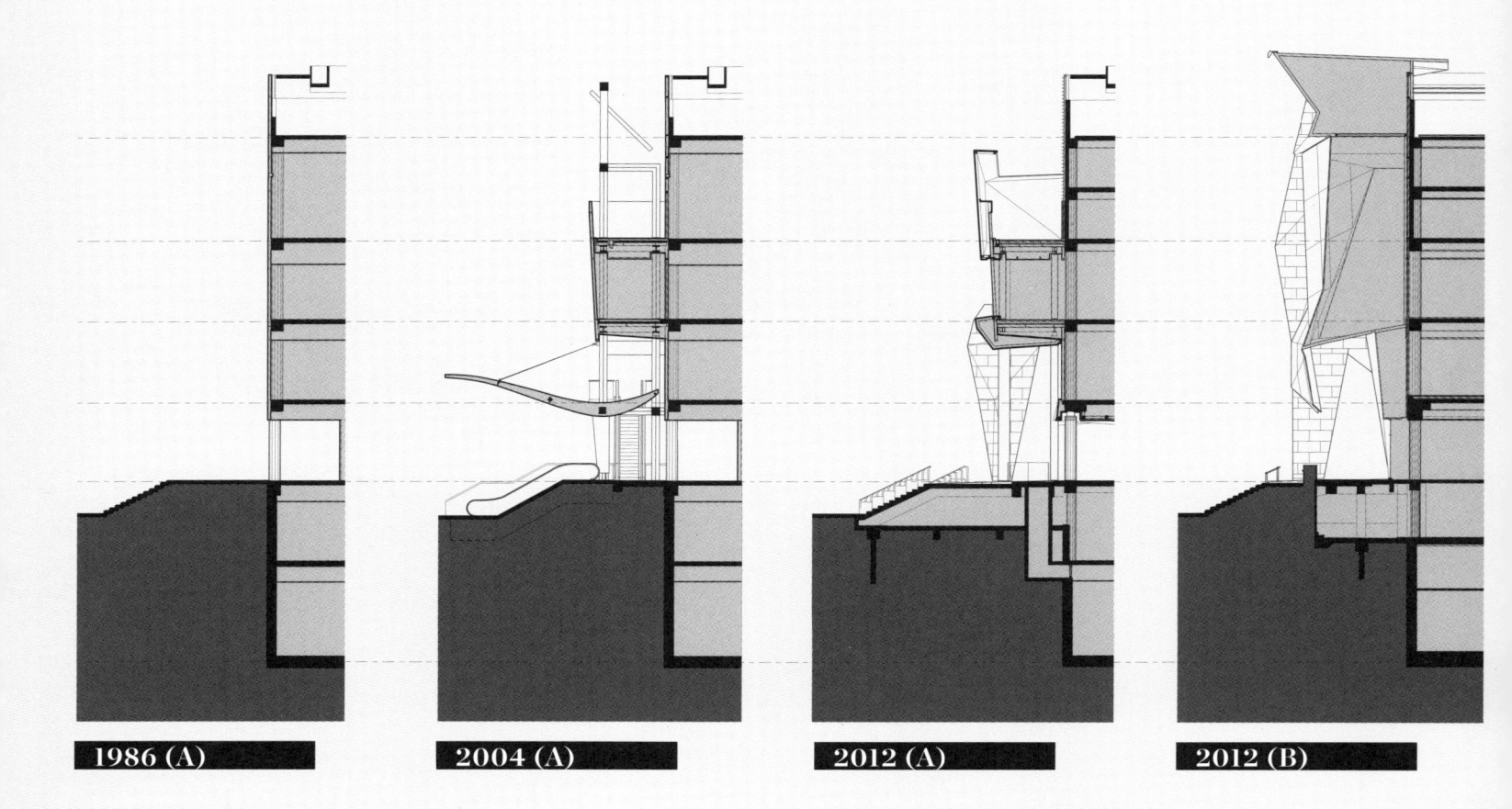

Wisma Façade Evolution

DP Architects has reworked the façade of Wisma Atria three times since 1986, each reincarnation further increasing the connectivity between the activities of the pedestrian promenade and the internal commercial retail shops. By manipulating the same structure as a host to a variety of frontages, the mall's personality has been periodically refreshed to retain a strong customer draw over a span of 30 years.

FEATURE PROJECTS – WISMA ATRIA   CHAPTER TWO   99

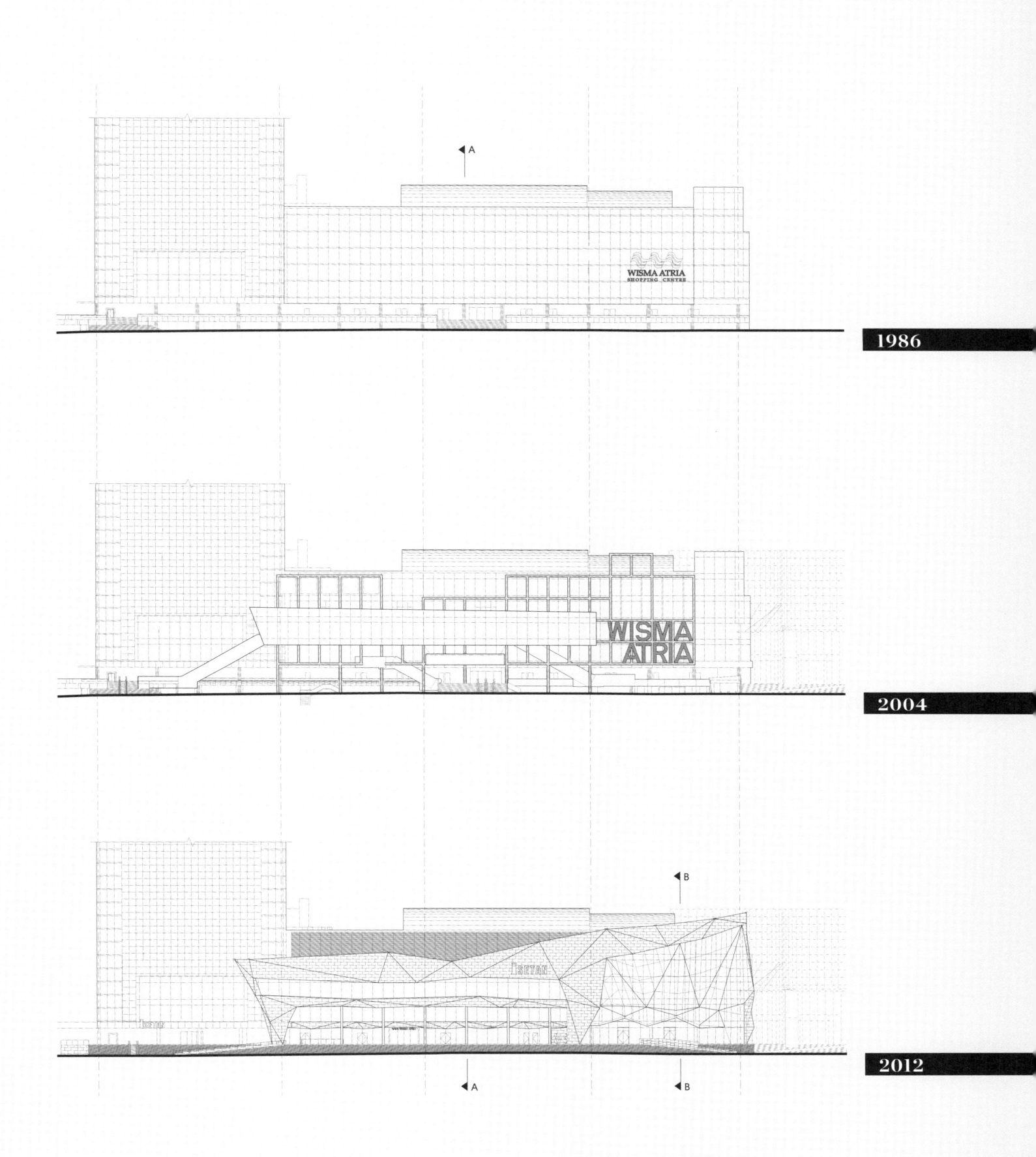

1986

2004

2012

100   PART 2   CONTRIBUTIONS OF DP ARCHITECTS

A

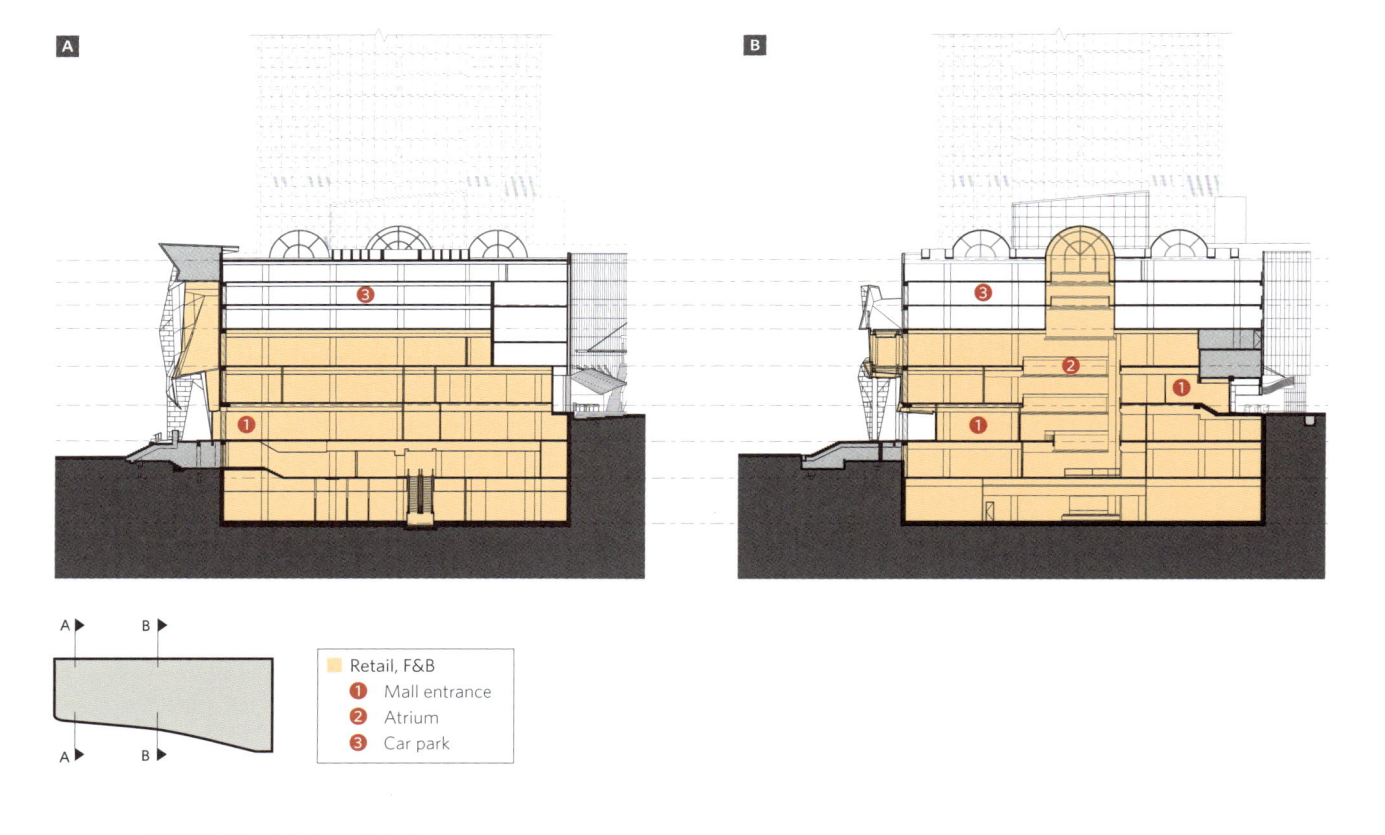

B

Retail, F&B
1. Mall entrance
2. Atrium
3. Car park

ABOVE
Transverse sections, 2012

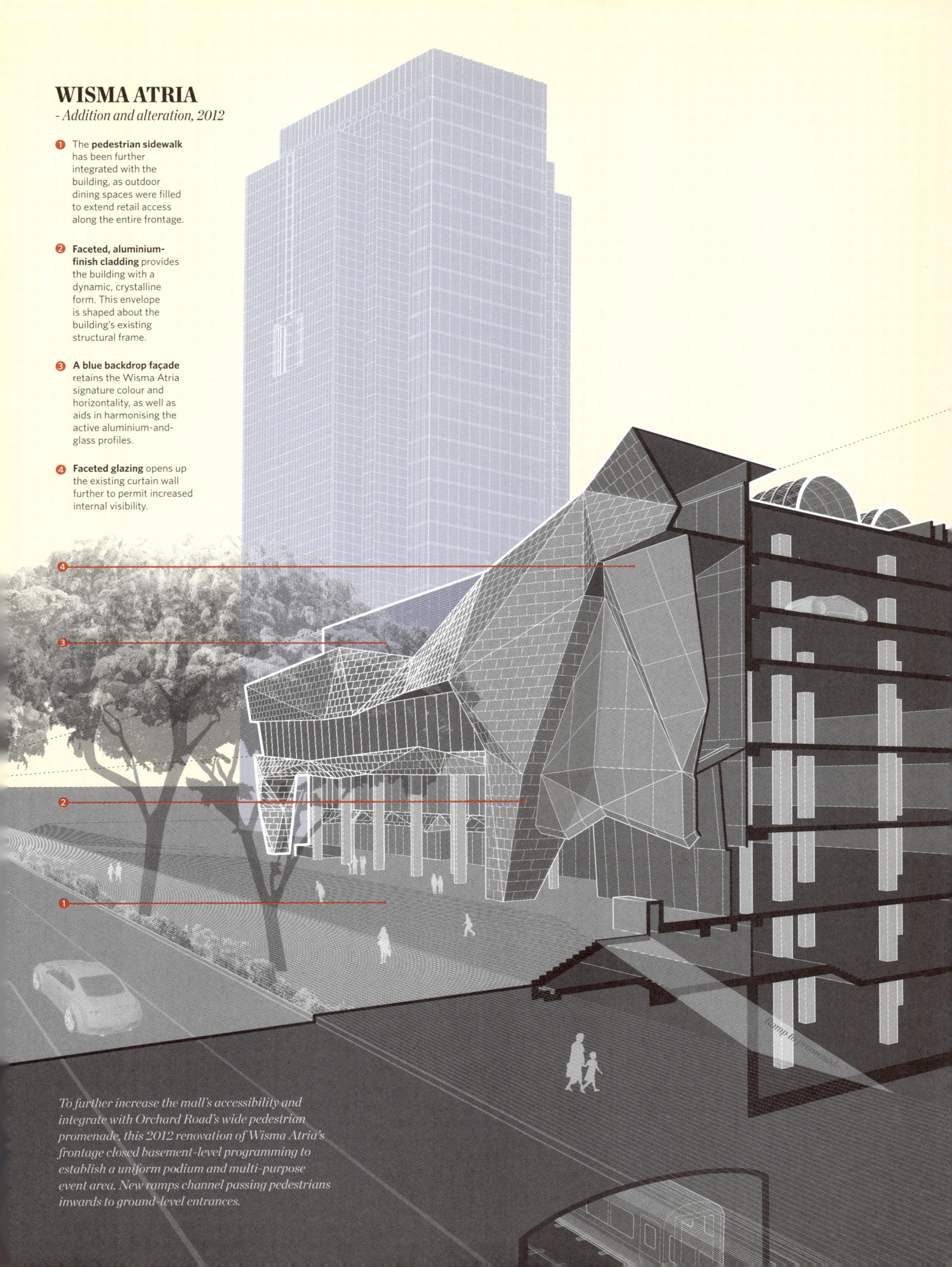

WISMA ATRIA
- Addition and alteration, 2012

1. The **pedestrian sidewalk** has been further integrated with the building, as outdoor dining spaces were filled to extend retail access along the entire frontage.

2. **Faceted, aluminium-finish cladding** provides the building with a dynamic, crystalline form. This envelope is shaped about the building's existing structural frame.

3. **A blue backdrop façade** retains the Wisma Atria signature colour and horizontality, as well as aids in harmonising the active aluminium-and-glass profiles.

4. **Faceted glazing** opens up the existing curtain wall further to permit increased internal visibility.

To further increase the mall's accessibility and integrate with Orchard Road's wide pedestrian promenade, this 2012 renovation of Wisma Atria's frontage closed basement-level programming to establish a uniform podium and multi-purpose event area. New ramps channel passing pedestrians inwards to ground-level entrances.

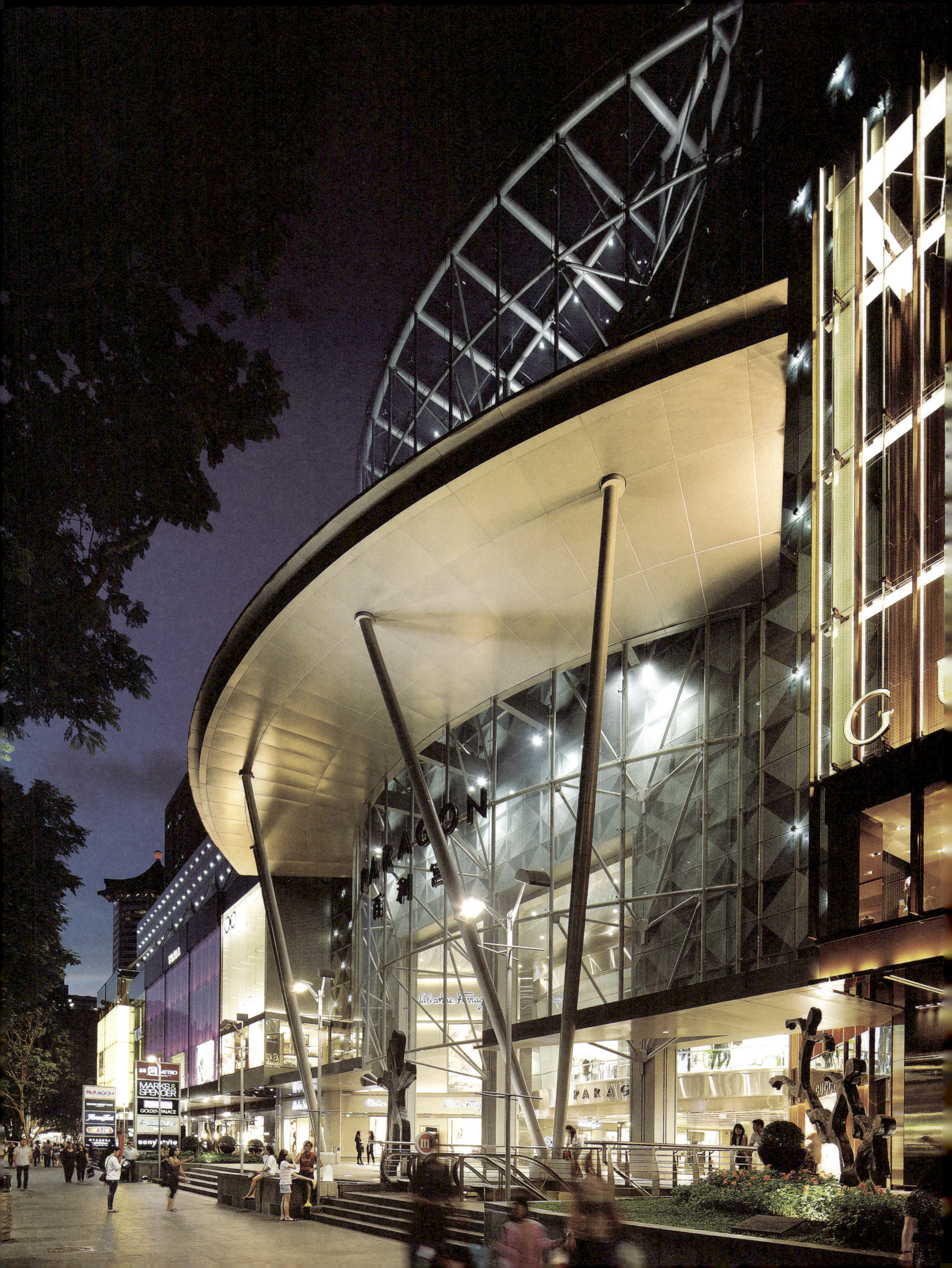
PARAGON
MARKS & SPENCER
GOLDEN PALACE
sony style
PARAG

Feature Projects
Paragon
Shopping Centre

Year Completed : 1999, 2003, 2009
Project Type   : Addition and alteration
Area   : 68,200 square metres (1999);
                   85,600 square metres (2003);
                   94,500 square metres (2009)

As a commodity goods centre, it is perhaps axiomatic that the malls of Orchard Road have been subject to a host of alterations since the region's earliest commercial development in the first years of the 20th century. Located at the geographical midpoint of Orchard Road, the site of what is now Paragon Shopping Centre has had a particularly diverse and active history of reconfiguration. Since the late 1990s, DP Architects has designed three phases of additions and alterations in 1999, 2003 and 2009. Each project re-established the mall's relationship with Orchard Road by means of increasing levels of transparency, façade articulation and circulatory connectivity.

A number of urban-scale adjacencies developed over the last century have played critical roles in the site's regional presence: first the construction of Bideford Road in the early 1900s transformed this land plot into a corner site with extended connectivity; corner condition visibility on Orchard Road has proved hugely significant for land value and store viability; the erection of a medical hospital immediately to the north of the site in the 1970s became a regional focal point; and, in the late 1990s, the construction of two Mass Rapid Transit stations centred pedestrian traffic on this segment of Orchard Road.

OPPOSITE
Paragon Shopping Centre's façade exhibits full glazing up to the fifth level, and three glazed blocks emphasise the storefronts of upscale retailers.

> Located at the geographical midpoint of Orchard Road, the site of what is now Paragon Shopping Centre has had a particularly diverse and active history of reconfiguration.

Numerous alterations to the site's commercial spaces reflect the changing nature of the Orchard Road region as a whole. With Orchard Road's mid-century evolution as a car distribution centre, the Orchard-Bideford junction became home to Orchard Motors, the nation's General Motors showroom – a structure converted into The Orchard shopping mall in the 1970s. Additionally, Singapore's first supermarket, Fitzpatrick's, was erected adjacent to the car showroom in 1958.[1] Both The Orchard and Fitzpatrick's eventually gave way to larger commercial malls: the six-storey Paragon Shopping Centre and the Promenade Shopping Centre.

In 1999 DP Architects completed its first addition and alteration of Paragon Shopping Centre. While most of the structural frame was left intact, this development included an extensive refurbishment to house a new concentration of premier fashion outlets, restaurants and a supermarket; a 14-storey tower was added atop the shopping podium, functioning as home to medical office spaces contiguous with Mount Elizabeth Hospital. The alterations featured a six-storey, naturally lit central atrium inserted within the podium. This major activity space operated to functionally and visually unify the shopping levels. Façade cladding in stone, glass and aluminium provided the mall with a new character, and allowance was made for a curved-glass entrance structure on axis with the primary atrium. The projecting element read as juxtaposed to the stone surface beyond, endowing the mall's frontage with a new degree of transparency and formal hierarchy.

Second-phase additions followed shortly after the 2002 Urban Redevelopment Authority (URA) amendments encouraging articulation overhead the sidewalk. The 2003 alteration also included the redevelopment and integration of the adjacent Promenade Shopping Centre first built in 1980, into a seven-storey extension including two basement levels. The insertion of a central atrium within this block established a secondary focal point for the mall – a terracing profile with transparent glass balustrades expanded the space upwards, and a span of clerestory windows offered the atrium natural indirect daylight. A wide corridor on every level connected the new atrium to that of the existing Paragon Shopping

ABOVE
The Paragon Shopping Centre façade, as designed by DP Architects in 1999 (left), 2003 (middle) and 2009 (right).

FAR RIGHT
A partial section through the glazed entrance structure and promenade.

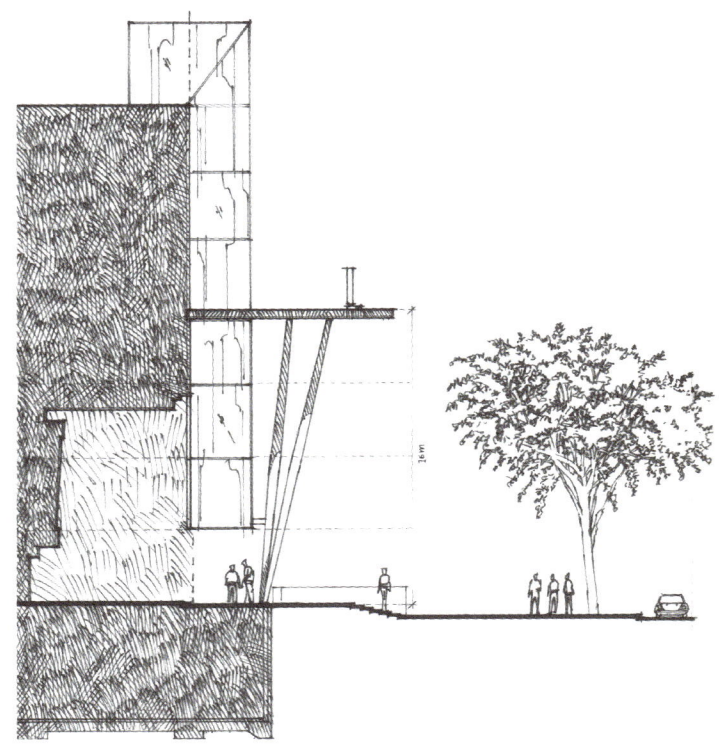

Centre. The dual atria provided a strong quality of openness and internal visibility.

With increasing land value and real estate premiums, Paragon Shopping Centre underwent a third alteration in 2009. This included an additional three storeys of offices, medical spaces and a gym to further strengthen the capacity of the retail podium. Capitalising on URA guidelines encouraging façade articulation with leasable floor area incentives, a new façade restructured the mall by means of articulation and transparency: the building's frontage now exhibits full glazing up to the fifth level, and three glazed blocks project four metres beyond the original elevation line. Two of these blocks are implemented at the building's corners to augment transparency and internal exposure of the spaces most visible to the street. The existing curved glazed entrance element was further enlarged and supported by a structural steel frame, and remaining regions of stone façade have been re-clad in layers of aluminium panels and fritted glass – drawing from the 'Paragon' namesake, these were patterned to reflect a multi-faceted diamond.

The design responded to the demands of the mall's upmarket tenants – Gucci, Salvatore Ferragamo, Prada, Tod's, Miu Miu – and their requirements for grand street displays. As the commercial components driving the mall's visibility, façade articulations were concentrated in blocks to showcase these brands. An architectural harmony was developed through materiality and massing: articulated blocks translate as individual elements projected outward from a unifying base façade while conforming to a larger compositional whole. The architecture expresses clearly both local difference and overall unity.

Paragon Shopping Centre's periodic transformation is communicative of Orchard Road's widespread evolution in retail architecture. Single-function stores became multi-shop buildings, which were later removed to make way for larger commercial shopping centres characterised by internal circulation spaces and attached high-rise structures. Today, phased designs continue to reinvent the building, reconfiguring its composition in plan and section.

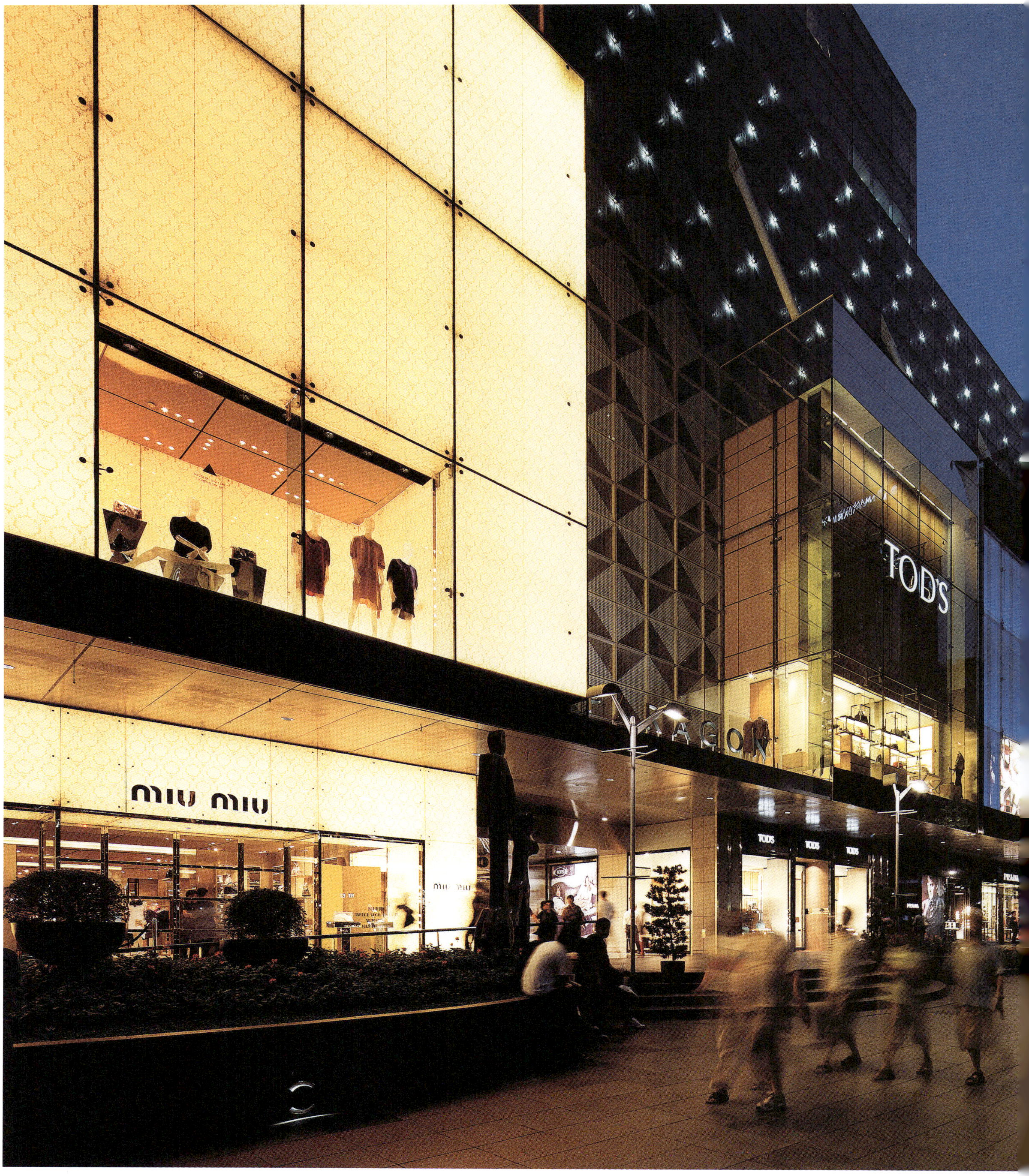
miu miu
TOD'S

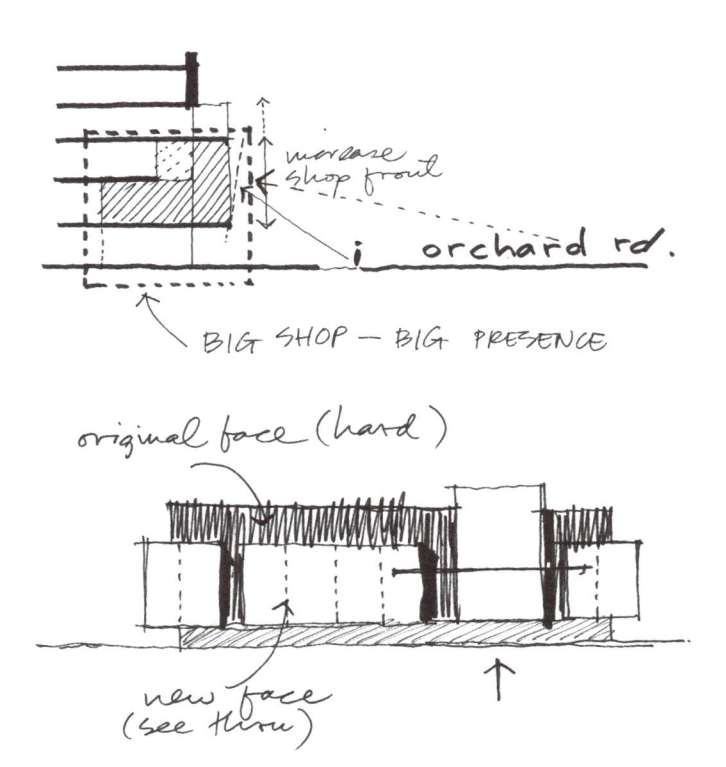

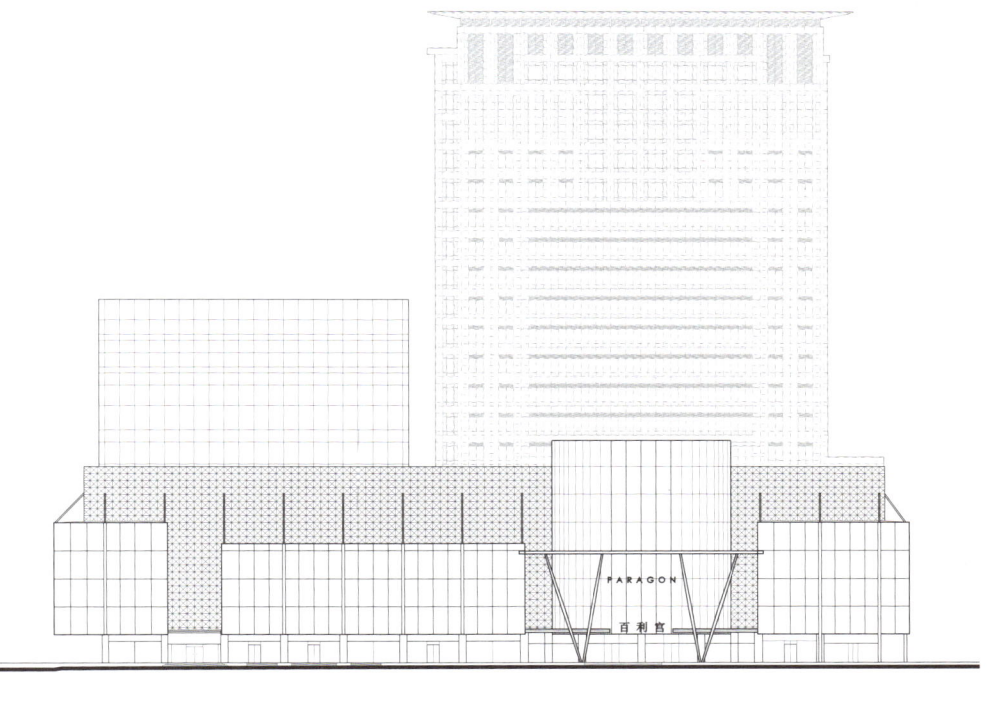

FEATURE PROJECTS PARAGON SHOPPING CENTRE   CHAPTER TWO   107

LEFT
At night, the projecting storefronts are illuminated, standing out from the base façade pattern.

TOP
Concept sketches of the 2009 façade alteration.

BOTTOM
Elevation fronting Orchard Road, 2009.

> Dual connected atria and a glass entrance structure provide a strong quality of openness and internal visibility.

TOP
The steel-supported glass entrance structure enters into the large atrium.

BOTTOM
Interior of the large atrium.

OPPOSITE
Interior of the small atrium.

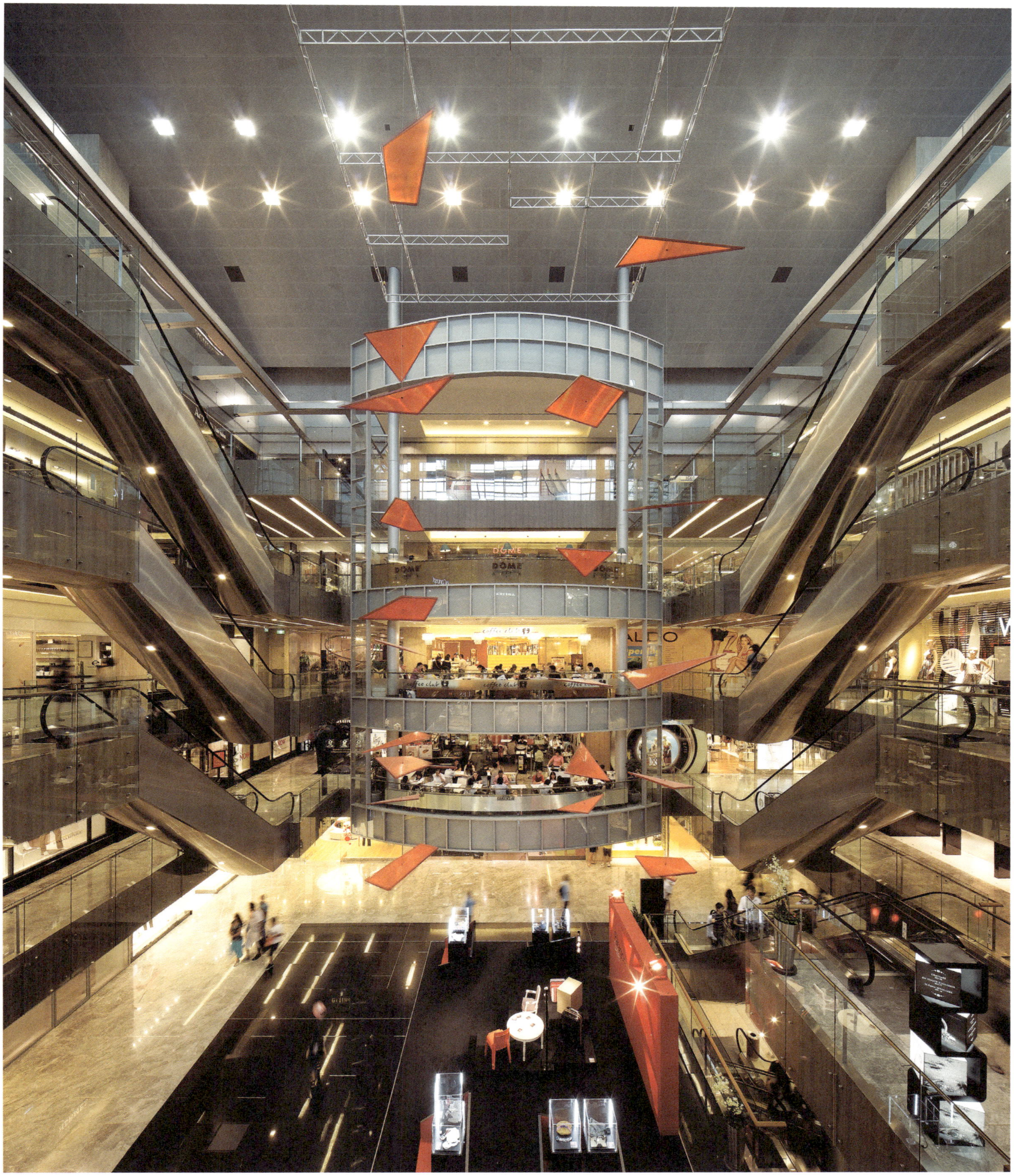
DÔME

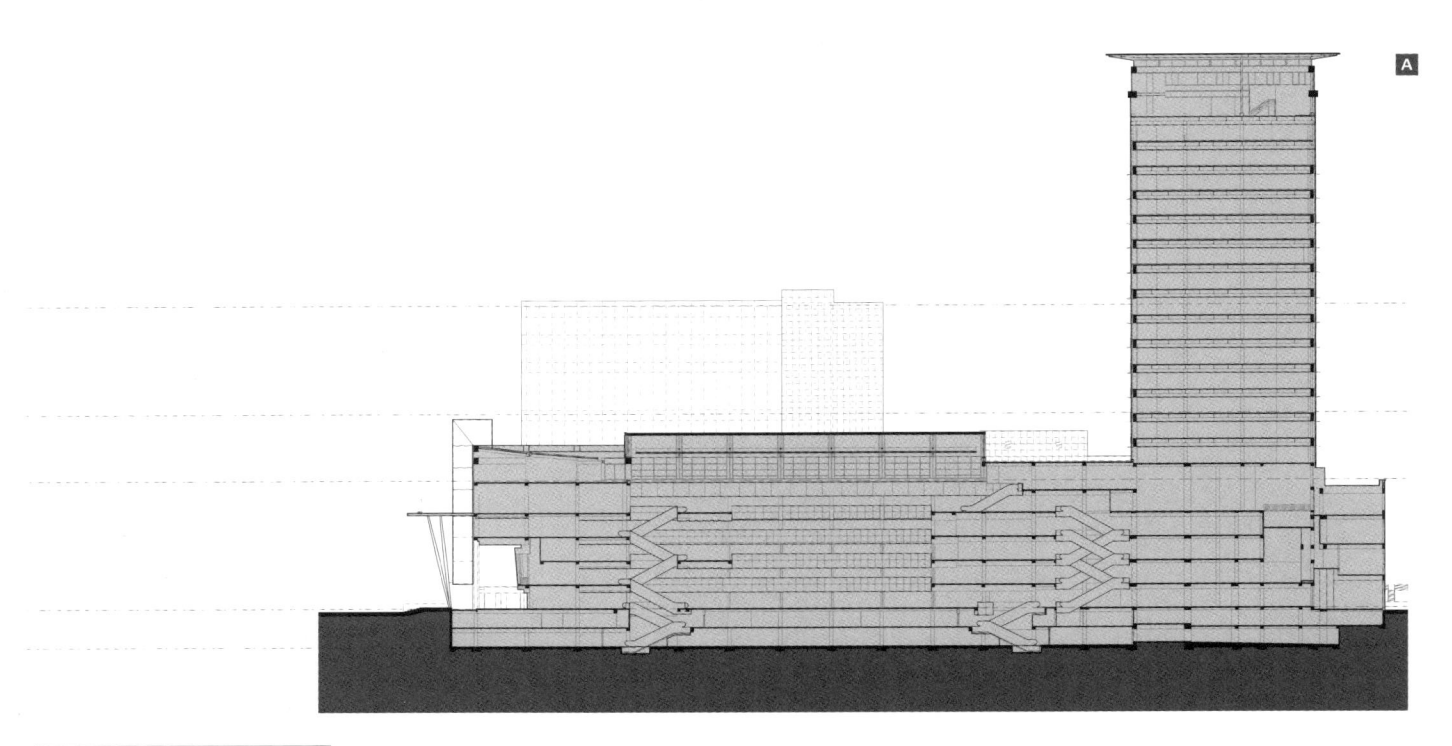

Section through entrance structure,
large atrium and tower, 2009

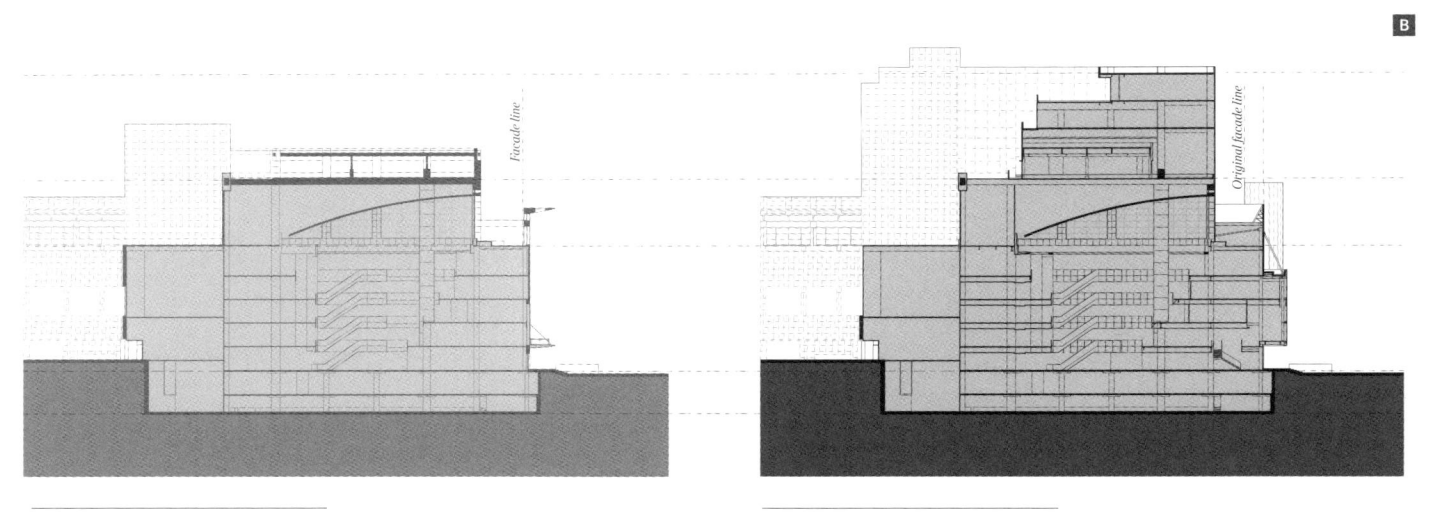

BEFORE
Section through small atrium, 2003

AFTER
Section through small atrium, 2009

Ground level and site plan, 2009

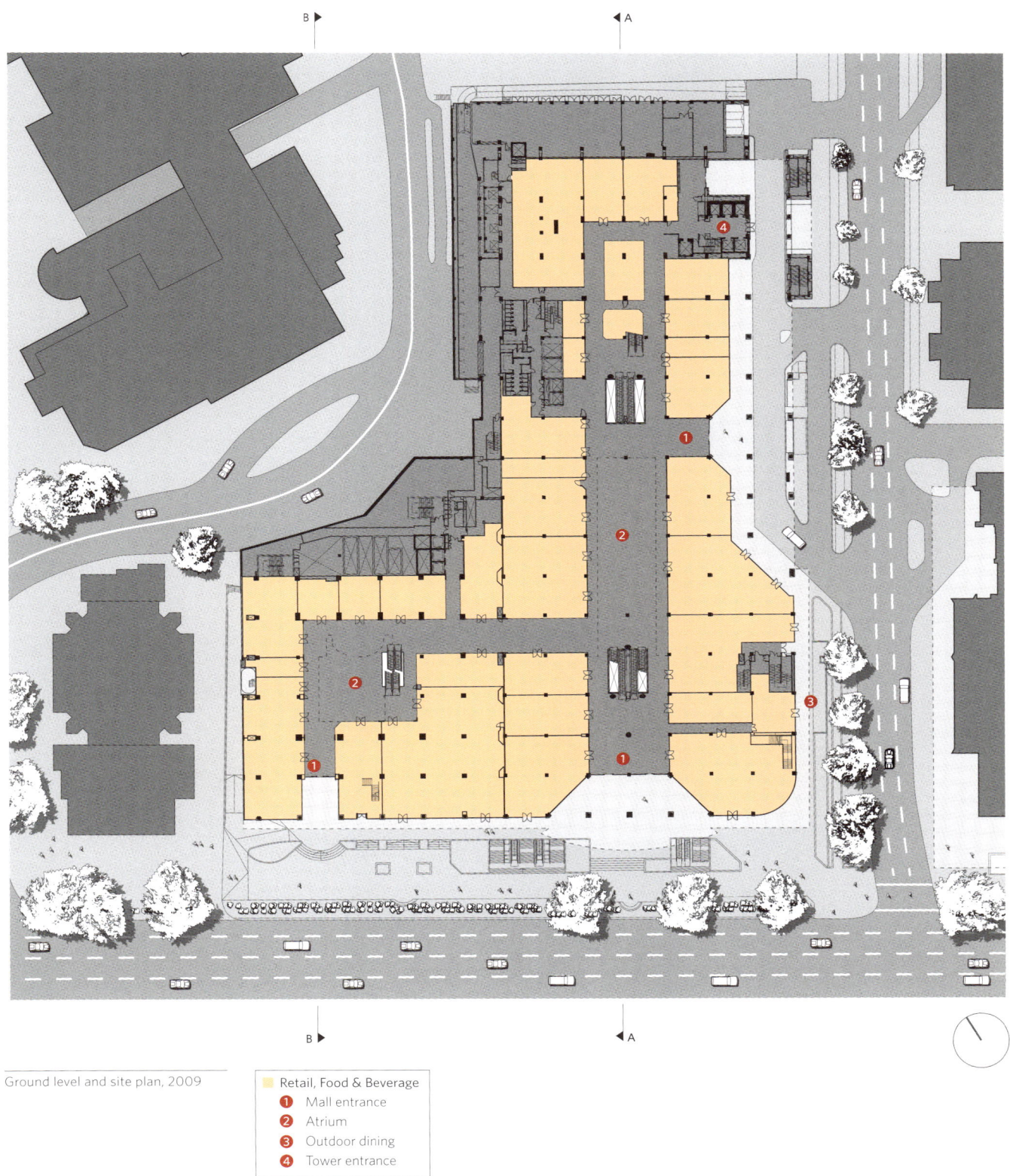

Retail, Food & Beverage
1. Mall entrance
2. Atrium
3. Outdoor dining
4. Tower entrance

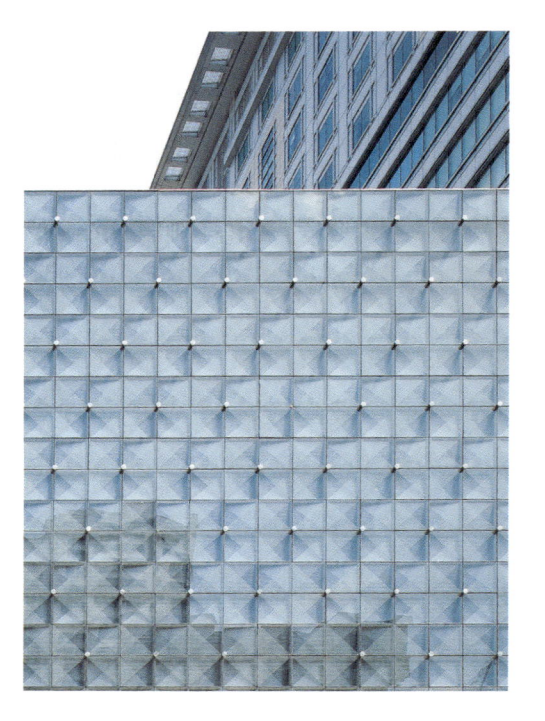

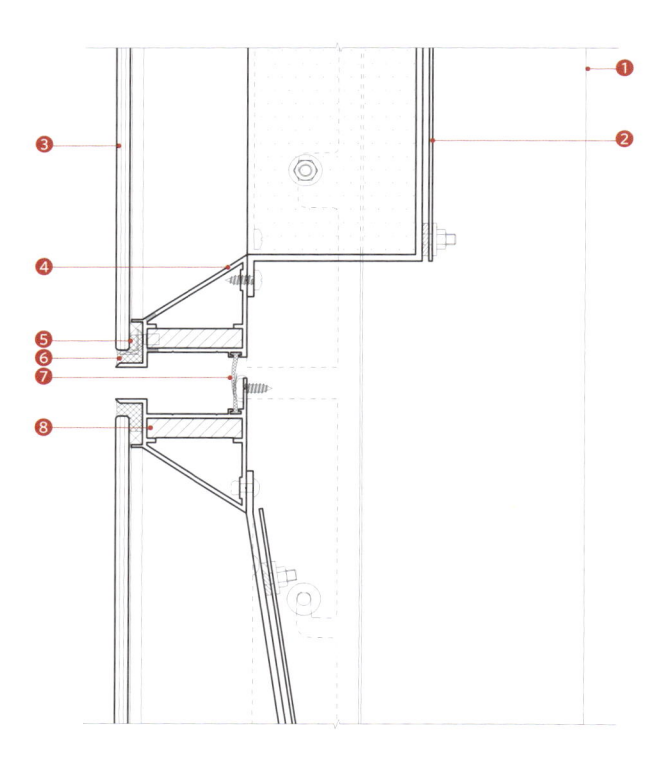

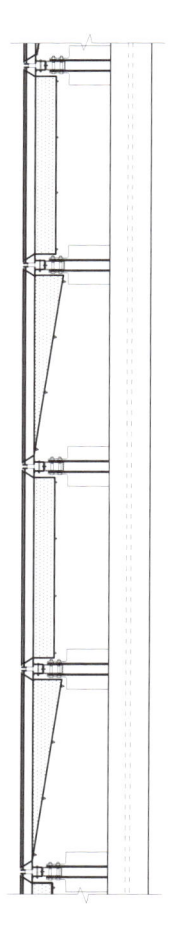

Section detail, aluminium and glass façade panels
1. Galvanised steel mullion/runner
2. Aluminium cladding in PVDF finish
3. Fritted glass
4. Aluminium affixed frame
5. Structural silicone sealant
6. Weatherseal silicone sealant
7. EPDM gasket
8. Aluminium corner bracket

ABOVE & OPPOSITE
Aluminium and fritted façade panels are detailed to reflect the mall's namesake – 'Paragon', a multi-faceted diamond.

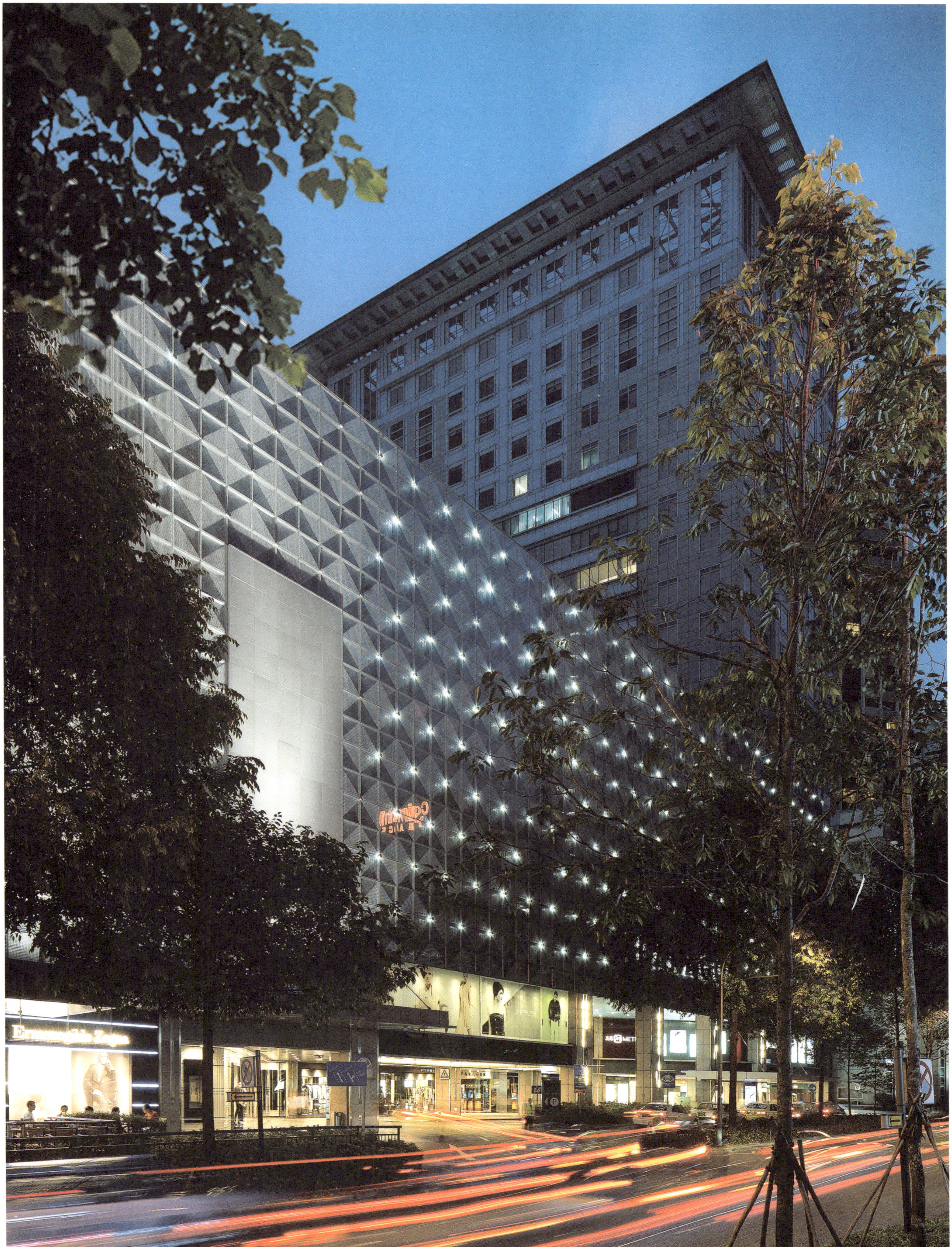

> Three glazed blocks project four metres beyond the original elevation line. Two of these blocks are implemented at the building's corners to augment transparency and internal exposure of the spaces most visible to the street.

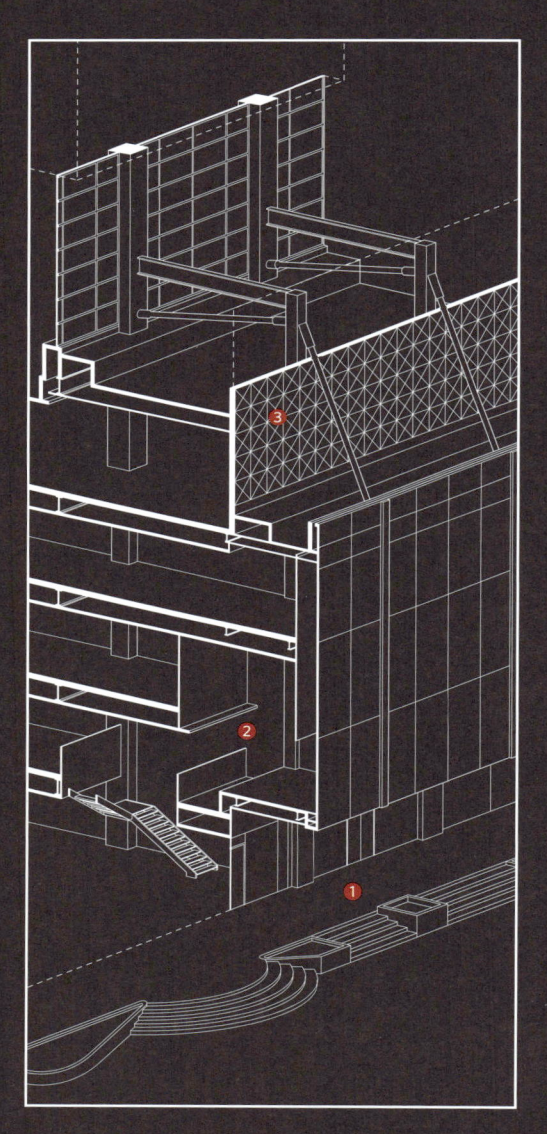

Partial section through retail block

① A four-metre covered corridor is created by the articulated façade.

② Each projected block houses a multi-storey flagship storefront.

③ The glazing-and-aluminium patterning provides a unifying base façade from which individual storefronts are projected.

PARAGON SHOPPING CENTRE
- Addition and alteration, 2009

❶ Glazed blocks project four metres beyond the existing building's elevation line. Each contains a flagship storefront.

❷ A glazing-and-aluminium patterning provides a unifying base façade.

❸ A glazed entrance opens into the large atrium.

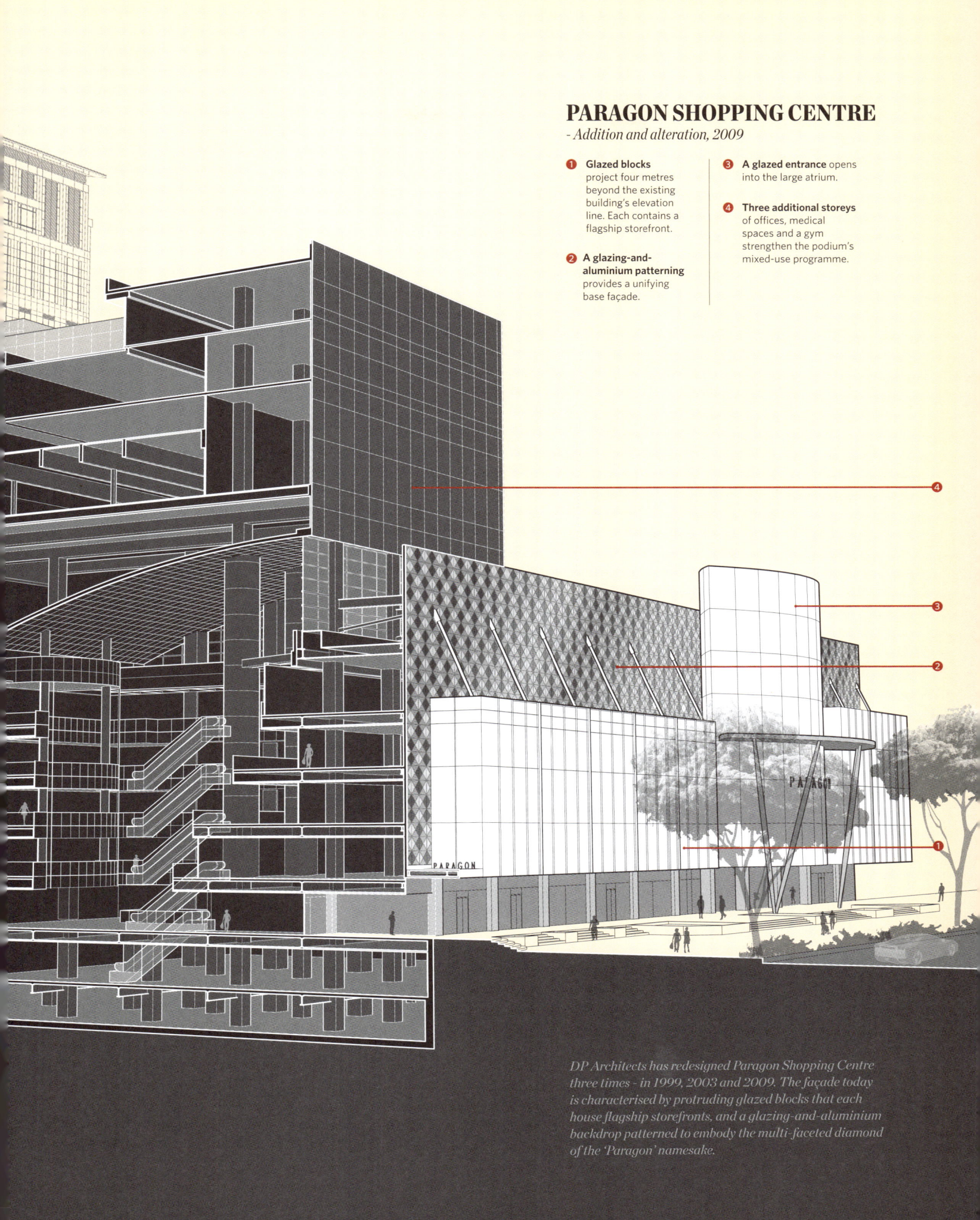

❹ Three additional storeys of offices, medical spaces and a gym strengthen the podium's mixed-use programme.

DP Architects has redesigned Paragon Shopping Centre three times - in 1999, 2003 and 2009. The façade today is characterised by protruding glazed blocks that each house flagship storefronts, and a glazing-and-aluminium backdrop patterned to embody the multi-faceted diamond of the 'Paragon' namesake.

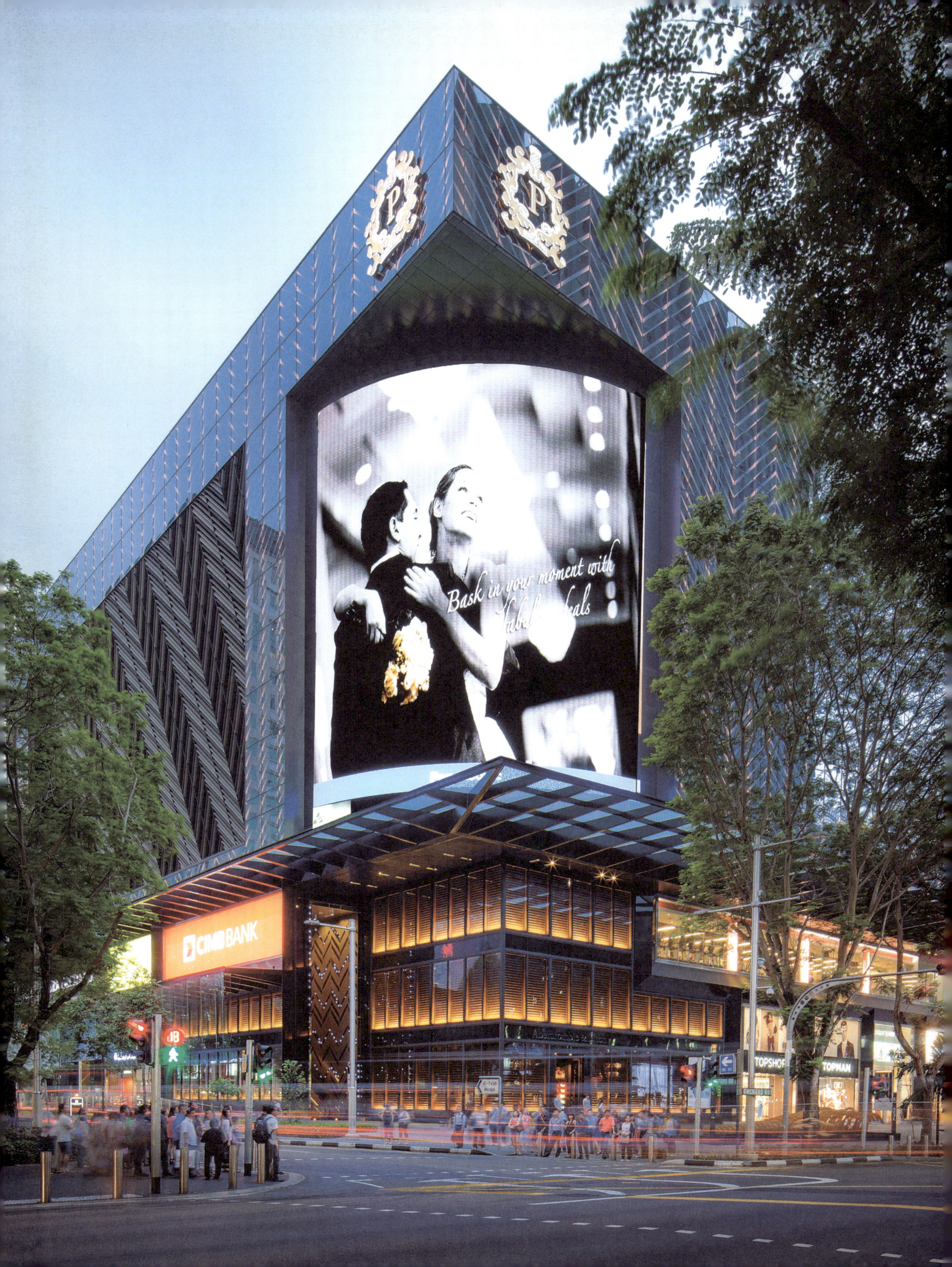
Bask in your moment with
CIMB BANK
TOPSHOP
TOPMAN

Feature Projects
Grand Park Orchard

Year Completed : 2010
Project Type   : Retrofit
Area   : 23,200 square metres

This existing hotel proved too slender in section to accommodate the internal mall circulation spaces common to Orchard Road's shopping centres. As a result, the architects of Grand Park Orchard were required to design a mall of independent shops accessible only from the street. In order to attain the inter-connectivity that render the malls of this shopping corridor so successful, these semi-autonomous storefronts are unified by a grand common space along the promenade, characterised by the building's deep canopy.

Established originally as Prince's Hotel Garni in the 1950s, this site formed by the junction of Bideford Road and Orchard Road at the heart of the commercial shopping belt has long been utilised for hospitality purposes. Though Prince's Hotel Garni was demolished in 1980, the plot later became home to the Crown Prince Hotel, a building whose label has undergone many transformations, but whose structure remains intact.

OPPOSITE
Grand Park Orchard at the corner of Orchard Road and Bideford Road.

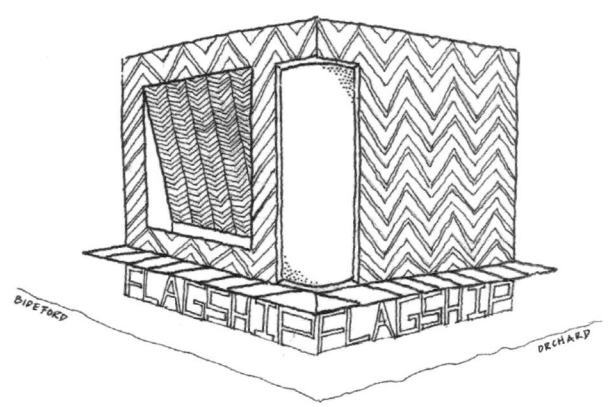

As a retrofit project to introduce a retail base into the building's programme, the design for Grand Park Orchard is respectful of the structure's modernist form, with 11 storeys of tiered blocks leaning in the direction of the road and an external elevator cab recessed at the corner addressing the street junction. This original composition effectively highlighted the movement and machine-like nature of the elevator as its signature feature. While the elevators were relocated in plan, the new design retains the building's corner focus on mechanical movement, reinstated by an eight-storey, 28-metre-high media LED screen.

The building's overall form has been simplified to a cube with sheer faces. Compositionally and materially, this strategy has rendered the screen an even clearer point of focus for the building. Programmatically, seven storeys of hotel function sit atop a three-storey retail base. The tapering blocks that house the hotel guestrooms have been overlaid with a sunshading screen, inserted at an angle to break the building's flat edge and reflect the structure's tiered form. The hotel lobby has been relocated to the fourth storey and is accessible by means of a street-level elevator landing. Meanwhile, a sidewalk escalator connects visitors directly to the third-storey gym and bank.

The promenade fronting the hotel has been transformed into a grand shared space. Due to existing narrow floor plates that constrain shops to sidewalk-only access, storefronts were to be provided with more frontage than typical on Orchard Road. Additionally, short storey-to-storey heights required a special consideration for this frontage. To accommodate these conflicting factors and to develop a common space to unify the mall, an extensive canopy system was designed above the third level. Codes require that canopies or projecting façades provide adequate sun-shading and rain protection starting from a 45-degree angle extended from the point where the building meets the sidewalk. Due to this building's atypical floor heights, narrow floor plate depth and structural limitations, a conditional construction waiver permitted a shortened canopy, cantilevered without additional support. The resulting uninterrupted, planar façade produces a unified mall frontage, beneath which marble-clad pillars perform as robust frames to give each storefront a degree of autonomy.

Architectural Branding Strategies

It is worth highlighting the use of architectural form for branding purposes, as retail mall success is often heavily dependent upon urban legibility. At Grand Park Orchard, a system of double-glazing units envelop the upper hotel levels, protecting the interior spaces from street noise and heat gain; these are provided with a ceramic fritting embossed on both layers to reduce thermal transfer and pick up the light from the unit's LED-embedded aluminium frame. The resultant superimposed patterning works day and night to segment the monolithic single plane of the façade. It provides the building with an easily recognisable architectural motif that recalls a herringbone stitch as used in the production of textiles.

ABOVE LEFT
The building as Crown Prince Hotel in the 1980s.
ABOVE RIGHT
Grand Park Orchard's massing scheme with superimposed herringbone façade pattern.

OPPOSITE TOP
The façade's herringbone pattern via LED-embedded glazing units.
OPPOSITE BOTTOM
The 10-metre deep canopy permits visibility to all three storeys of retail.

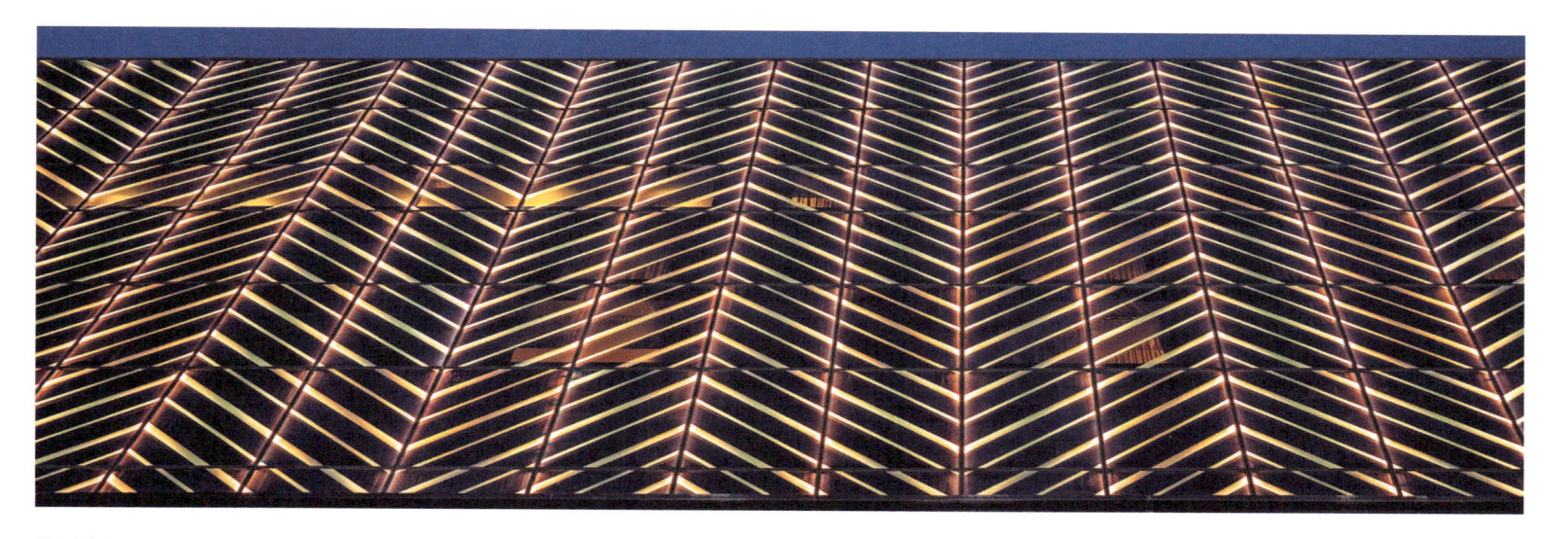

FEATURE PROJECTS GRAND PARK ORCHARD   CHAPTER TWO   119

The tapering blocks that house the hotel guestrooms have been overlaid with a sunshading screen, inserted at an angle to break the building's flat edge and reflect the structure's tiered form.

TOP
A partial section through the storefront and canopy.

BOTTOM
The mall's 28-metre-high media LED screen at the site's prominent street corner.

OPPOSITE
The sunshading screen overlaid onto the tapered hotel guestroom blocks.

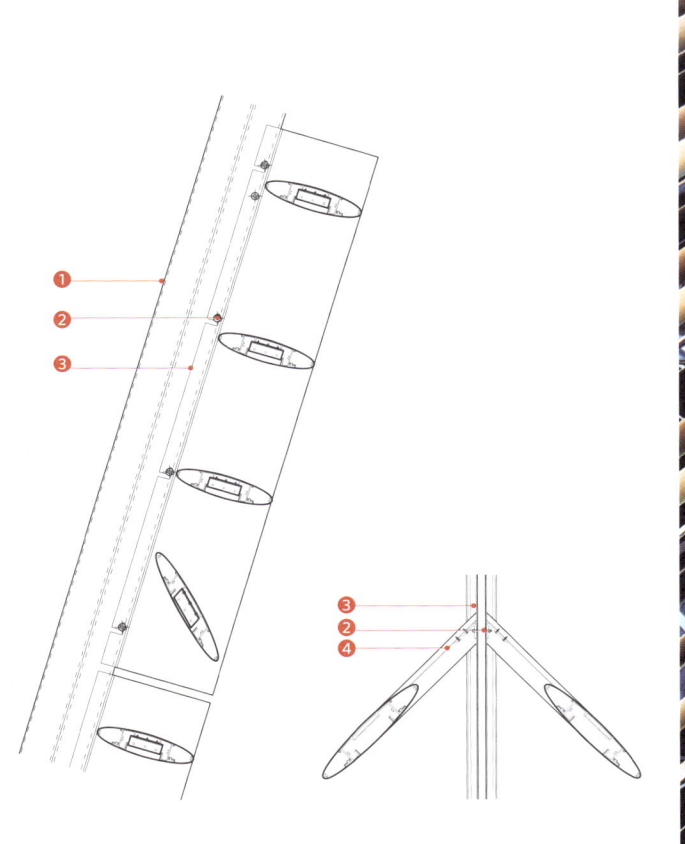

Section detail, inclined sunshading screen
- ① Galvanised mild steel, rectangle section
- ② Stainless steel bolt and nut
- ③ Aluminium end plate with hook-on slot
- ④ Aluminium angle cleat

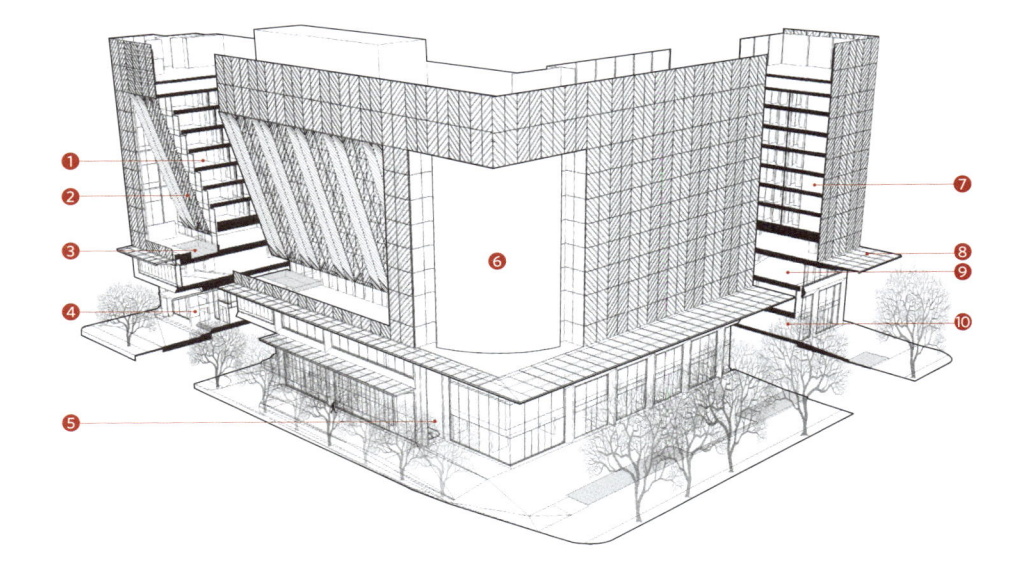

Sectional perspective
1. Stacked suites
2. Louvred sunscreen
3. Hotel pool
4. Hotel entry
5. External escalator
6. Media LED screen
7. Hotel - Levels 4-11
8. Extended canopy
9. Gym and bank - Level 3
10. Retail - Levels 1-2

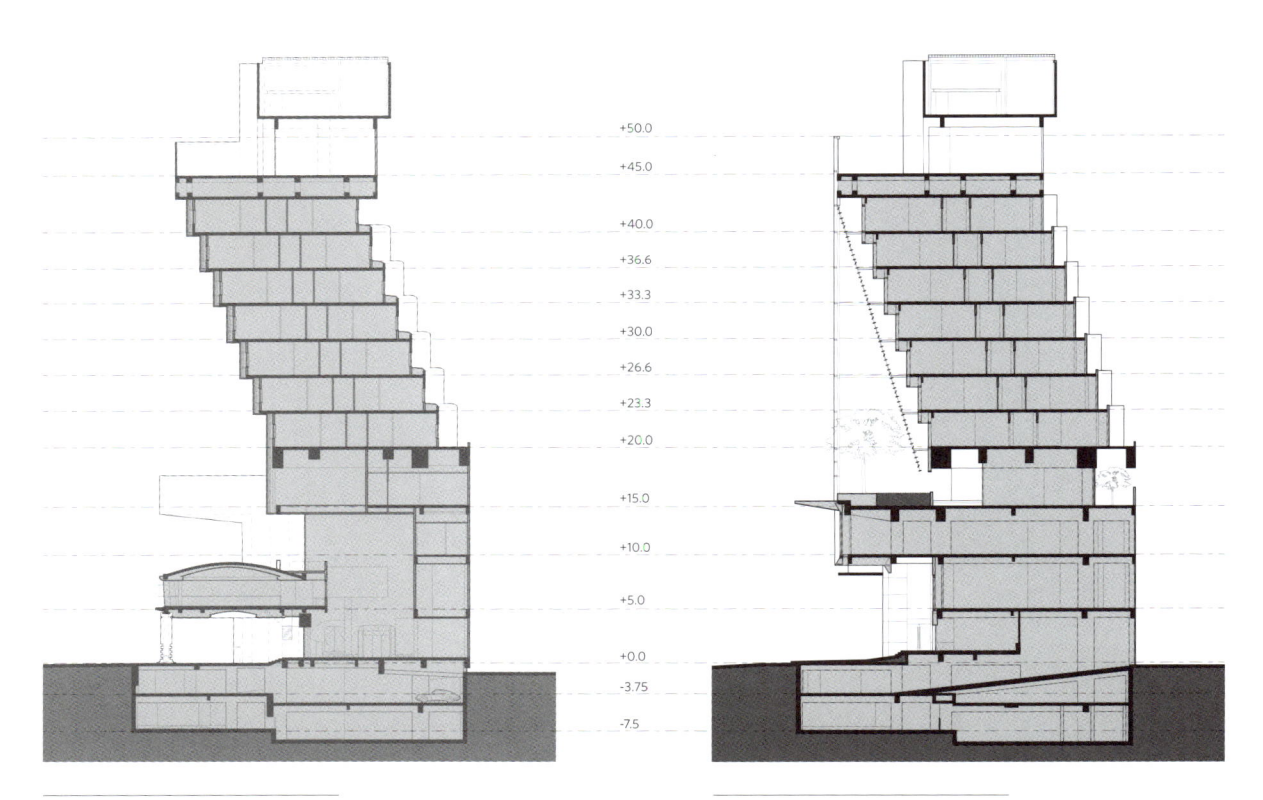

BEFORE
Transverse section through the hotel

AFTER
Transverse section through the hotel and retail base

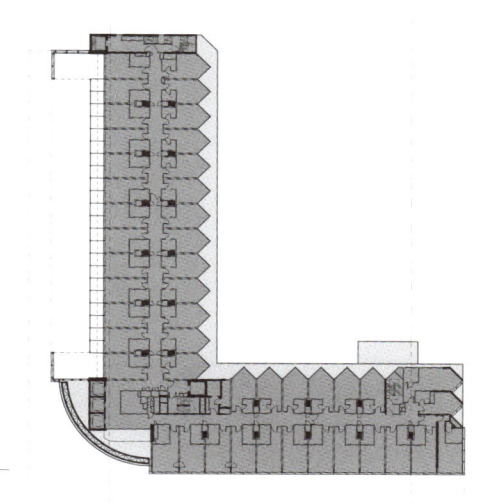

FEATURE PROJECTS — GRAND PARK ORCHARD CHAPTER TWO 123

Level 5 plan

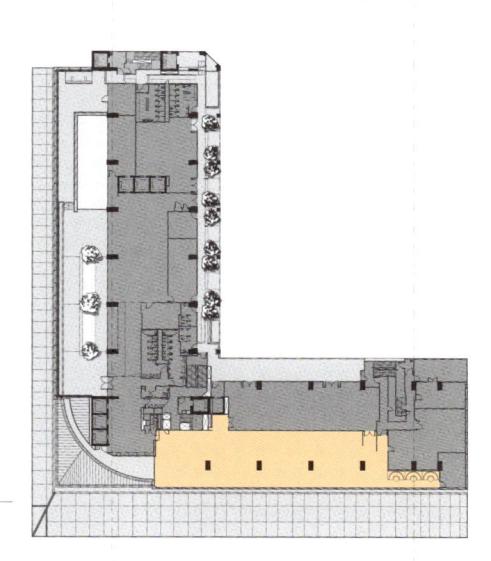

Level 4 plan

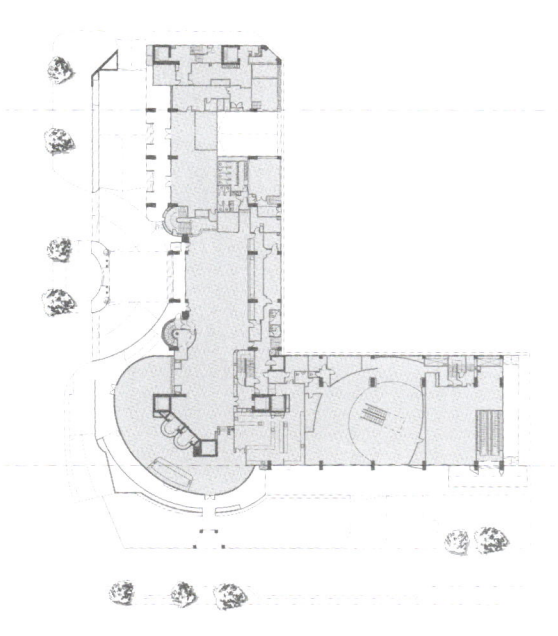

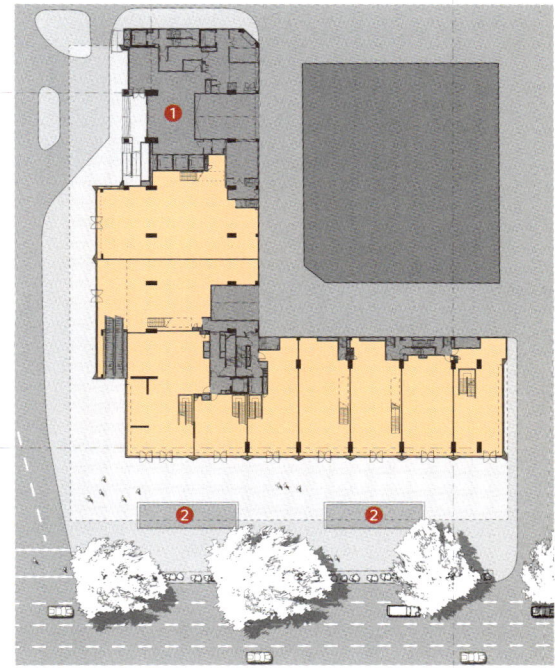

■ Retail, Food & Beverage
① Hotel lobby
② Water feature

BEFORE
Ground level and site plan

AFTER
Ground level and site plan

The building's LED-embedded glazing system and louvred sunshading screen, both patterned to reflect a herringbone stitch, provide Grand Park Orchard with a distinctive architectural motif.

A Behind the fritted glass at the fourth-storey hotel restaurant B Escalators lead from the sidewalk to a third-storey gym and bank C The fourth-storey hotel lobby and pool deck D The hotel's pool at night

FEATURE PROJECTS　GRAND PARK ORCHARD　　CHAPTER TWO　127

D

126   PART 2   CONTRIBUTIONS OF DP ARCHITECTS

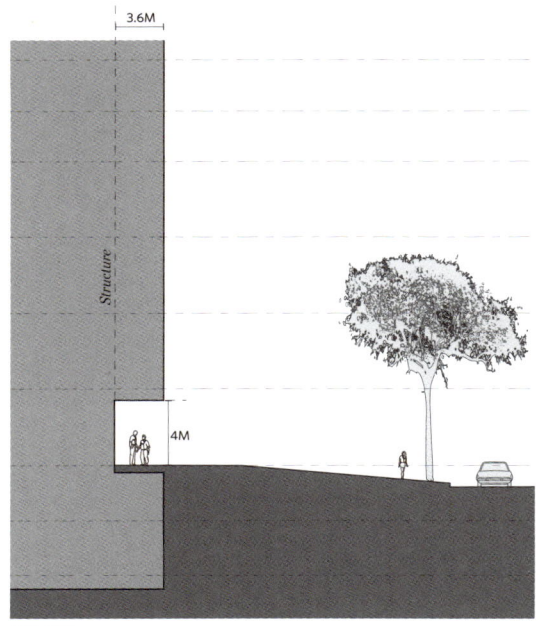

BEFORE

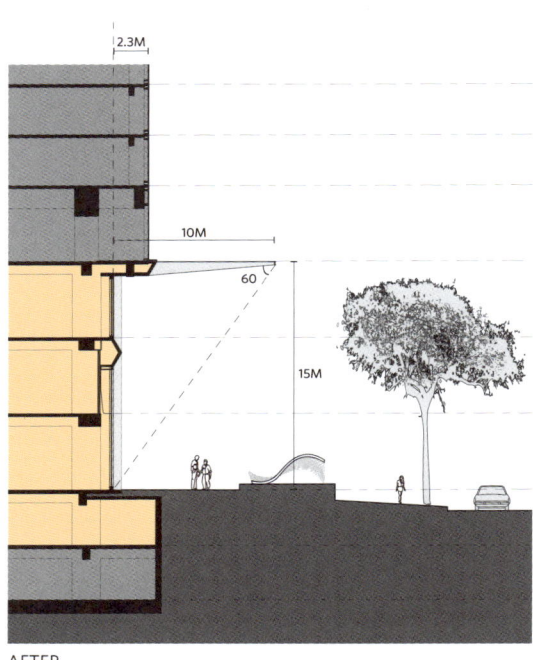

AFTER
A building waiver permits less coverage due to structural constraints and design intent for a simple, uninterrupted façade

DESIGN INTENT	STRUCTURAL CONSTRAINTS	RESOLUTION A	RESOLUTION B
Simple façade	Capacity of existing structure limited to 10m, below minimum coverage	A lowered canopy interrupts the pedestrian sight line to third-level retail	Added structure interrupts the façade and/or promenade

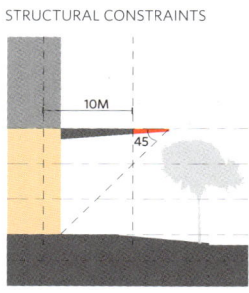

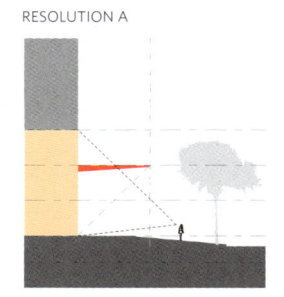

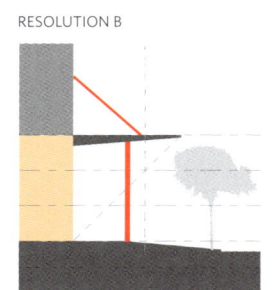

▮ New retail base

ABOVE
Canopy design rationale

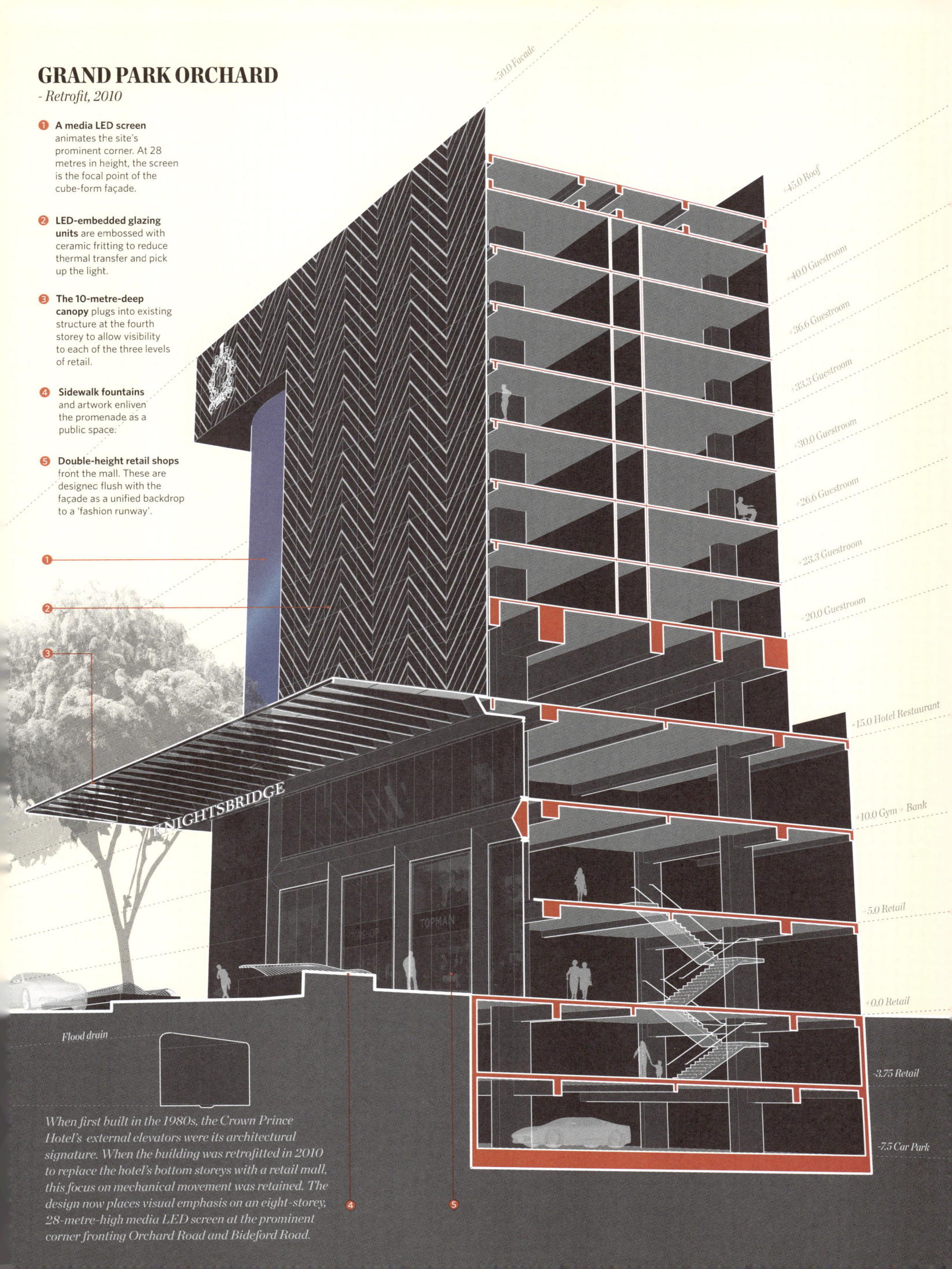

GRAND PARK ORCHARD
- *Retrofit, 2010*

1 **A media LED screen** animates the site's prominent corner. At 28 metres in height, the screen is the focal point of the cube-form façade.

2 **LED-embedded glazing units** are embossed with ceramic fritting to reduce thermal transfer and pick up the light.

3 **The 10-metre-deep canopy** plugs into existing structure at the fourth storey to allow visibility to each of the three levels of retail.

4 **Sidewalk fountains** and artwork enliven the promenade as a public space.

5 **Double-height retail shops** front the mall. These are designed flush with the façade as a unified backdrop to a 'fashion runway'.

Flood drain

When first built in the 1980s, the Crown Prince Hotel's external elevators were its architectural signature. When the building was retrofitted in 2010 to replace the hotel's bottom storeys with a retail mall, this focus on mechanical movement was retained. The design now places visual emphasis on an eight-storey, 28-metre-high media LED screen at the prominent corner fronting Orchard Road and Bideford Road.

+50.0 Façade
+45.0 Roof
+40.0 Guestroom
+36.6 Guestroom
+33.3 Guestroom
+30.0 Guestroom
+26.6 Guestroom
+23.3 Guestroom
+20.0 Guestroom
+15.0 Hotel Restaurant
+10.0 Gym + Bank
+5.0 Retail
+0.0 Retail
-3.75 Retail
-7.5 Car Park

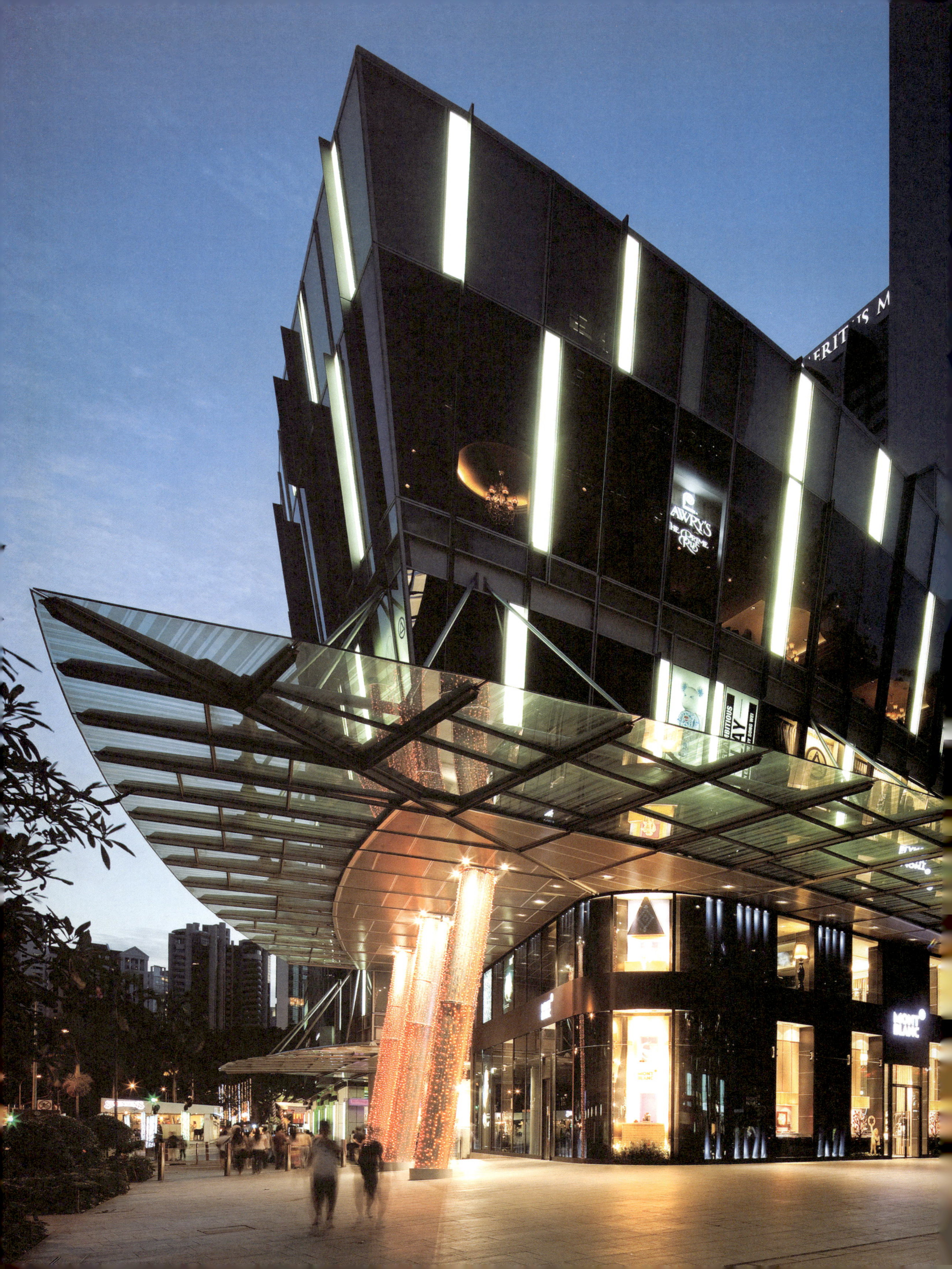

Feature Projects
Mandarin Gallery

Year Completed : 2009
Project Type : Retrofit
Area : 18,200 square metres (retail);
92,000 square metres (hotel)

The Mandarin Singapore hotel was erected in 1971 as a 4-storey lobby podium topped by a 40-storey tower and a second 37-storey tower was added to the complex in 1980. With more than 1000 guestrooms and a site frontage 150 metres in length, the hotel continues to exhibit a commanding presence on Orchard Road. On the corner of a major intersection and pedestrian crossing, the site is bordered on three sides by vehicular streets. This 2009 retrofit project converted the primary hotel lobby along Orchard Road into a four-storey retail podium.

Significantly reconfigured site conditions have established the building's new pedestrian accessibility. By relocating the hotel's vehicular drop-off lanes along Orchard Road to Orchard Link Road at the site's western boundary, the promenade has been widened and opened to pedestrian-only traffic. The main hotel lobby, originally on ground level, has also been repositioned to the fifth level in the process of reprogramming, permitting new retail spaces to interface with sidewalk foot traffic.

OPPOSITE
Mandarin Gallery at the corner of Orchard Road and Grange Road.

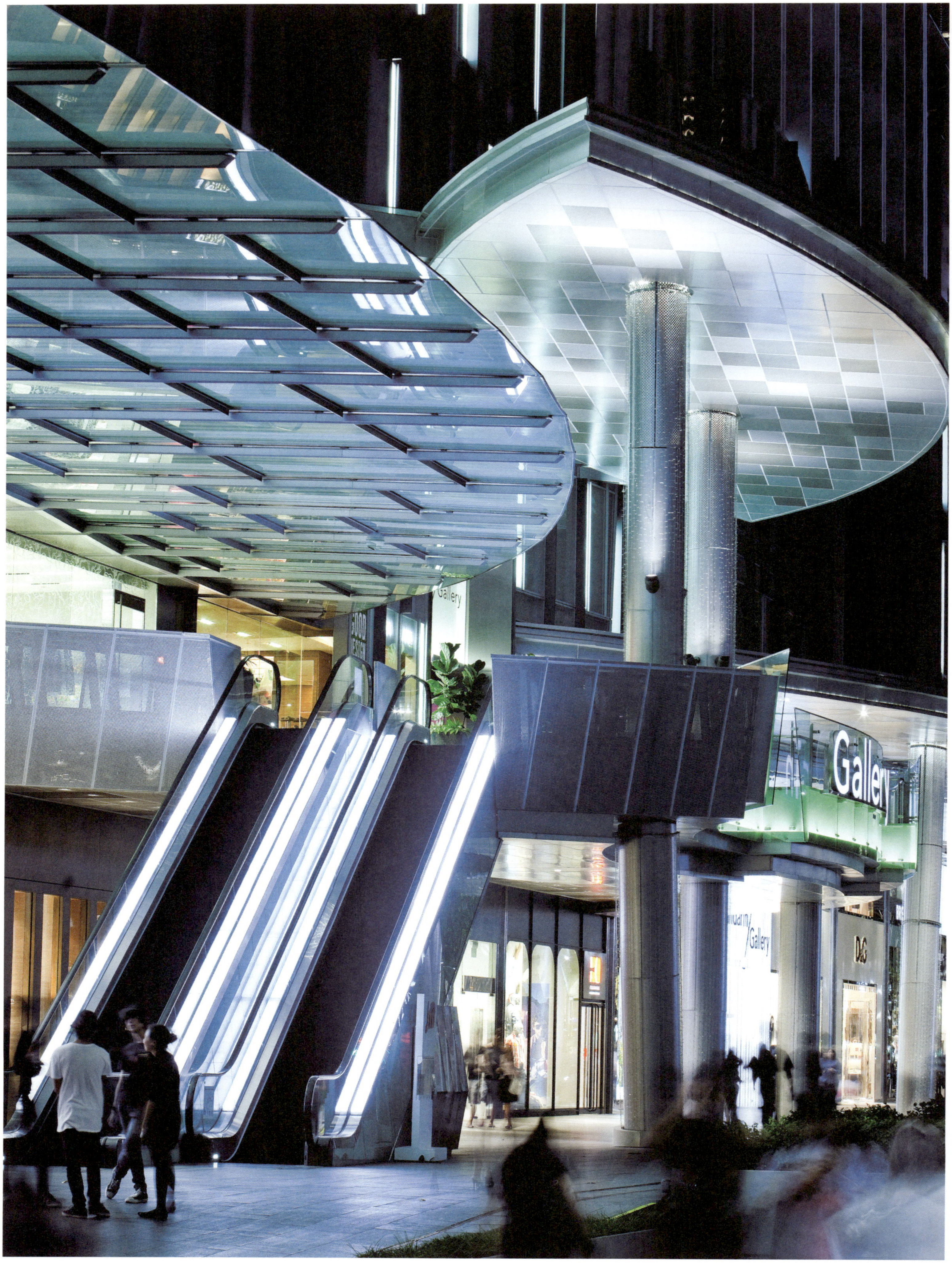
Gallery
D&G

> **Significantly reconfigured site conditions have established the building's new pedestrian accessibility.**

Two primary functional elements in the design of Mandarin Gallery exemplify the extroversion of the closed form mall. First, an 8-metre-deep canopy shelters a covered public promenade with double-volume shopfronts 8.5 metres in height. Secondly, an escalator blends the horizontal movement of pedestrian traffic with vertical movement, connecting the promenade directly with an elevated landing and mall entrance on the second storey.

Form and articulation work both at large and small scales to engage pedestrian flows. At the scale of the building, the architects have implemented organic form to jointly mitigate the existing structure's monumentality and further establish continuity between retail space and street space—Mandarin Gallery's gentle glass curves can be described dually as a carving from the mall's exterior and a bulging from the retail space within. The effect is a visual and programmatic conflation of the two, the dissolution of a boundary line. Mandarin Gallery's new façade and canopy project toward the street corners for extended presence within high-frequency circulation patterns.

Façade detailing techniques adapt the materiality of the building to the scale of the passerby. Repetitive glass units segment the curves of the façade's double skin; these are inset with white light boxes, spandrel panels and dark vertical fins for further articulation of the surface. This strategy is followed through to the curved canopy, where deep steel members support modules of fritted-glass units. The canopy is suspended by tension cables from a fourth-level datum, detailed to balance the verticality of the façade's mullion system with an element of strong horizontality.

OPPOSITE
Escalators extend from a second-storey landing.

ABOVE
Mandarin Singapore hotel in the 1980s.

Section detail, glazed canopy system
1. CHHF pipe truss tie rod
2. Mild steel tie-rod bracket
3. Fillet weld
4. Tie rod bracket in direction of tubular section
5. Pipe truss
6. Stiffener plate weld to trusses
7. Fillet weld with truss below
8. Universal beam truss
9. Silicone sealant with backer rod
10. Ceramic-fritted laminated glass
11. Bent sheet weld to I-beam
12. Aluminium angle weld to aluminium bent sheet

ABOVE & OPPOSITE
The eight-metre-deep glazed canopy is supported by a system of steel trusses and cables.

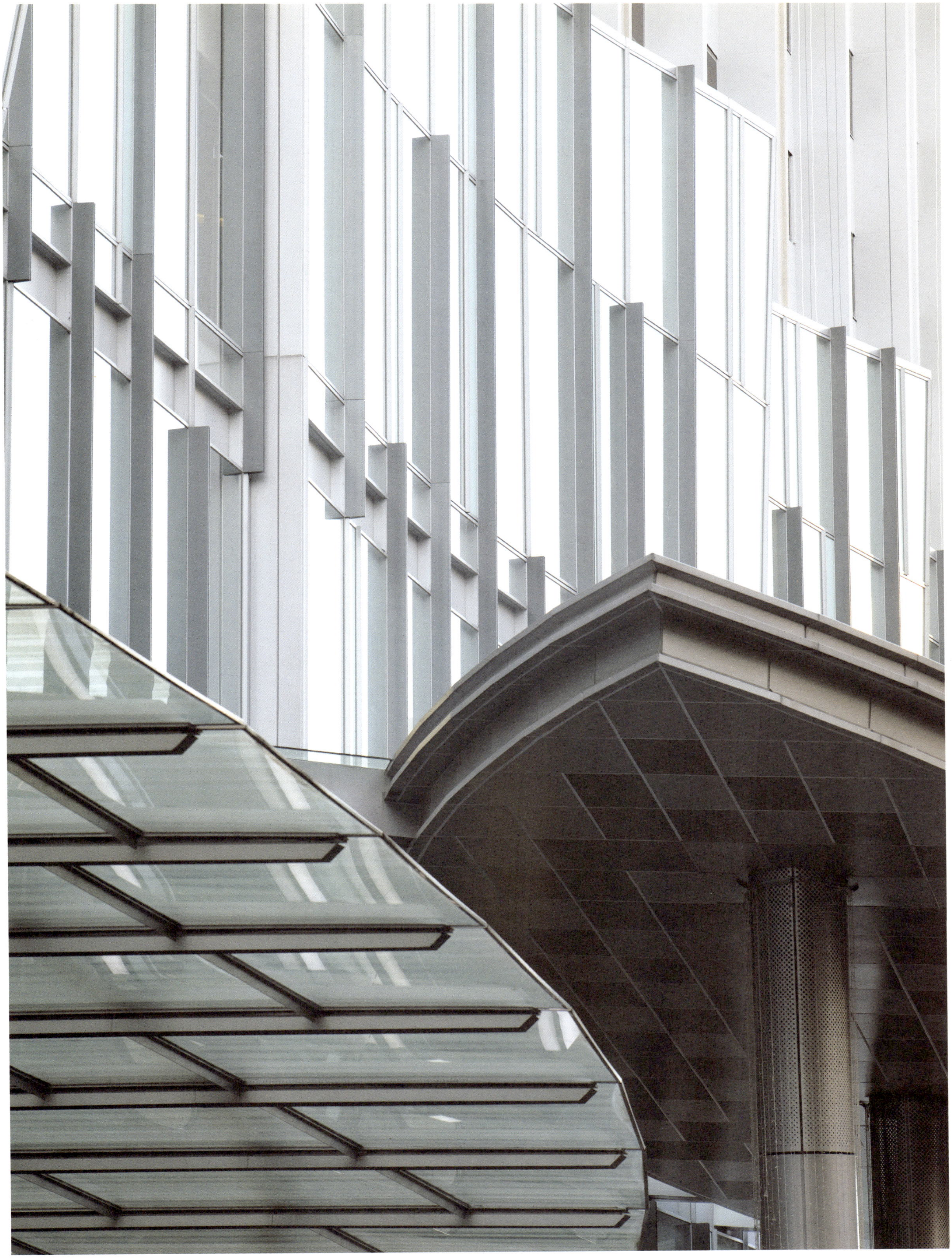

ABOVE
Mandarin Gallery at the corner of Orchard Road and Orchard Link. The hotel entrance is to the far right.

RIGHT
A partial section through the storefont.

FAR RIGHT
The landing offers direct access to upper-storey retail shops from the promenade.

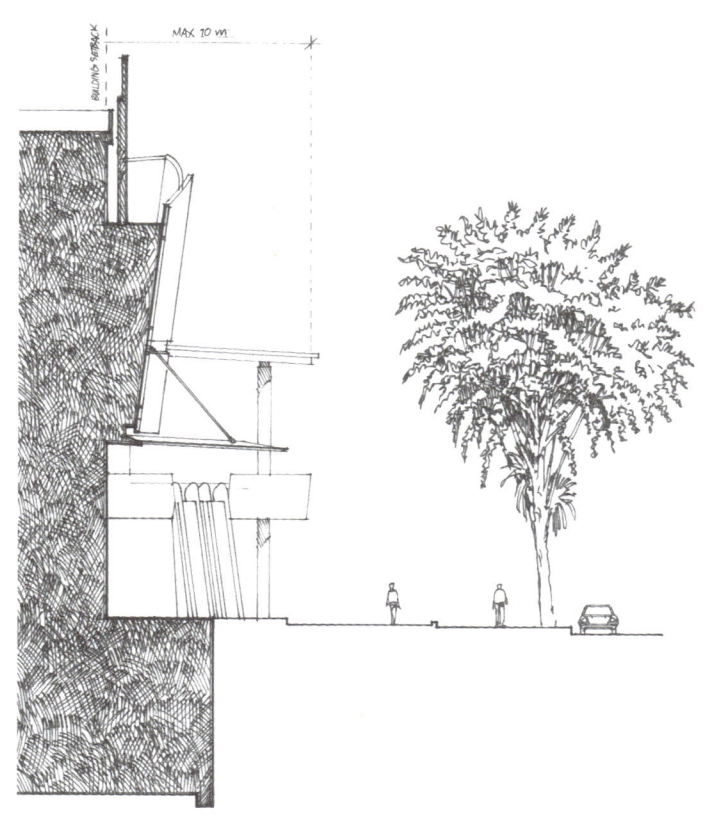

FEATURE PROJECTS MANDARIN GALLERY CHAPTER TWO 135

> By relocating the hotel's vehicular drop-off lanes along Orchard Road to Orchard Link Road at the site's western boundary, the promenade has been widened and opened to pedestrian-only traffic.

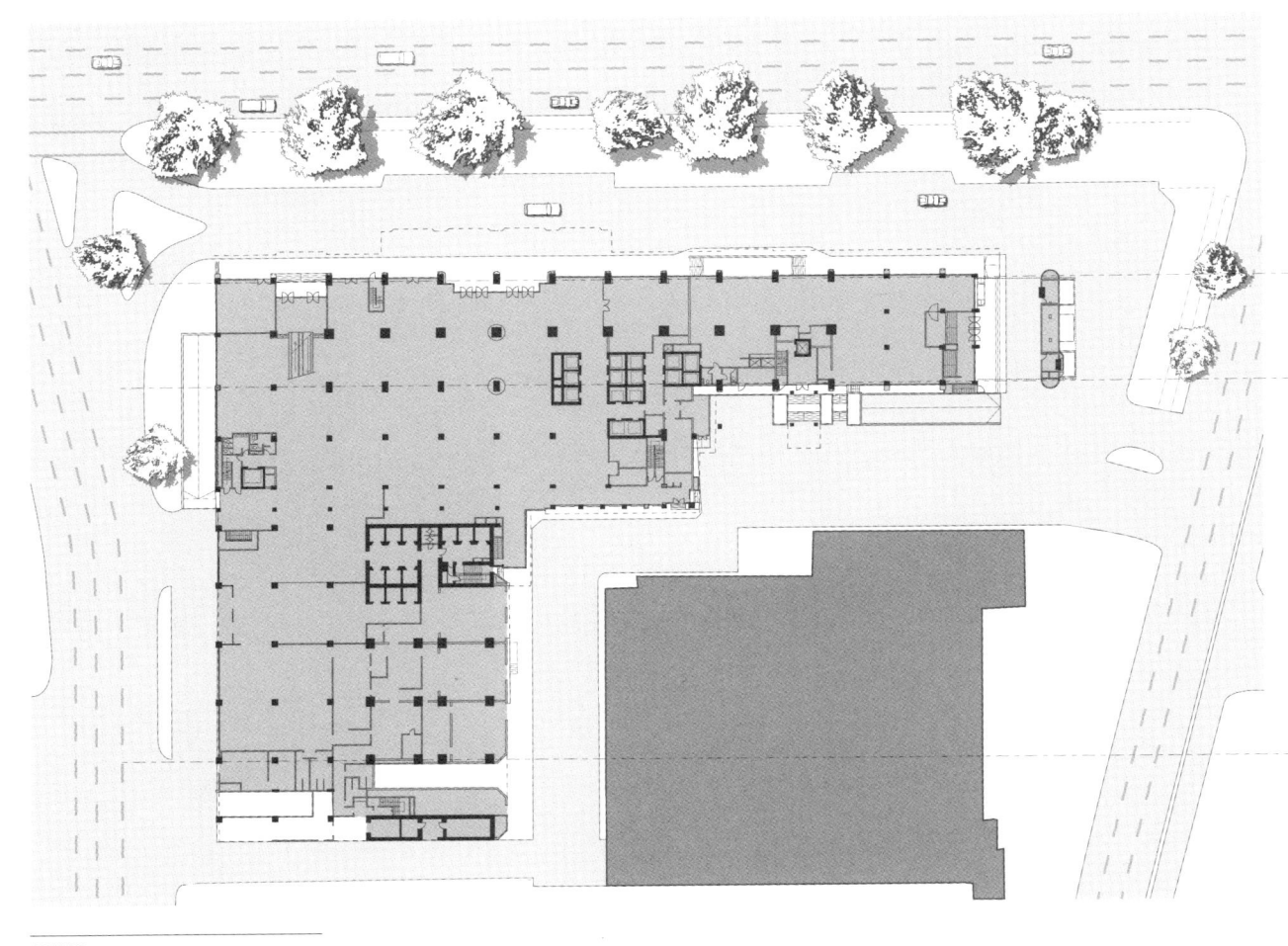

BEFORE
Ground level and site plan

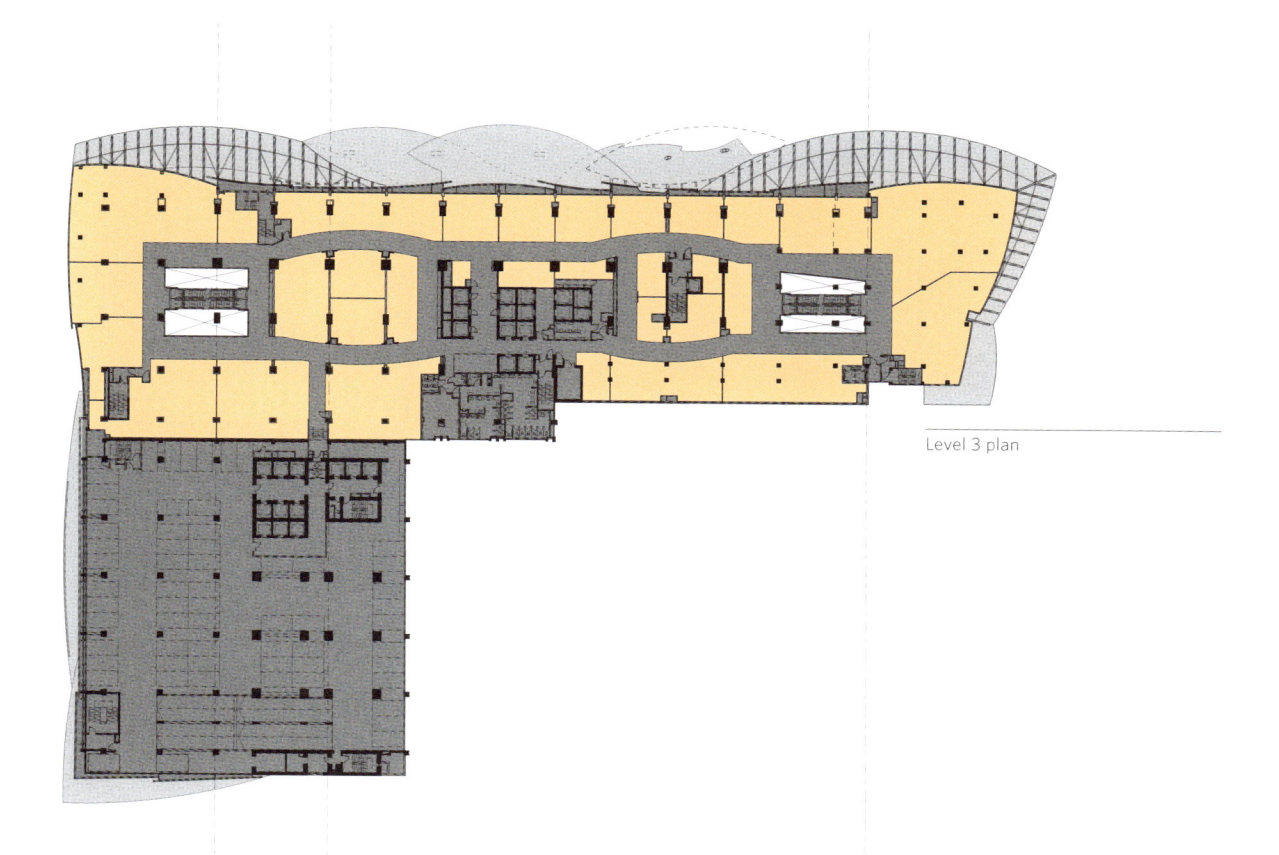

FEATURE PROJECTS MANDARIN GALLERY   CHAPTER TWO

Level 3 plan

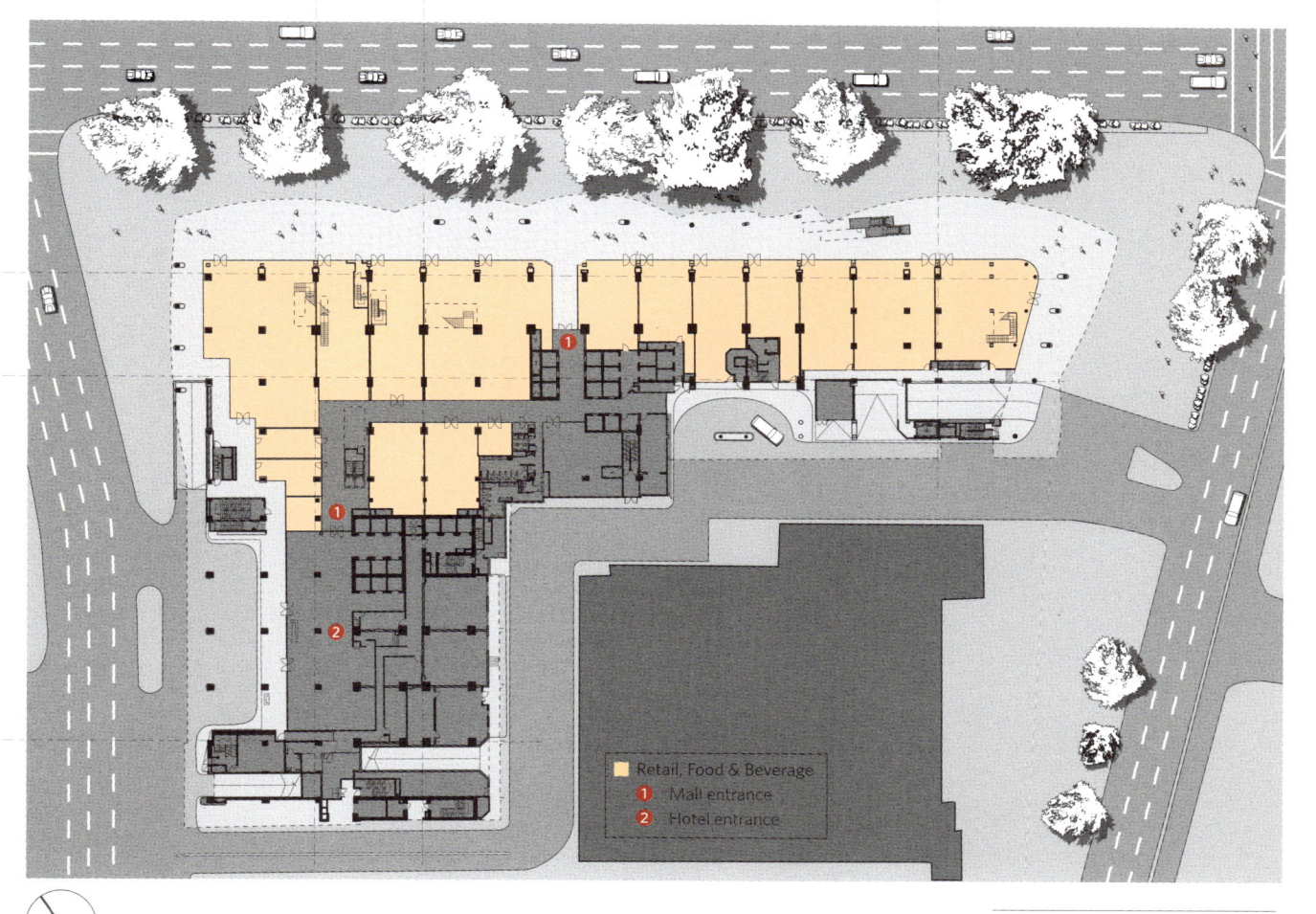

- Retail, Food & Beverage
- ① Mall entrance
- ② Hotel entrance

AFTER
Ground level and site plan

length!   *texture*   *texture / animation*

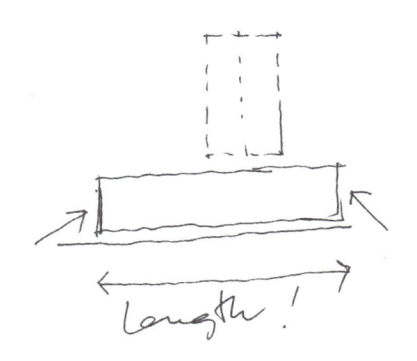

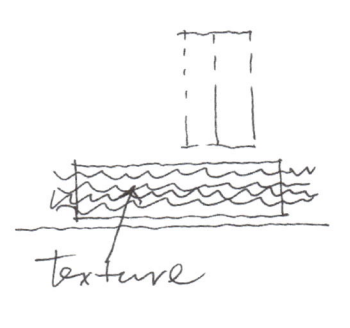

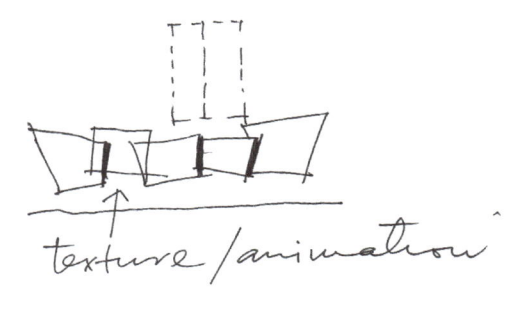

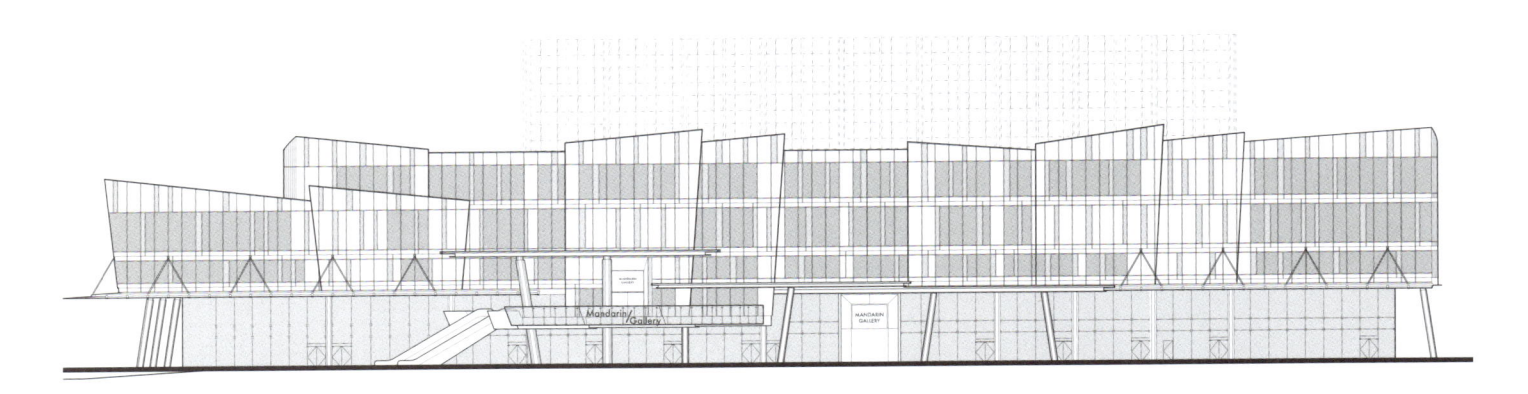

TOP & MIDDLE
Elevation design.

BOTTOM
The mall's new elevation breaks from the monotony of the existing concrete-shell podium with a series of dynamic curvilinear masses.

OPPOSITE
A The mall's main entrance at ground level.
B & C The escalator and landing.

FEATURE PROJECTS – MANDARIN GALLERY   CHAPTER TWO

PART 2   CONTRIBUTIONS OF DP ARCHITECTS

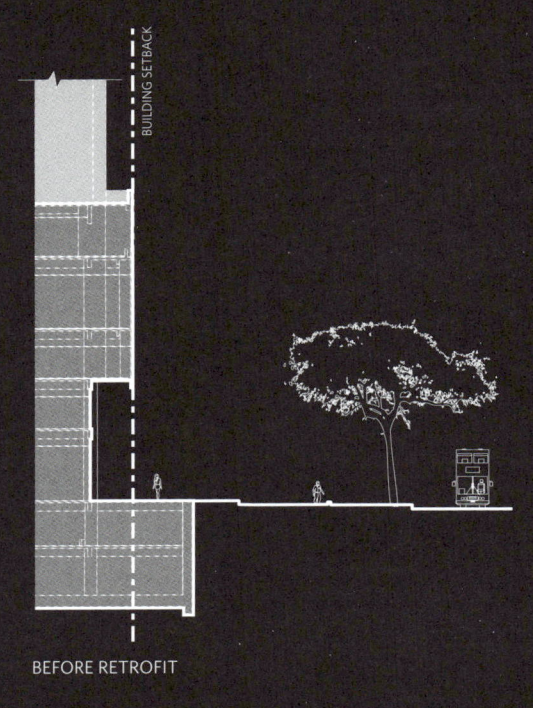

BEFORE RETROFIT

AFTER RETROFIT

ABOVE
A partial section through the retail podium and storefront.

MANDARIN GALLERY
- Retrofit, 2009

1 **Outdoor escalators** link passersby directly to upper-storey retail space.

2 **A second-storey entrance** enhances mall access.

3 **A double façade** lightens the existing concrete shell with transparent glazing and a dynamic mullion system.

4 **The existing hotel** lobby is relocated from the podium to the fifth storey.

This 2009 retrofit converted a four-storey podium of an existing hotel built in 1971 to a retail mall. Sidewalk escalators and a second-storey landing enhance mall accessibility. The original closed-form building has been redesigned with a dynamic, segmented façade that increases visibility and breaks up the form's monumentality. This series of design moves is intended to further engage the pedestrian.

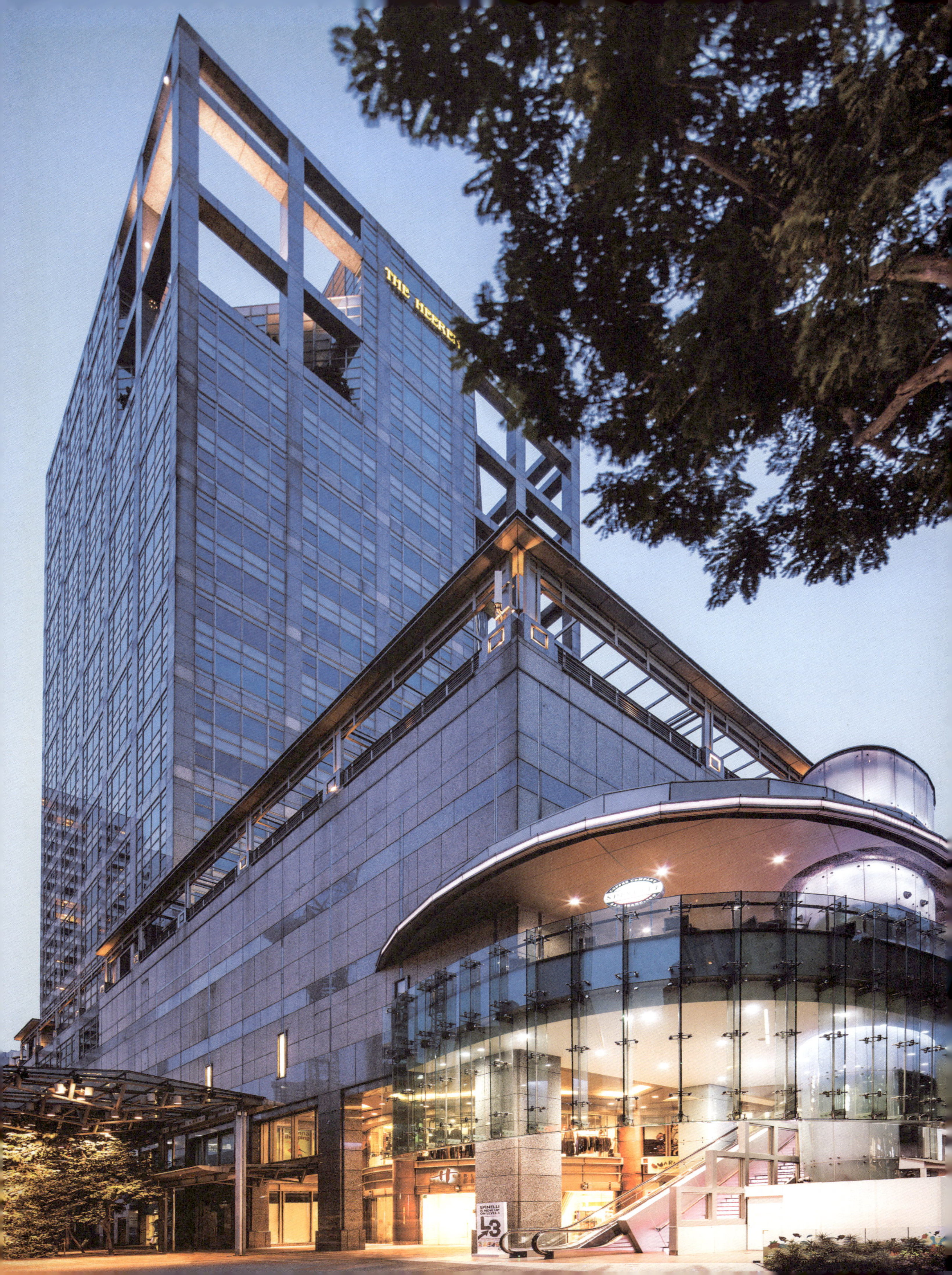
SPINELLI
L3

Feature Projects
The Heeren

Year Completed : 2009. Phased, work ongoing.
Project Type : Façade extension
Area   : 465 square metres

With a youth park and the National Youth Centre located one block to the south, The Heeren and its site at the corner of Orchard Road and Cairnhill Road have served for many years as a recreational and social magnet for young consumer populations. In addition, its location at a prime pedestrian crossing makes it a dynamic haven of activity. The Heeren, a 14-storey office tower atop a six-storey retail podium, was built in 1997 specifically to house stores catering to youths. In 2009 DP Architects completed an extension hosting an outdoor refreshment area and urban verandah along the Orchard Road frontage to enhance the mall's presence at the level of the sidewalk. In keeping with the youth consumer trends and their corresponding shops, the addition offers a dynamic layout, form and material selection to augment pedestrian engagement.

The design is calibrated to offer an intimate relationship between pedestrian and architecture: the traveller does not pass by The Heeren; rather, he passes under it and through it as angled glass kiosks, an overhead urban verandah and an outer glass rain screen work together to encapsulate a triple-height sidewalk space.

OPPOSITE
The Heeren's façade extension is programmed with urban verandahs on two levels.

> The design is calibrated to offer an intimate relationship between pedestrian and architecture.

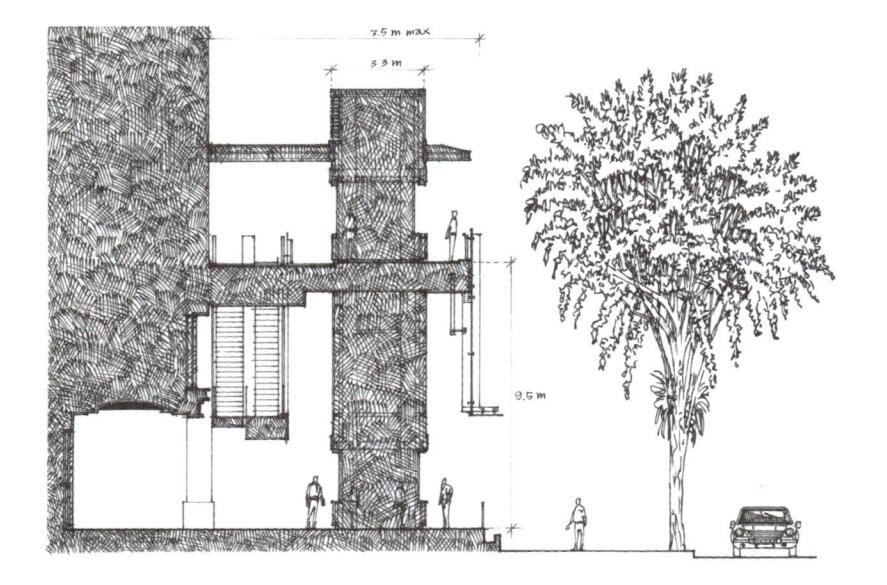

An undulating glass façade incorporates the fluidity and movement of foot traffic. Performing jointly as rail and rain screen, the glazing is segmented and detailed with glazed fins and point connections, relating the sweeping curves more acutely to the scale of the human body. It also strengthens the layered nature of The Heeren's frontage – the experience of walking through the façade's extension and ascending to its upper verandah by escalator introduces the visitor to a dynamic play between interior and exterior space.

A special tectonic solution plays a major role in shaping this project – by condensing vertical supports in three clusters to enclose food and beverage kiosks serviceable to the sidewalk and upper verandah, the

TOP LEFT
A partial section through the façade extension and promenade.
BOTTOM
The building's façade before the addition.

TOP RIGHT
The building's frontage along Orchard Road. LED-backed glazed panels are programmed with multi-coloured light displays.

architects have freed the sidewalk space. The kiosks are angled, clad in LED-backed glass, and mounted with plasma screens to produce a visual dynamism directed towards the regional youth population.

A compilation of functional elements are designed to take advantage of the site's heavy patterns of human movement. The kiosks inject mall programme directly into the promenade's pedestrian flows. Façade additions have worked to enhance the building's original plan as designed by Architects 61, in 1997, in which two internal diagonal corridors lead from the mall's central atrium to the street corner and a bus stop, channelling pedestrians from the site's highest-frequency nodes directly into the heart of the building's programme. Perhaps most importantly, an external escalator extends, like the oblique internal corridors, from the upper verandah towards the bus stop and eastbound crowds, linking pedestrians directly with an additional stretch of mall frontage on the third storey. This last design component has worked to universally transform the retail typology characteristic to the Orchard Road shopping corridor – it has been further developed with The Heeren, where the third-storey shop frontage extends the entire length of the façade.

The project has been segmented into multiple design phases led by DP Architects. Additional forthcoming work, will reconfigure the building at its corners to further target the bus stop and Orchard-Cairnhill junction.

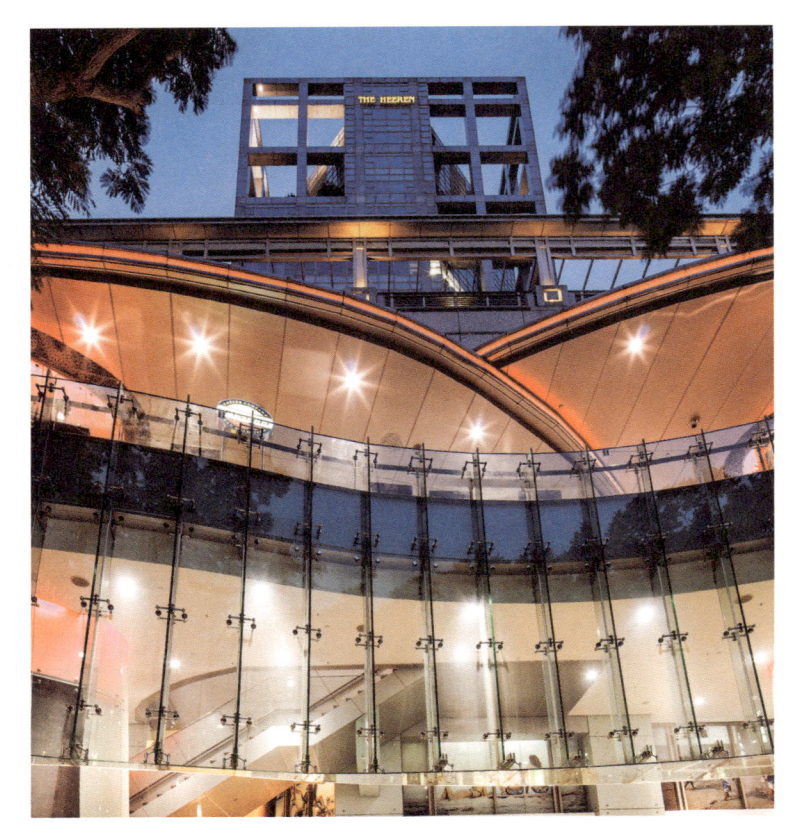

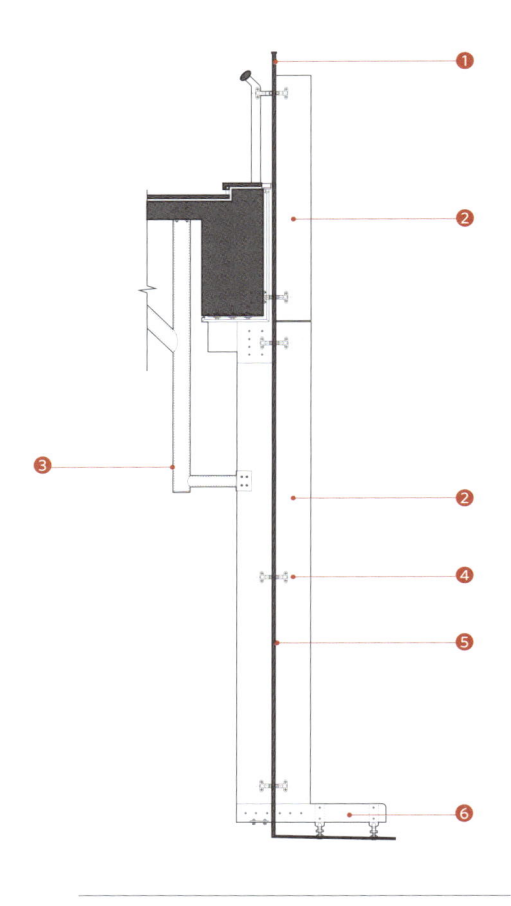

Section detail, downhang glass
1. Glass railing
2. Glass fin
3. Steel support structure
4. Clamp
5. Downhang glass
6. Glass fin supporting glass canopy

TOP & OPPOSITE
Undulating curves are detailed with glass fins and steel joints.

BOTTOM
Shop frontage opens to outdoor dining spaces on the third storey, with direct street access via an external escalator.

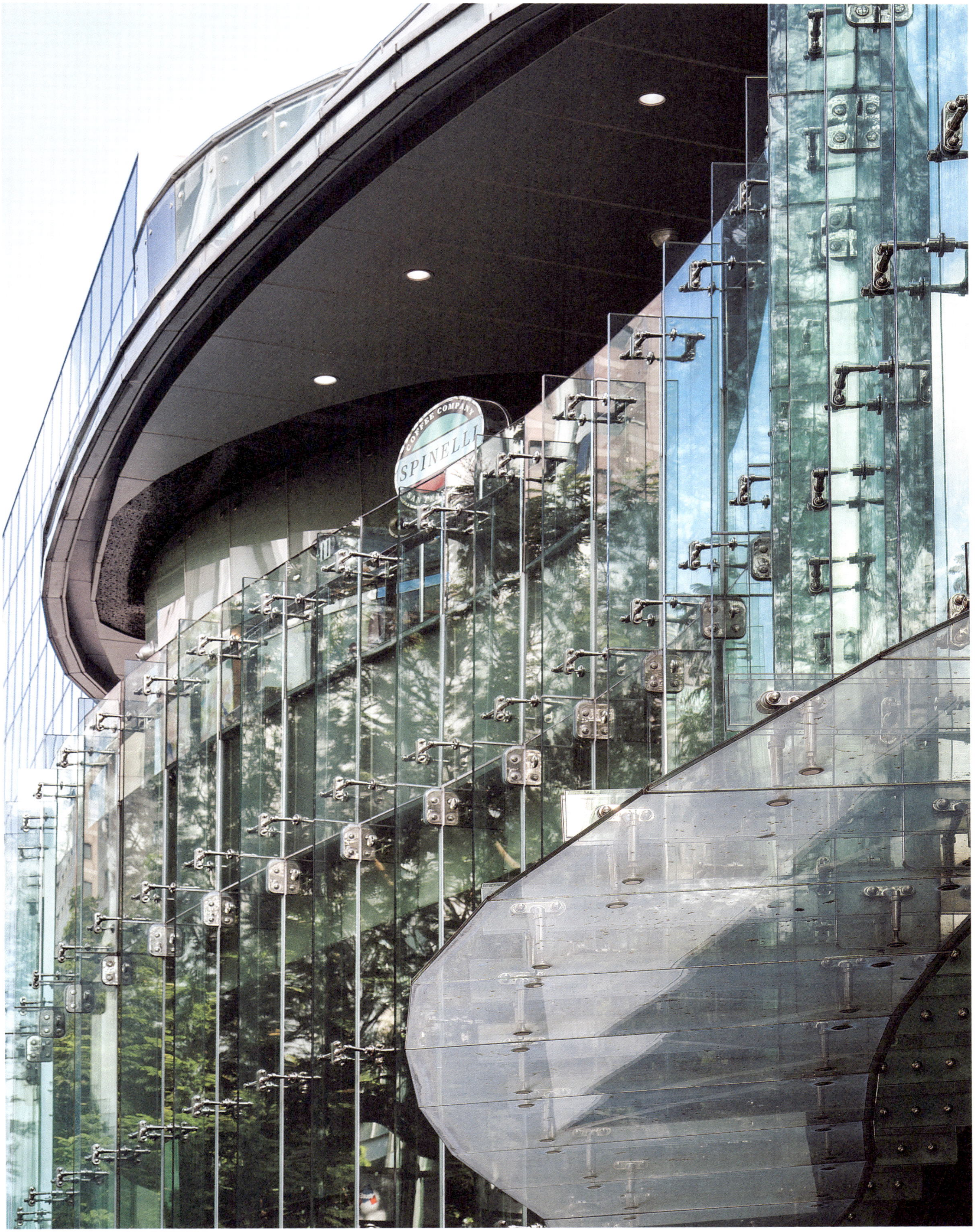
COFFEE COMPANY
SPINELLI

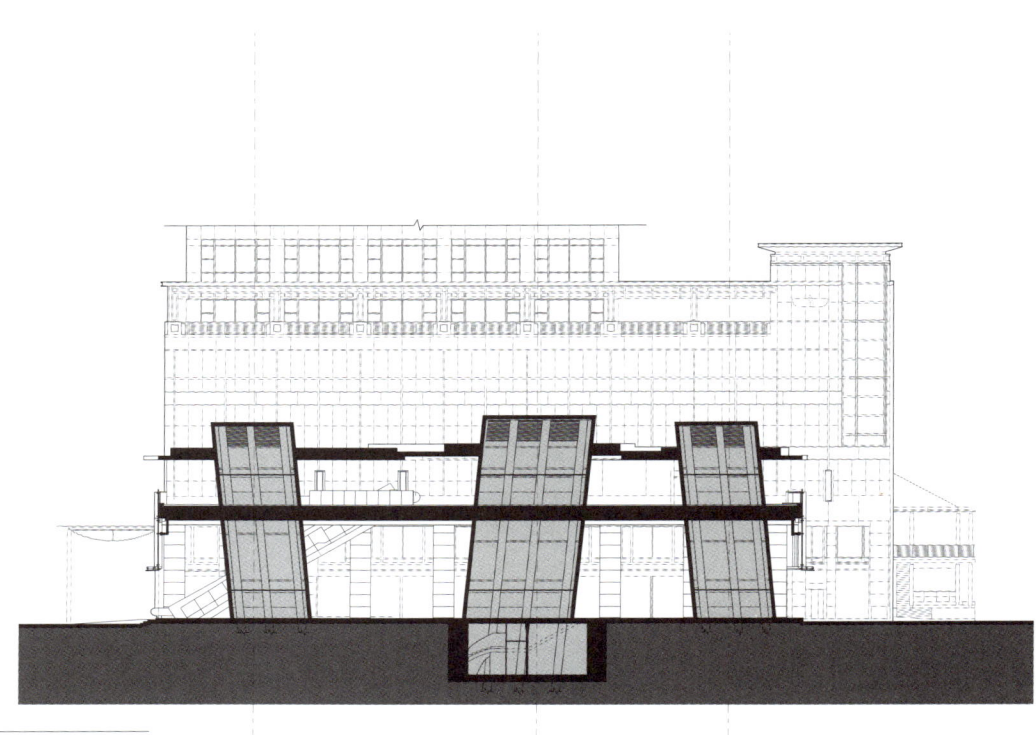

Longitudinal section through façade extension

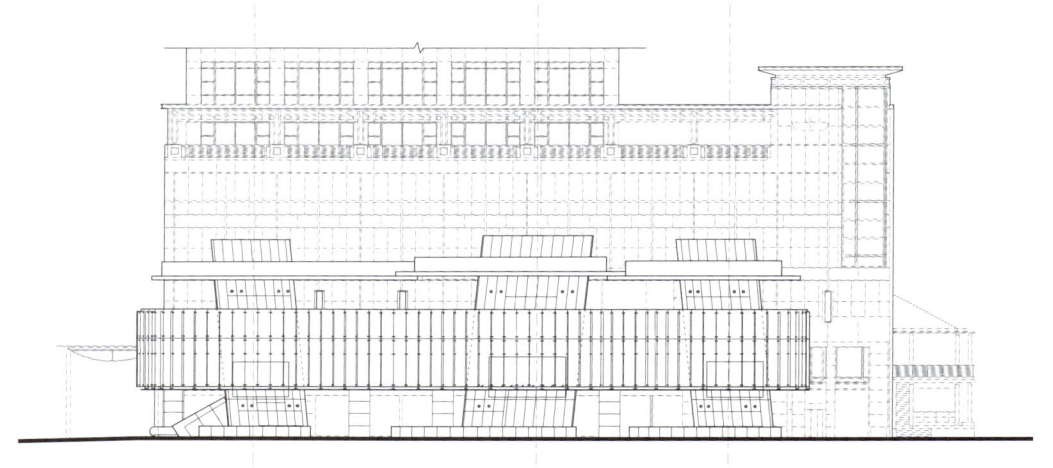

Elevation fronting Orchard Road

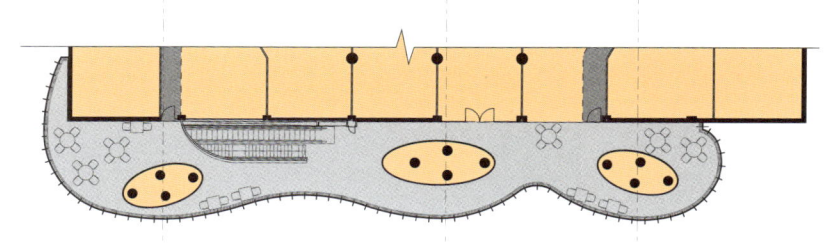

Level 3 plan of façade extension

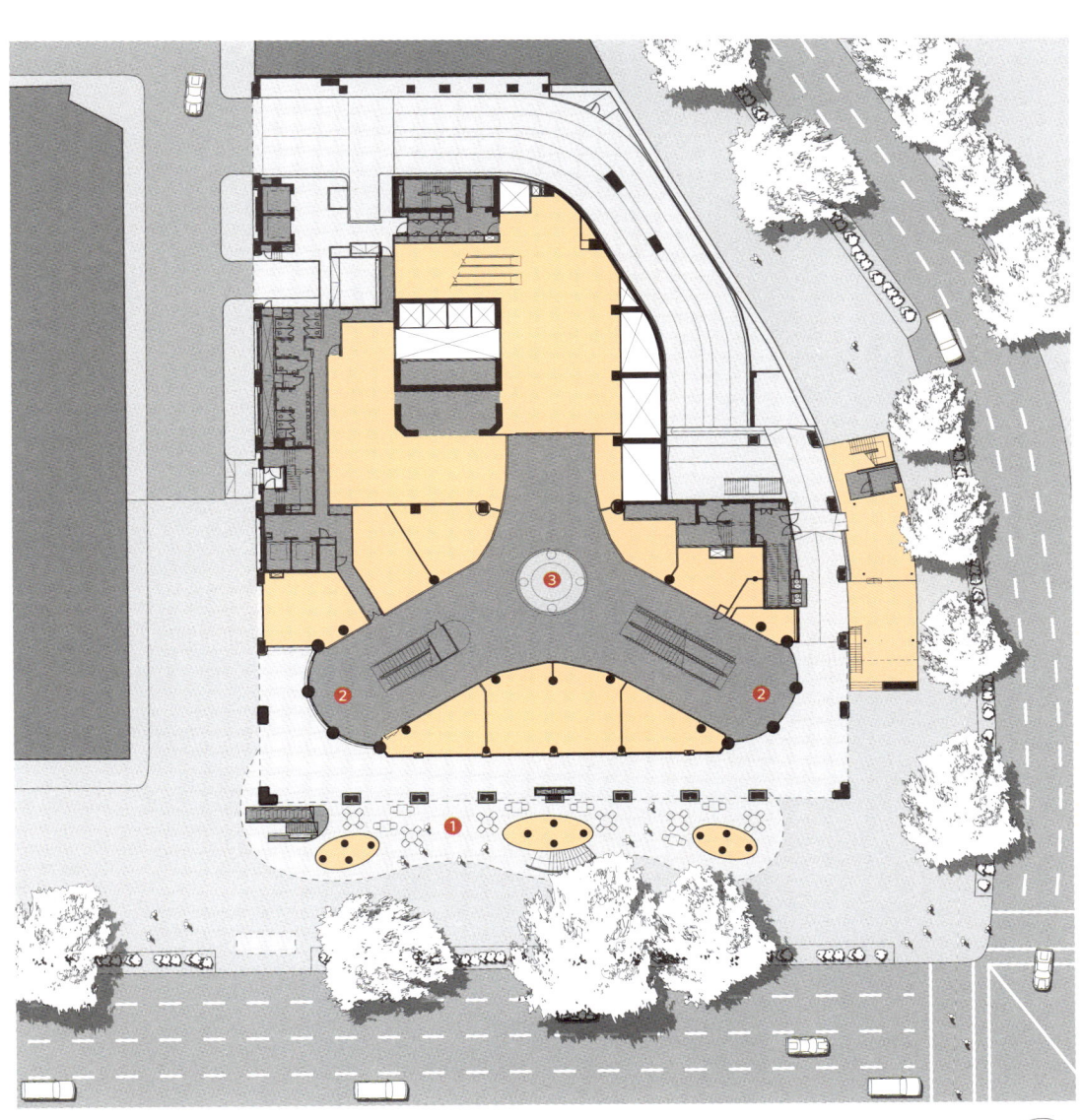

Ground level and site plan

Retail, Food & Beverage
1. Urban verandah
2. Mall entrance
3. Atrium

A compilation of functional elements are designed to take advantage of the site's heavy patterns of human movement. The kiosks inject mall programme directly into the promenade's pedestrian flows.

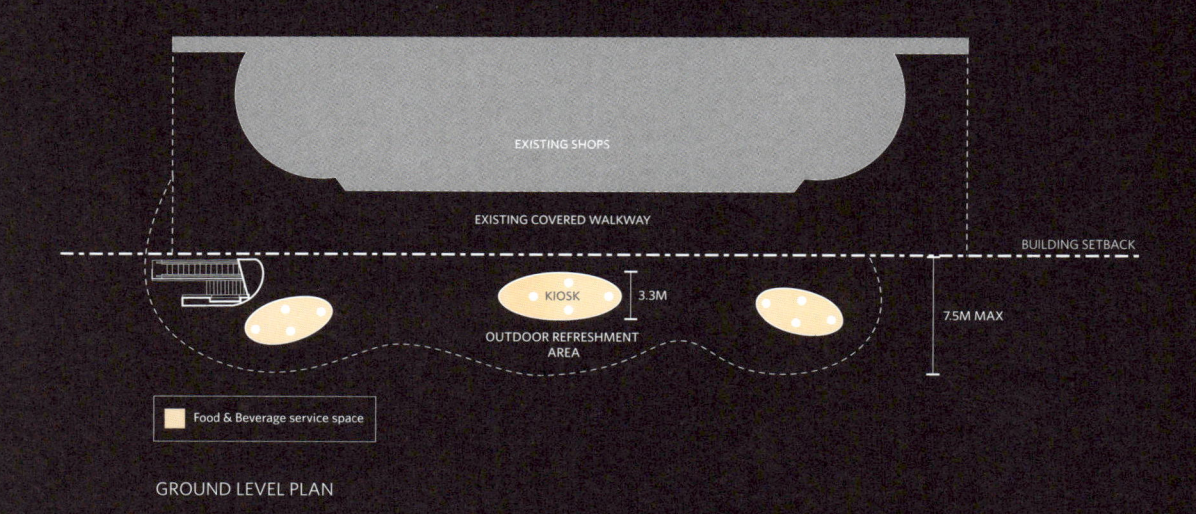

BEFORE EXTENSION

AFTER EXTENSION

3.3M

7.5M MAX

EXISTING SHOPS

EXISTING COVERED WALKWAY

BUILDING SETBACK

KIOSK

3.3M

OUTDOOR REFRESHMENT AREA

7.5M MAX

Food & Beverage service space

GROUND LEVEL PLAN

ABOVE
Façade design rationale

THE HEEREN
- *Façade extension, 2009*

❶ Outdoor escalators extend from the promenade to a third-storey verandah and storefronts.

❷ Kiosks clad in LED-backed glass and mounted with plasma screens serve outdoor dining spaces on two levels.

❸ A glazed rainscreen provides a dynamic curvilinear form aligned with the flows of pedestrian footfall.

❹ A third-storey landing with outdoor dining spaces expands the streetside to storefronts on multiple levels.

A triplet of kiosks injects retail programme directly into the pedestrian flows of Orchard Road's promenade. The kiosks, clad in LED-backed glass and mounted with plasma screens, work with the curvilinear design of the façade extension's third-storey rainscreen to produce a dynamic visual effect and engage the passing pedestrian.

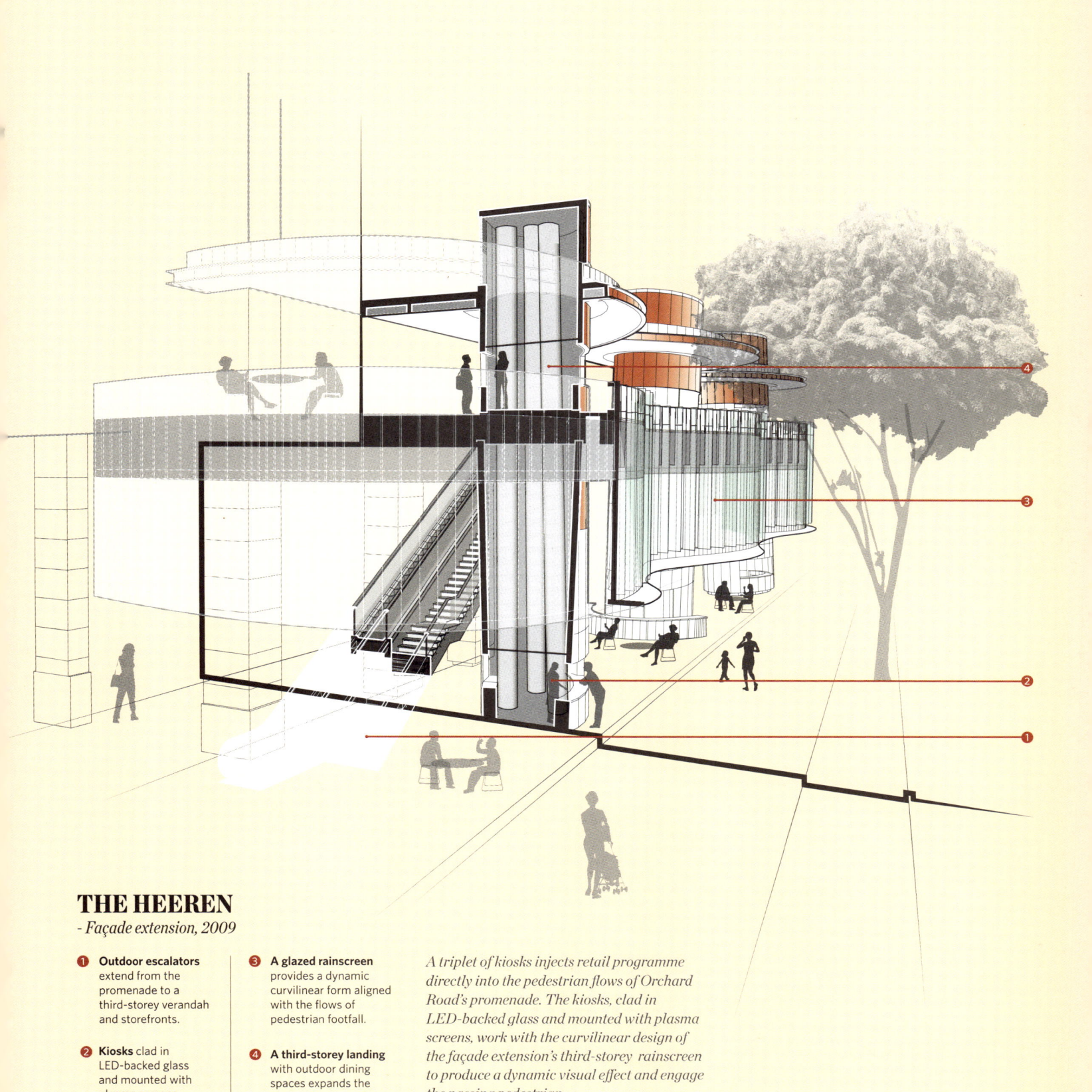

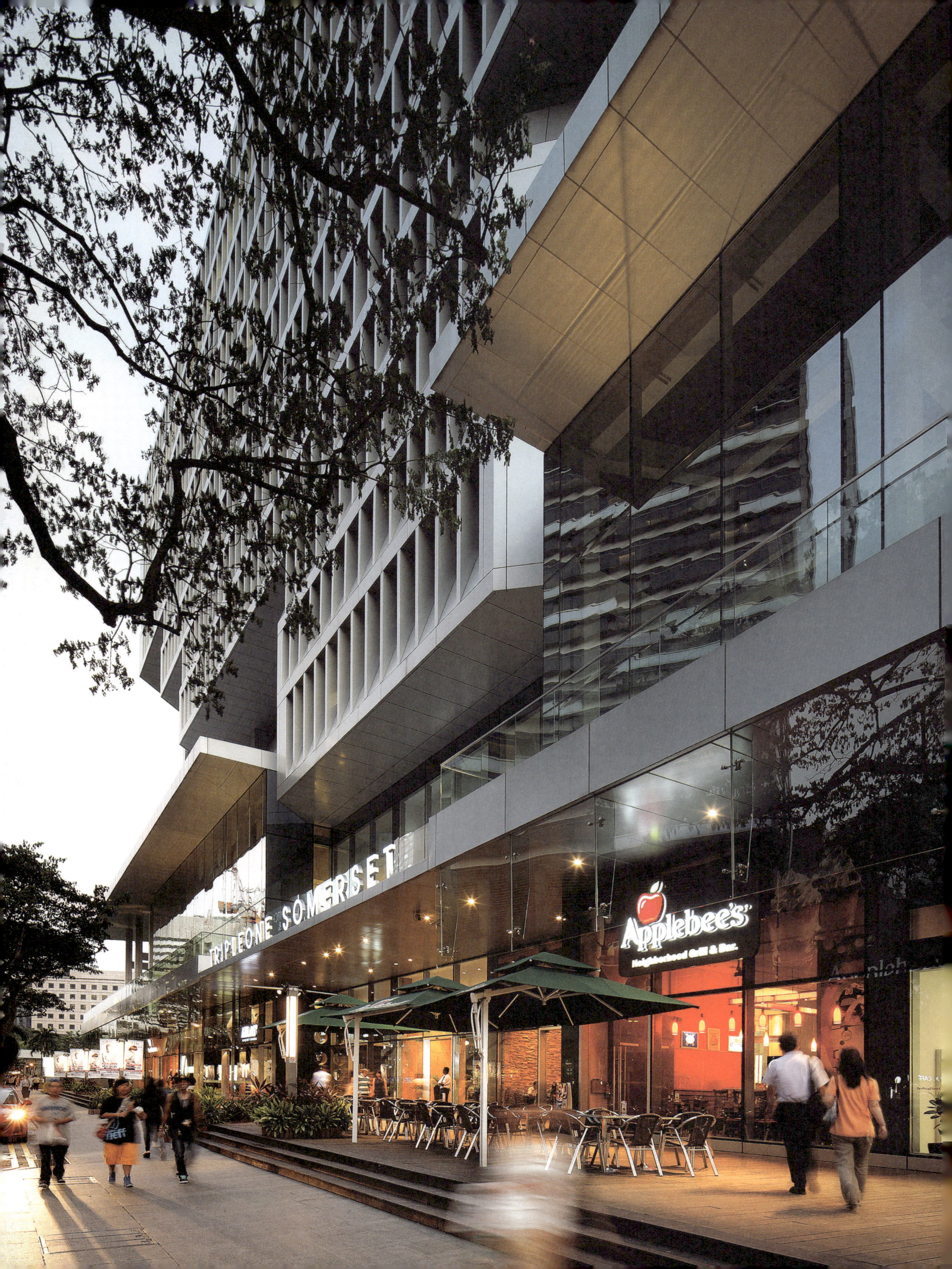
TRIPLEONE SOMERSET
Applebee's
Neighborhood Grill & Bar.

Feature Projects
TripleOne Somerset

Year Completed : 2009
Project Type : Retrofit
Area : 36,000 square metres

Aspects of social progressivism were critical to the Brutalist designs that popularised this movement in architecture worldwide from the post-war 1950s through to the 1970s. Retrofitting lower floors of the 1977 Public Utilities Board building at TripleOne Somerset to accommodate public retail spaces might be considered, then, a contemporary amplification of the building's original social pursuits.

TripleOne Somerset, now home to the headquarters of Singapore Power, was originally designed by Group 2 Architects in response to an architectural design competition in 1971. The 17-storey, 100-metre-high structure could be likened to projects including Gerhard Kallmann's 1962 Boston City Hall. It exhibits common Brutalist physical attributes, namely heavy block form and the structural exposure of functions and services. An H-shaped plan accentuates the building's two commercial wings, and an expressed central services core and stairwells stress verticality – this is balanced with a horizontality produced by a sectional tapering, a formal quality communicative of civic approachability and invitation. In this tropical setting, such a formal composition becomes particularly important as a mode of shading lower storeys.

OPPOSITE
TripleOne Somerset's covered walkway with outdoor dining spaces.

The site is located one block to the south of Orchard Road, a peripheral destination to the main retail corridor, yet one holding an important position adjacent to the Somerset Mass Rapid Transit (MRT) station; it is worth noting the building's unique functional authority as home to the Orchard Road regional power hub.

TripleOne Somerset preceded the MRT station's construction by a decade, and so the additions and alterations of this project in many ways reformulate functional and visual connectivity to this and other subsequently established elements of the urban fabric. An interruptive void exposing a basement-level car park was filled to establish continuity between the sidewalk and interior spaces; ground-level additions nearest the MRT entrance situate new shops closer to the station's pedestrian traffic; a plaza at the corner of Somerset Road and Grange Road was arranged with reference to a popular food court across the street; and municipal plans for the forthcoming conversion of an adjacent vehicular parking lot to a public recreational park were considered as an impending visibility link.

Internal rearrangements of existing lower-level plans have also facilitated new relationships between TripleOne Somerset and the surrounding fabric. The building's ground floors were initially dedicated to public programming and included a lobby, offices, a cafeteria and an auditorium. New partitions have replaced these spaces with 5600 square metres of retail space and 460 square metres of outdoor eateries. While renovations were respectful of existing structure, strategic alterations were made to augment some of the spatial qualities inherent to the original plan and section. For instance, a series of slabs were removed and columns reinforced with wrapped fibreglass to transform the double-height, 24-metre-wide auditorium into a ground-level atrium.

New architectural details are subtle and geometrically uniform, crafted as a backdrop to the prominent existing structure in which they are embedded. The façade is composed of a simple glass-and-steel framing system – large panels of glass achieve lightness and transparency, and shop signage is set interior to the glazing so as not to interrupt this sheen surface quality. A collection of natural materials complement the raw finishes of the exposed reinforced concrete beams and slabs, including timber and glass details, and flooring of composite Chinese bamboo. A metallic fluorocarbon finish retains the tile patterning of the original exterior cladding.

TOP
The Public Utilities Board building as erected in 1977.
BOTTOM
The building's retrofitted retail podium makes up TripleOne Somerset's first two storeys.

OPPOSITE
Elevation fronting Somerset Road.

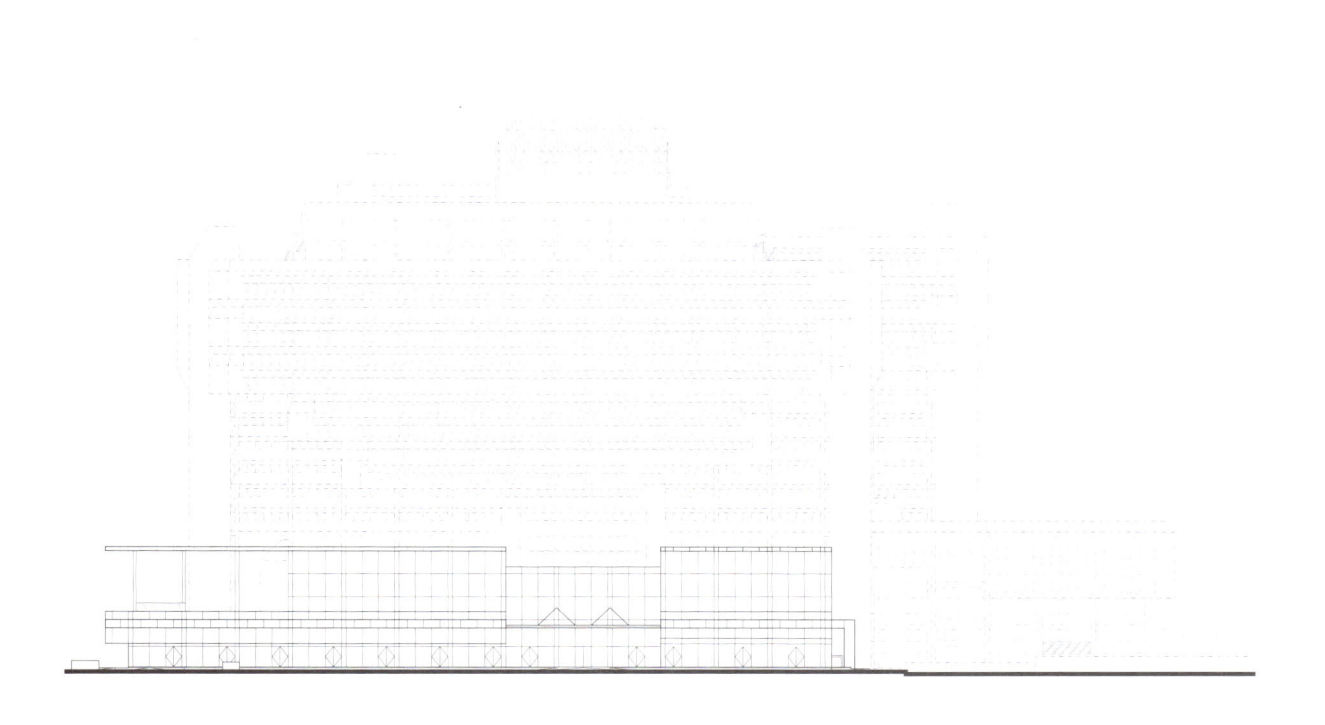

FEATURE PROJECTS — TRIPLEONE SOMERSET   CHAPTER TWO   155

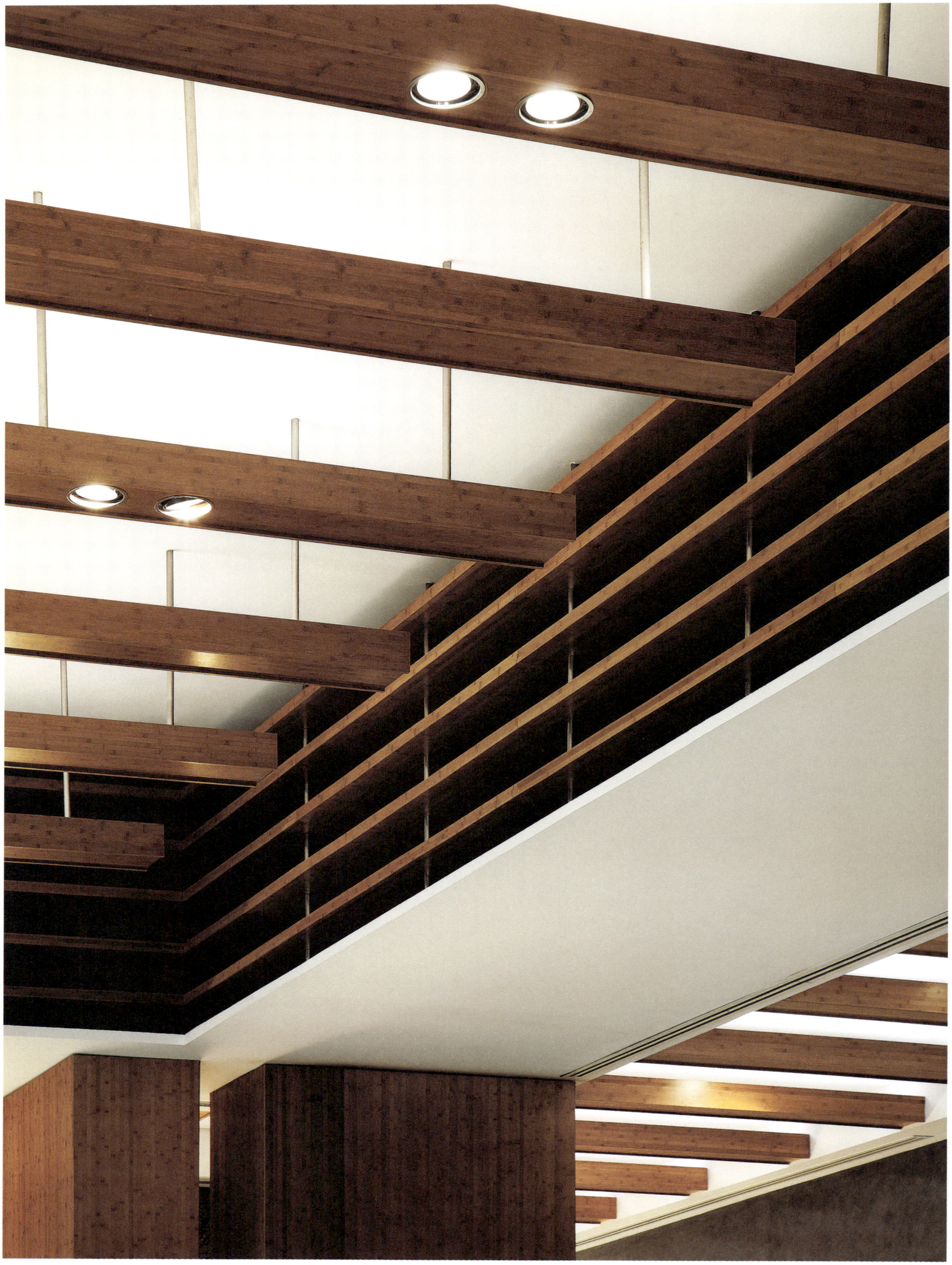

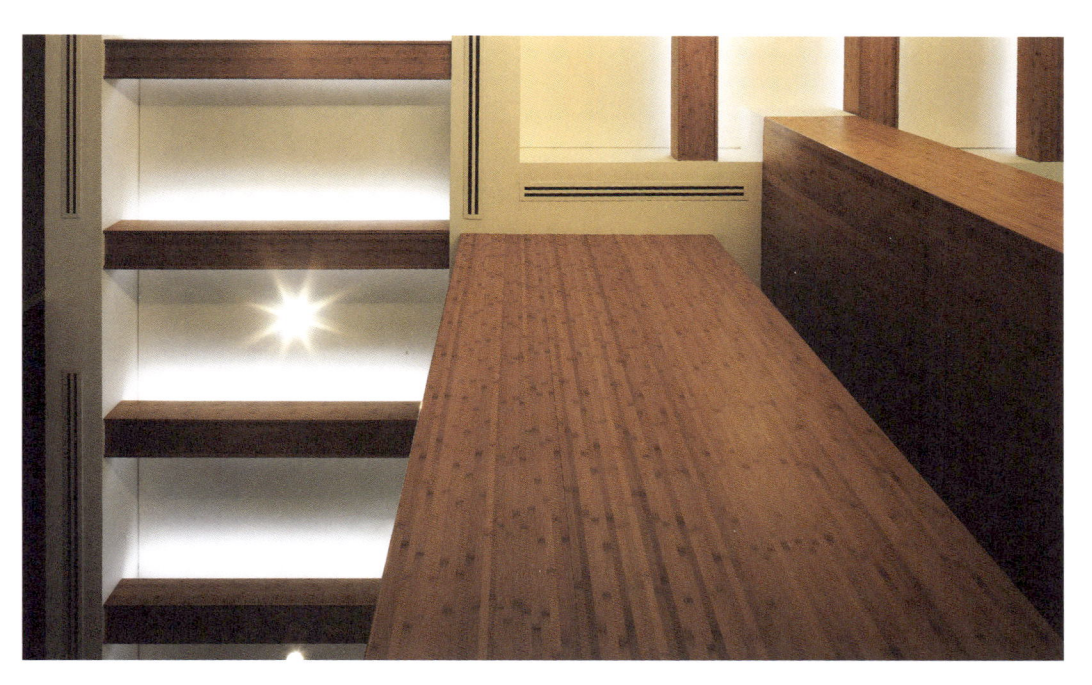

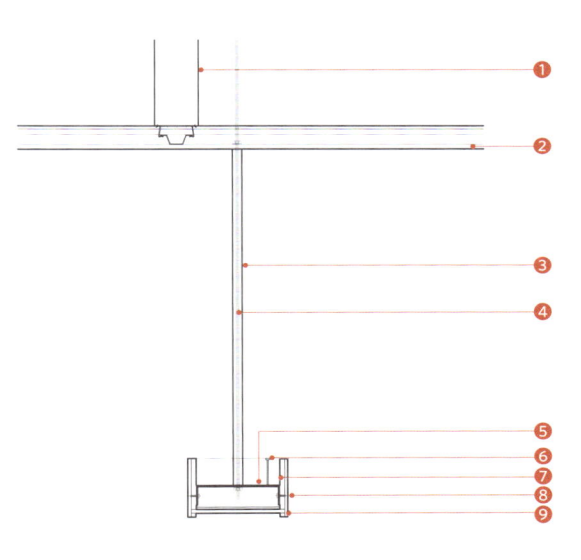

Section detail, atrium ceiling
1. Metal hanger
2. Plaster board in painted white finish
3. Hollow stainless steel pipe
4. Threaded cable support to structure
5. Metal frame painted white
6. Lighting on raiser
7. Plywood panel
8. Self-tapping screw
9. Bamboo veneer plywood

ABOVE & OPPOSITE
The atrium's ceiling is detailed in white plaster and bamboo veneer.

A

BEFORE
Section through the auditorium

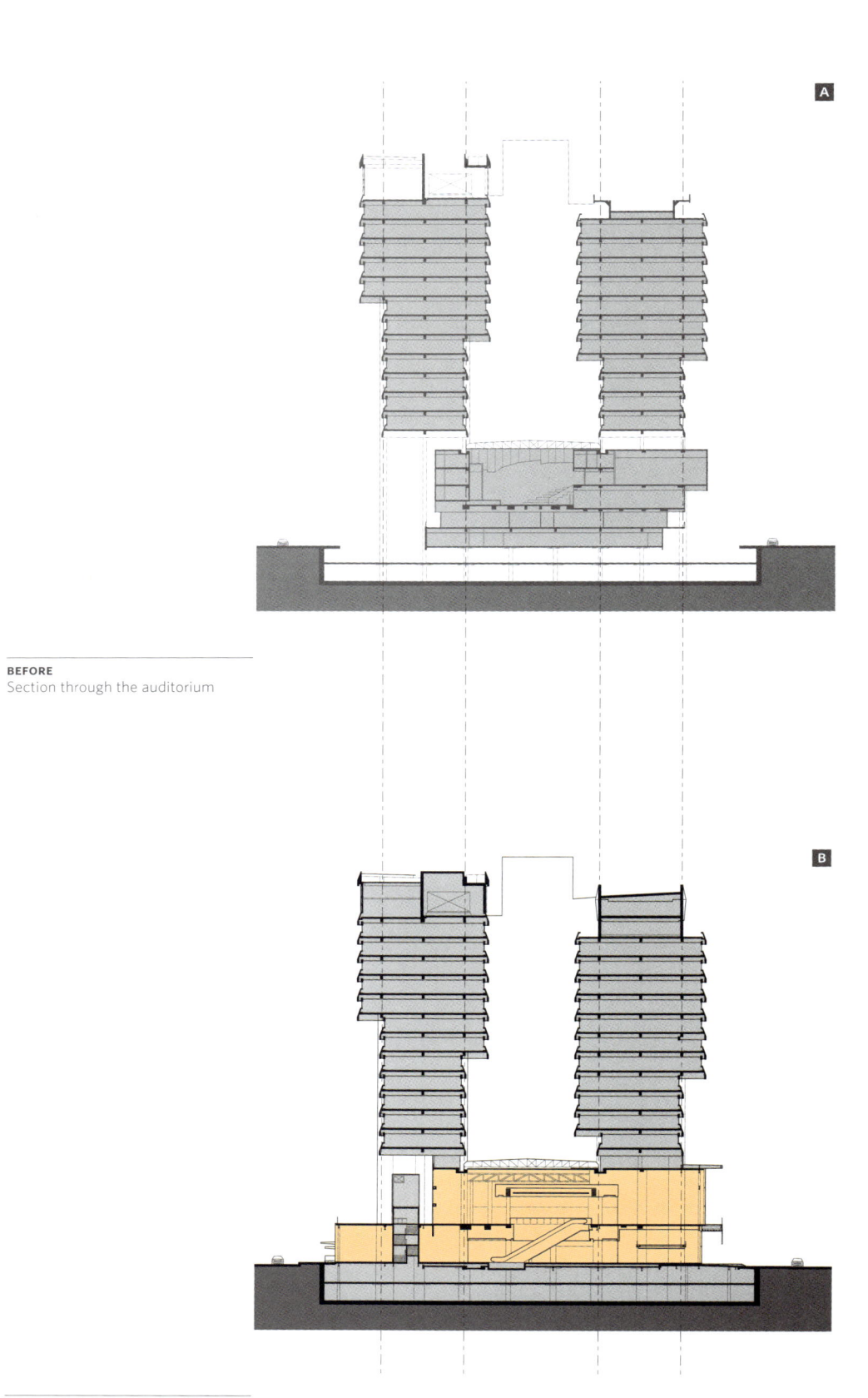

B

AFTER
Section through the converted atrium

BEFORE
Ground level and site plan

AFTER
Ground level and site plan with retail programme

■ Retail, Food & Beverage
❶ Mall entrance
❷ Atrium

A & B The transparent façade establishes new connectivity with the street.
C The atrium at ground level.
D A new metallic fluorocarbon finish retains the tile patterning of the original cladding.

New architectural details are subtle and geometrically uniform, crafted as a backdrop to the prominent existing structure in which they are embedded.

The façade is composed of a simple glass-and-steel framing system – large panels of glass achieve lightness and transparency, and shop signage is set interior to the glazing so as not to interrupt this sheen surface quality.

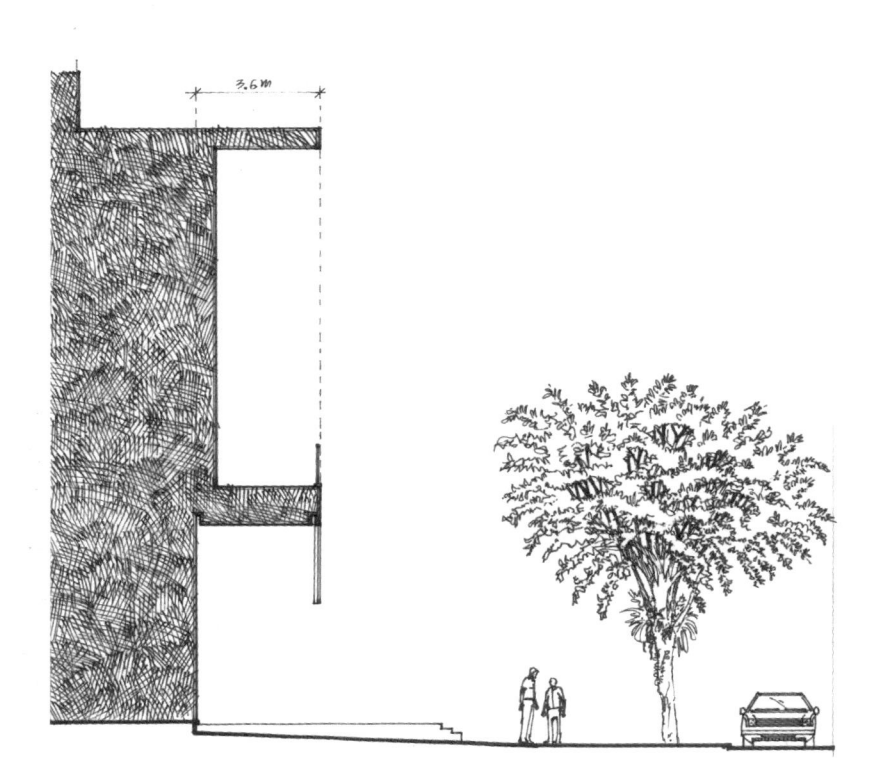

ABOVE
A partial section through the storefront

TRIPLEONE SOMERSET
- Retrofit, 2009

1. **Existing car parks** were covered to make way for a wide pedestrian promenade.

2. **Retail tenants** have the option to design single or double-storey shop spaces.

3. **Outdoor food and beverage spaces** integrate the retail podium with the public sidewalk.

4. **A retail atrium** is constructed within the shell of an existing auditorium.

5. **Metal cladding** in a fluorocarbon finish retains the building's original cladding pattern.

The podium of this 1970s, Brutalist-design Public Utilities Board building was converted into a retail shopping mall. By closing ground voids that opened to the basement-level car parks, and retrofitting an auditorium as a public atrium with food court, TripleOne Somerset establishes a new dialogue with the site and street.

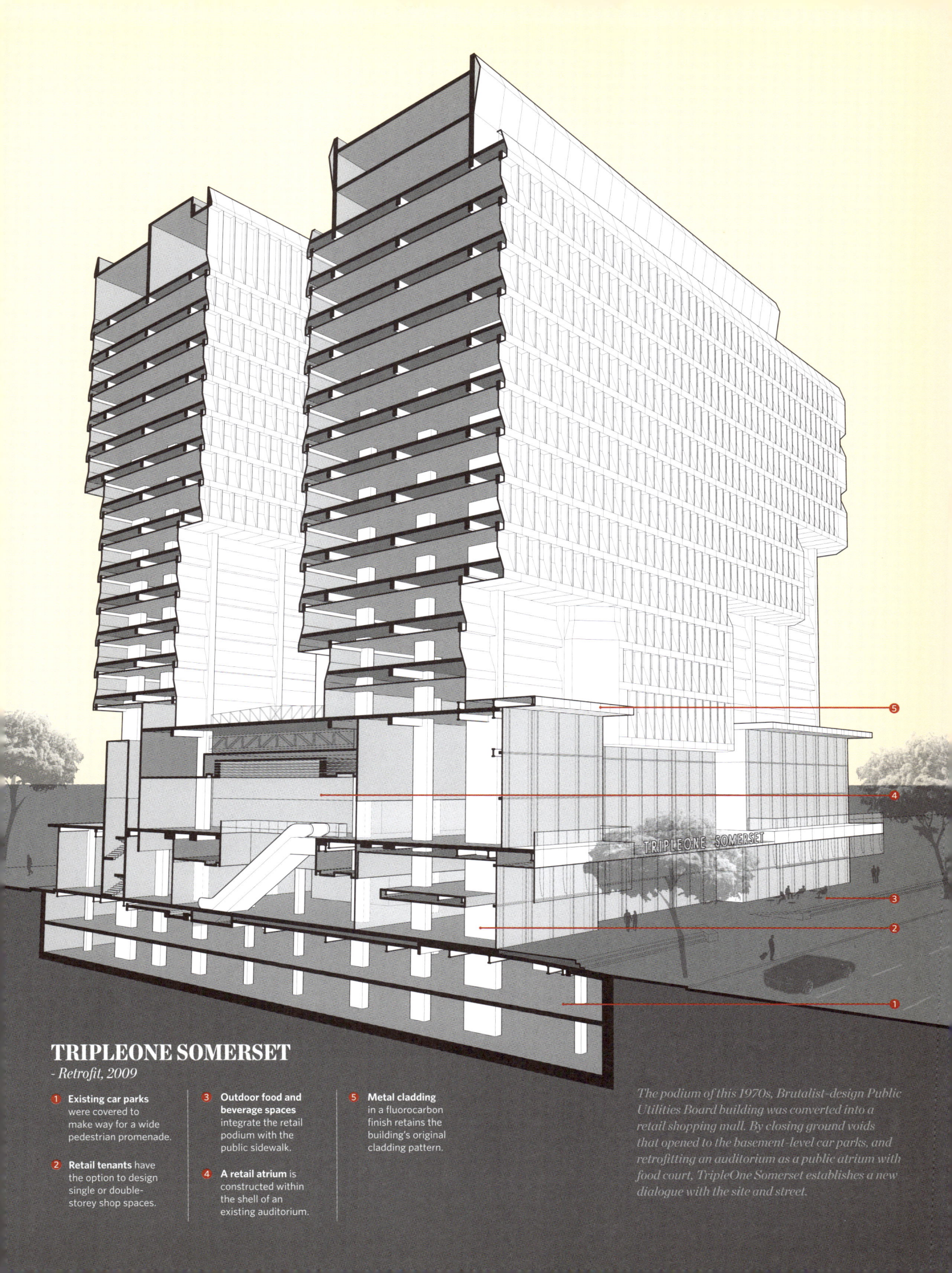

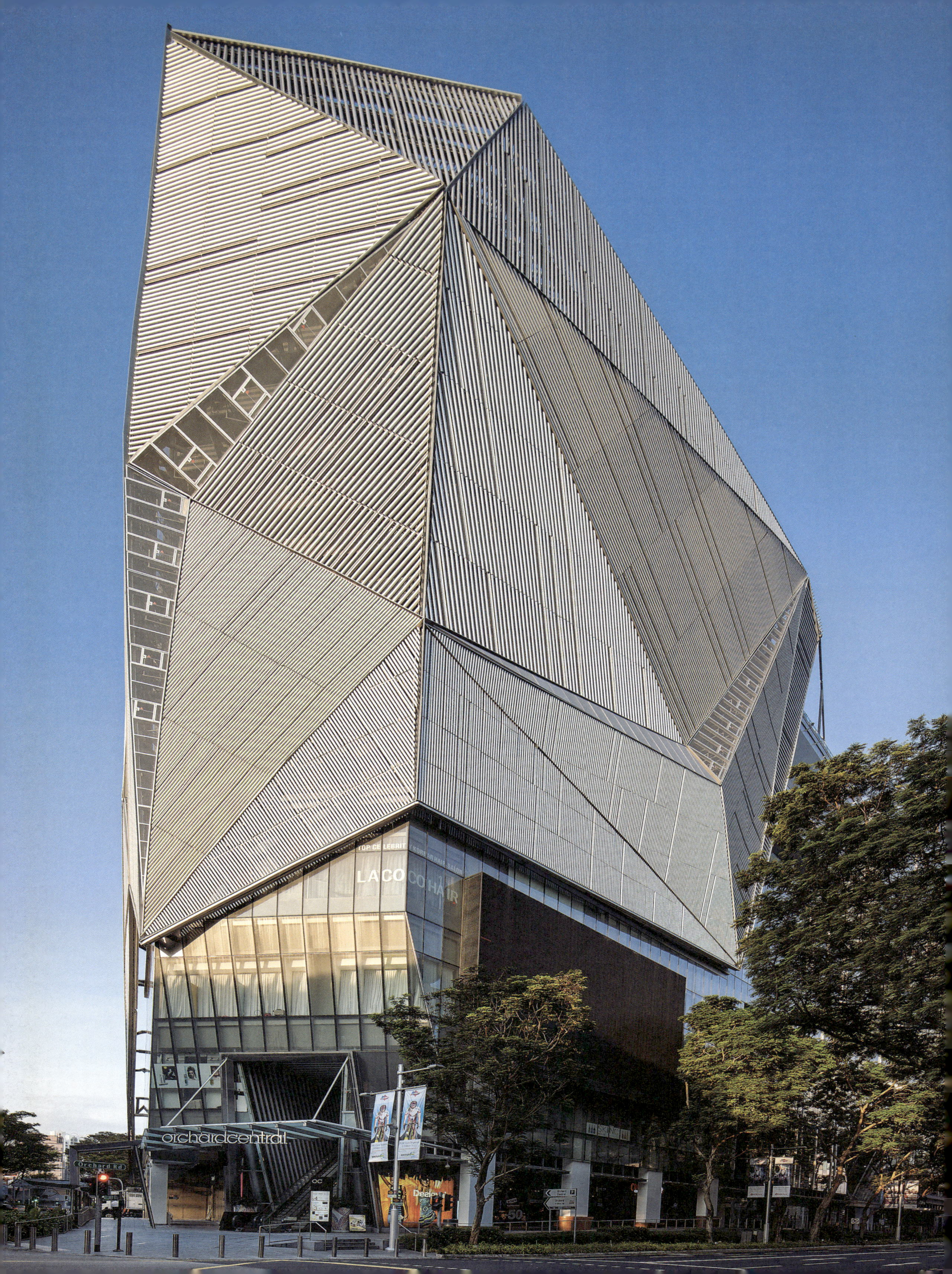
orchardcentral

Feature Projects
Orchard Central

Year Completed : 2009
Project Type : New build
Area : 36,000 square metres

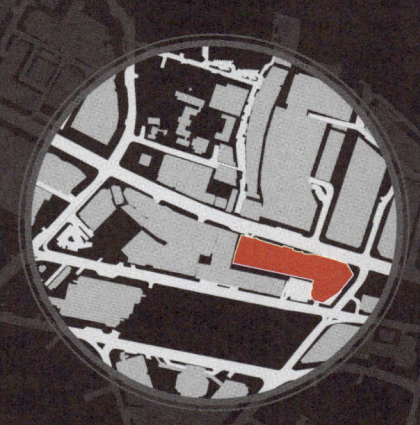

At 12 storeys, Orchard Central is Singapore's first high-rise shopping centre. The mall takes the place of an open-air car park once famous as the public space known as Glutton's Square, an after-hours congregation of hawker stalls. Unlike the other projects featured in this chapter, Orchard Central is a new build. As such, DP Architects incorporates many of the characteristics that have been developed in past Orchard Road mall renovation, while programmatic decisions push these explorations to new extents. In the ongoing evolution of Orchard Road's street-integrated mall architecture, Orchard Central makes great strides in the extroversion of retail space, communicating a new mode of connectivity with its urban site and environs.

The design of Orchard Central wraps and injects private commercial space with the public space of Orchard Road, activating all 12 storeys of the mall with street linkages. The façade hosts an exploratory circulation system that places the visitor in unique relationships with the surrounding city: a series of open-air escalators and landings extend the experience of the sidewalk at ground level onto landscaped roof decks on the 11th and 12th storeys.

OPPOSITE
The mall's main entrance opens to the corner of Orchard Road and Killiney Road.

Numerous vantage points designed within the façade encourage a surgical exploration of the city, as one travels upward and through the building's skin. The roof deck is a lushly landscaped outdoor setting that operates as a park – a new public space that offers views outward, conflating the mall with the space of the city. This enveloping circulatory system also extends inward, puncturing internal spaces of shops and restaurants.

The exploratory aspects of Orchard Central's façade work to slow the process of shopping. Rather than moving through retail spaces as an act of efficiency, shoppers are persuaded to engage with the shopping experience. Attributes of internal programming also serve this purpose: the structure is segmented into specialised clusters – youth shops, luxury goods stores, entertainment spaces – that are placed with visual links to core activated spaces – a five-storey rock-climbing wall in the atrium, transparent elevators and nearly US$10 million worth of public art displays – to form a clear internal hierarchy and fuel the building with life.

A variety of architectural elements differentiate these programmatic clusters. Externally, masses containing these zones protrude from the façade, and LED-embedded mullions are coupled with ceramic-fritted glazing units to articulate the forms at night. Internally, ceiling lighting and flooring systems are arranged in linear patterns that inform specialised axes of movement to further activate the internal spaces.

Traditionally, the cost of rental space is inversely related to floor height, as upper floors become

ABOVE LEFT
Escalators line the façade.
ABOVE RIGHT
View of the façade along Orchard Road.

OPPOSITE
Massing concept sketch describing a variety of programmatic clusters.

FEATURE PROJECTS – ORCHARD CENTRAL   CHAPTER TWO

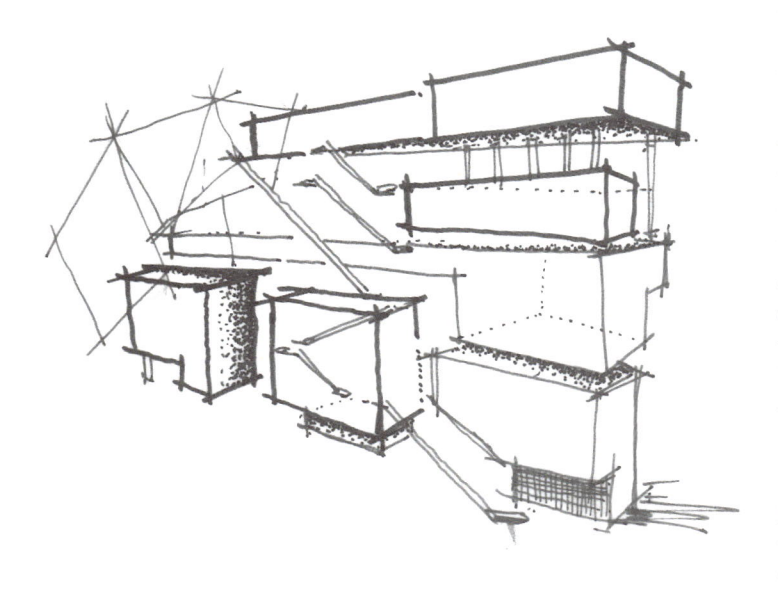

unlikely destinations for shoppers. In an effort to resolve this issue, the top levels of the building have been reconsidered. The roof hosts a series of dining spaces and gardens positioned to attract visitors to the uppermost level and transform the roof as high-value space. At the building's eastern end, the programme's required car park is concentrated on the upper storeys to avoid exhausting important space at street level, and a rear-winding ramp serves as the entrance. In many ways, the car park honours that which made the site famous in the 1960s — its upper-level location is an essential driver of the building's unique architecture: an extensive, segmented external rain screen wraps the space in elevation and at roof level. The screen is detailed to display a nightlong performance of light and colour, transforming Orchard Central into a prominent beacon for the Orchard Road region.

168 PART 2 CONTRIBUTIONS OF DP ARCHITECTS

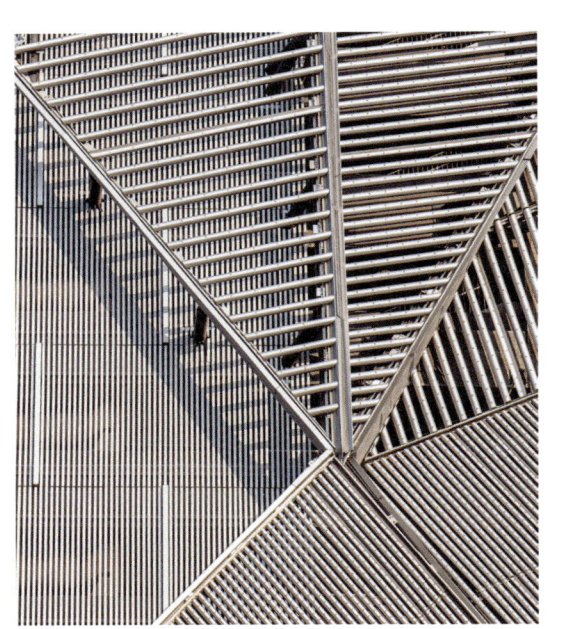

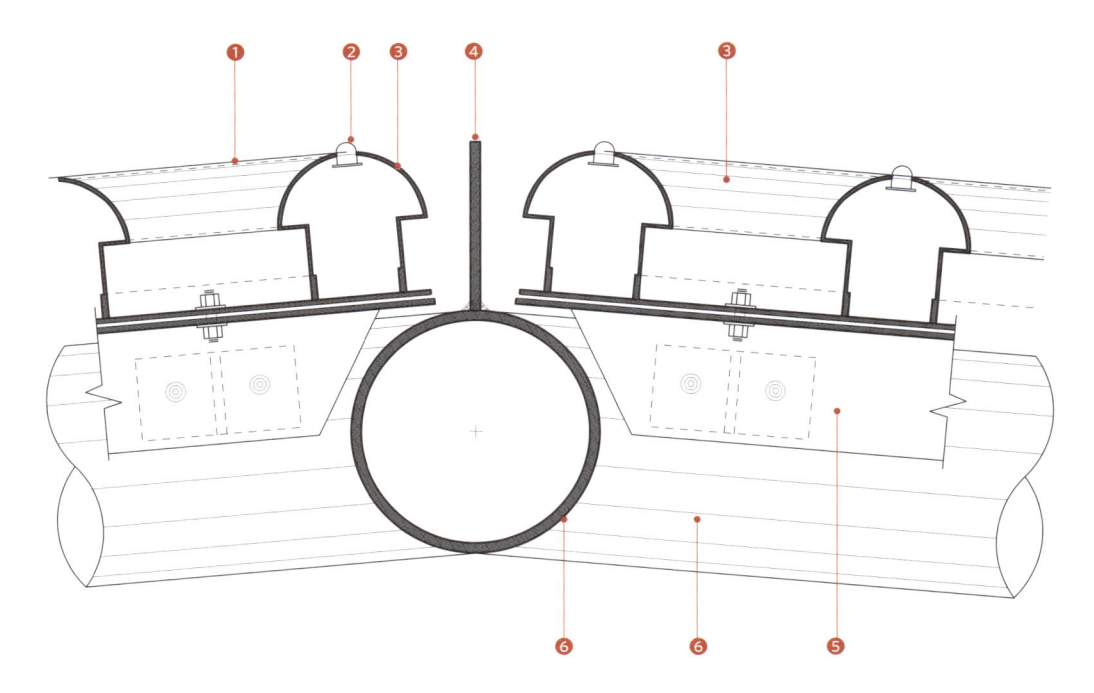

Section detail, steel framework with LED lighting
1. Unitised facet panel
2. LED light fitting
3. Extruded aluminium reflectors
4. Steel fin
5. Steel brackets fixed to cleats
6. Tubular steel frame

ABOVE LEFT & OPPOSITE
Details of the steel and aluminium framework.

ABOVE RIGHT
The faceted screen wraps the upper-level car park and extends to the ground.

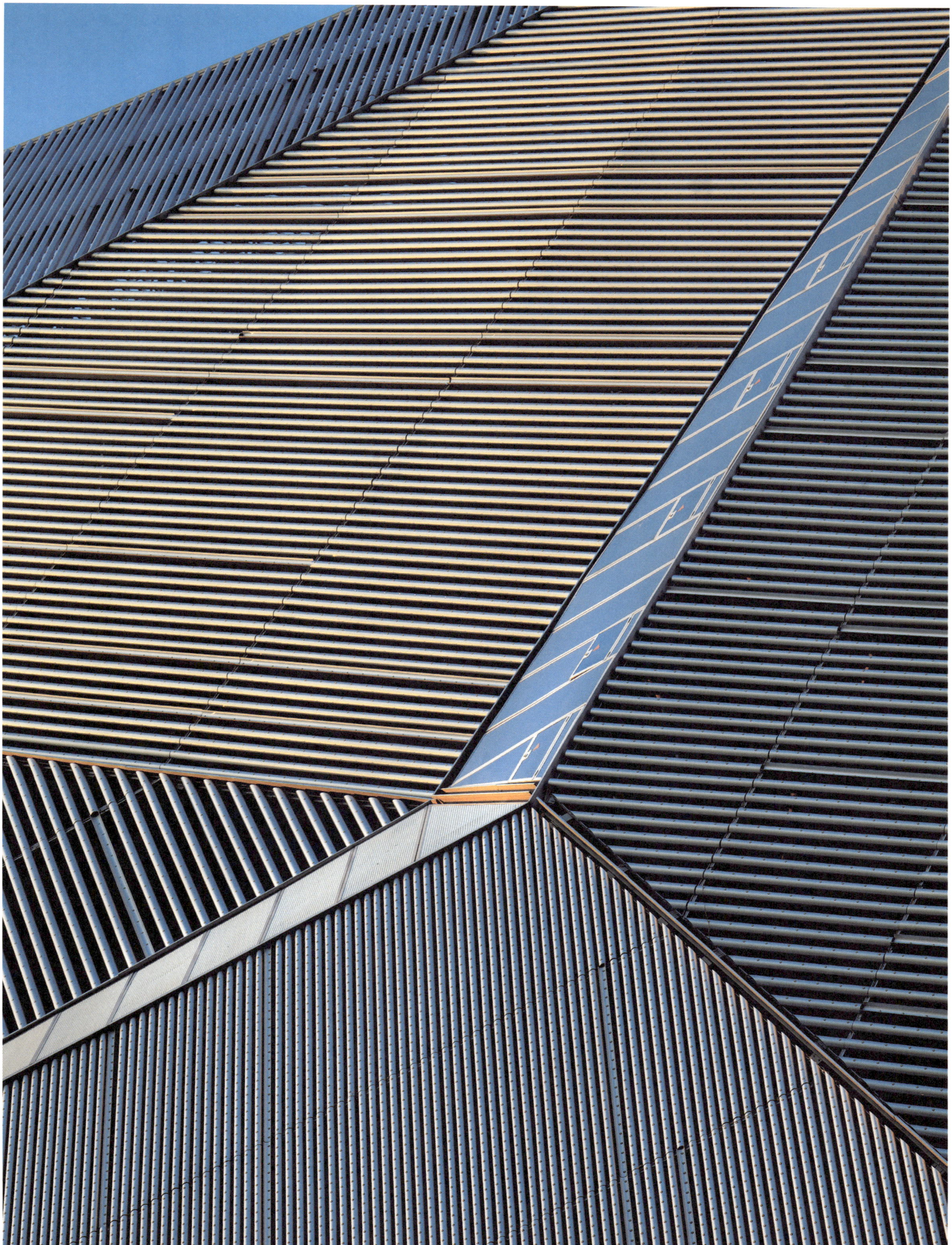

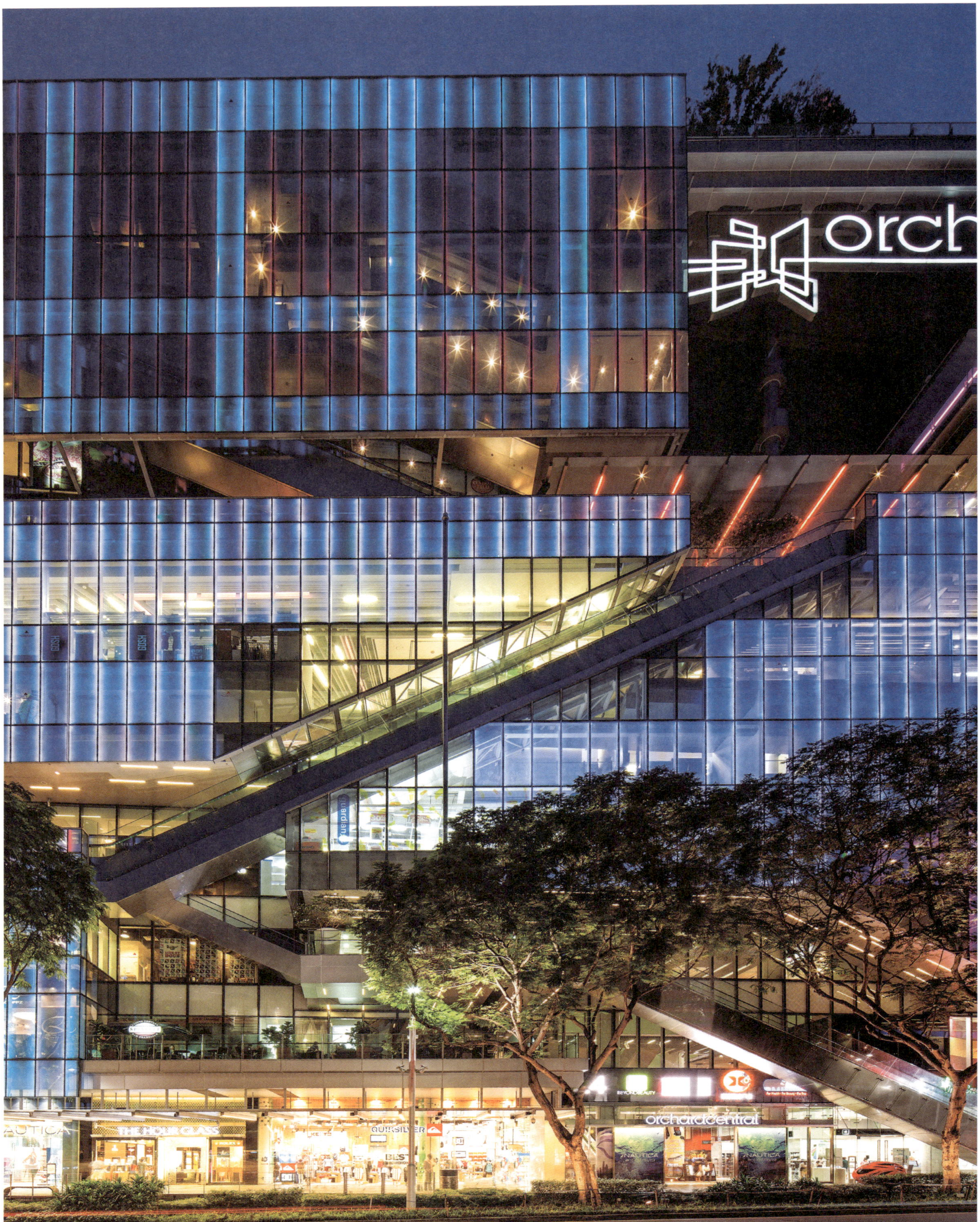
orch
orchardcentral

Numerous vantage points designed within the façade encourage a surgical exploration of the city, as one travels upward and through the building's skin.

OPPOSITE
LED-embedded mullions and ceramic-fritted glazing units illuminate the façade at night.

ABOVE LEFT
A partial section through the façade.

ABOVE RIGHT
The faceted external screen is fitted with LED lighting.

> The exploratory aspects of Orchard Central's façade work to slow the process of shopping. Rather than moving through retail spaces as an act of efficiency, shoppers are persuaded to engage with the shopping experience.

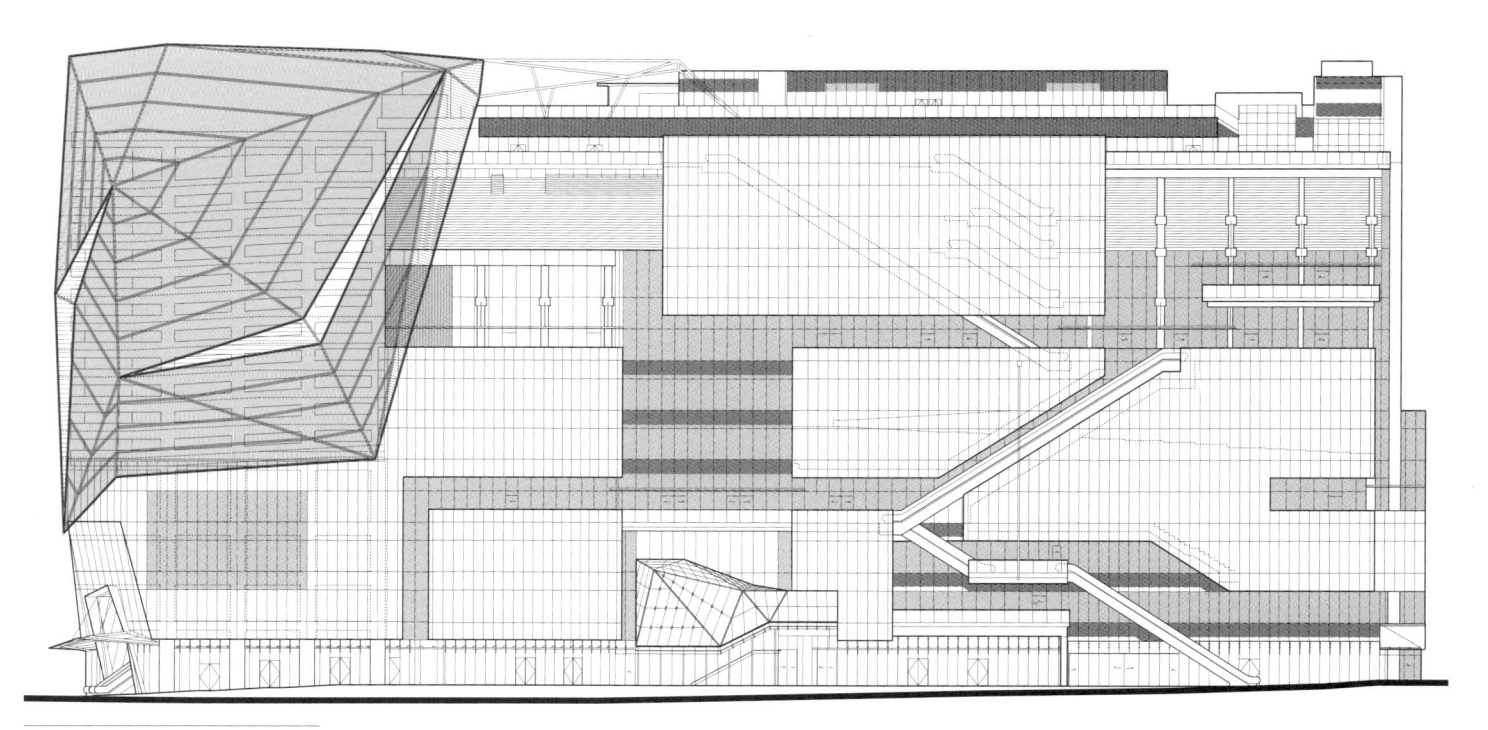

Elevation fronting Orchard Road

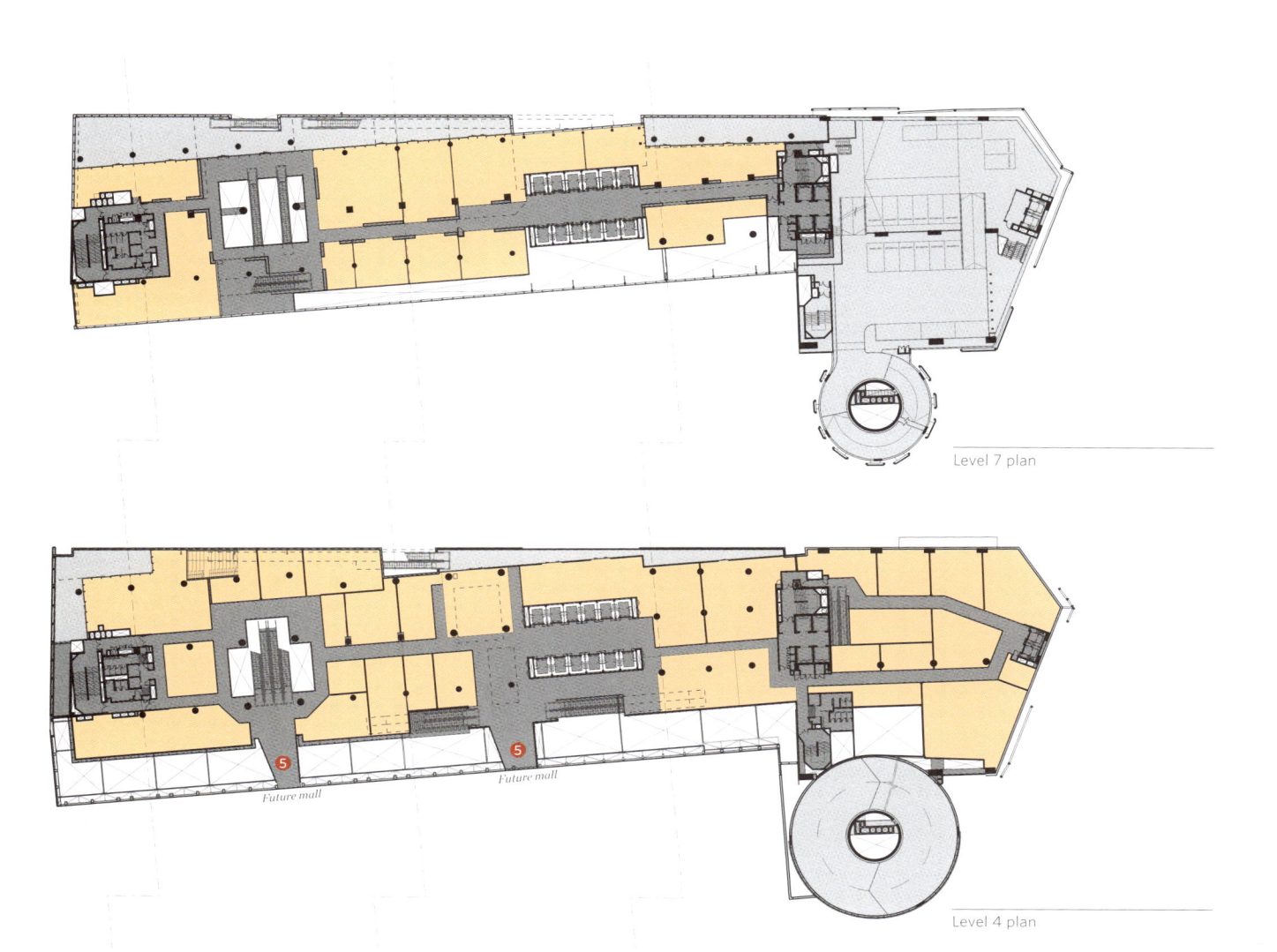

Level 7 plan

Future mall *Future mall*

Level 4 plan

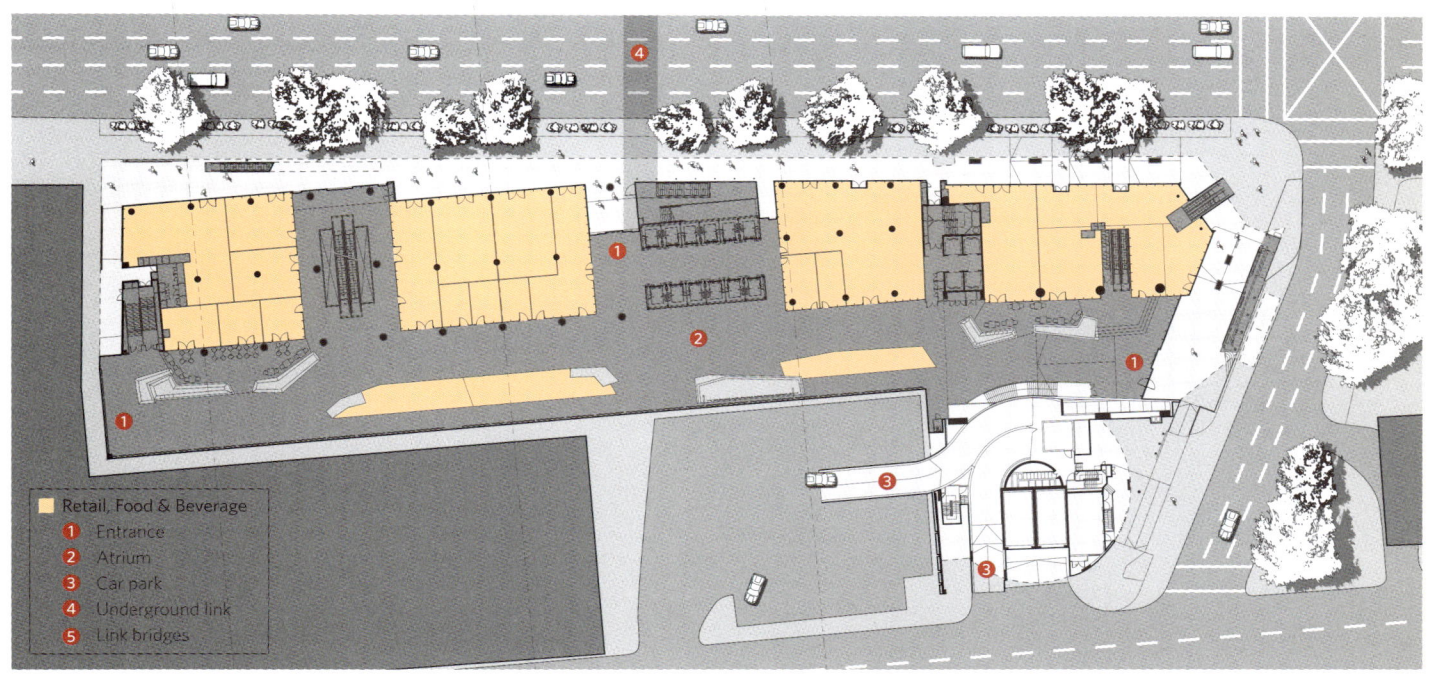

Retail, Food & Beverage
1. Entrance
2. Atrium
3. Car park
4. Underground link
5. Link bridges

Ground level and site plan

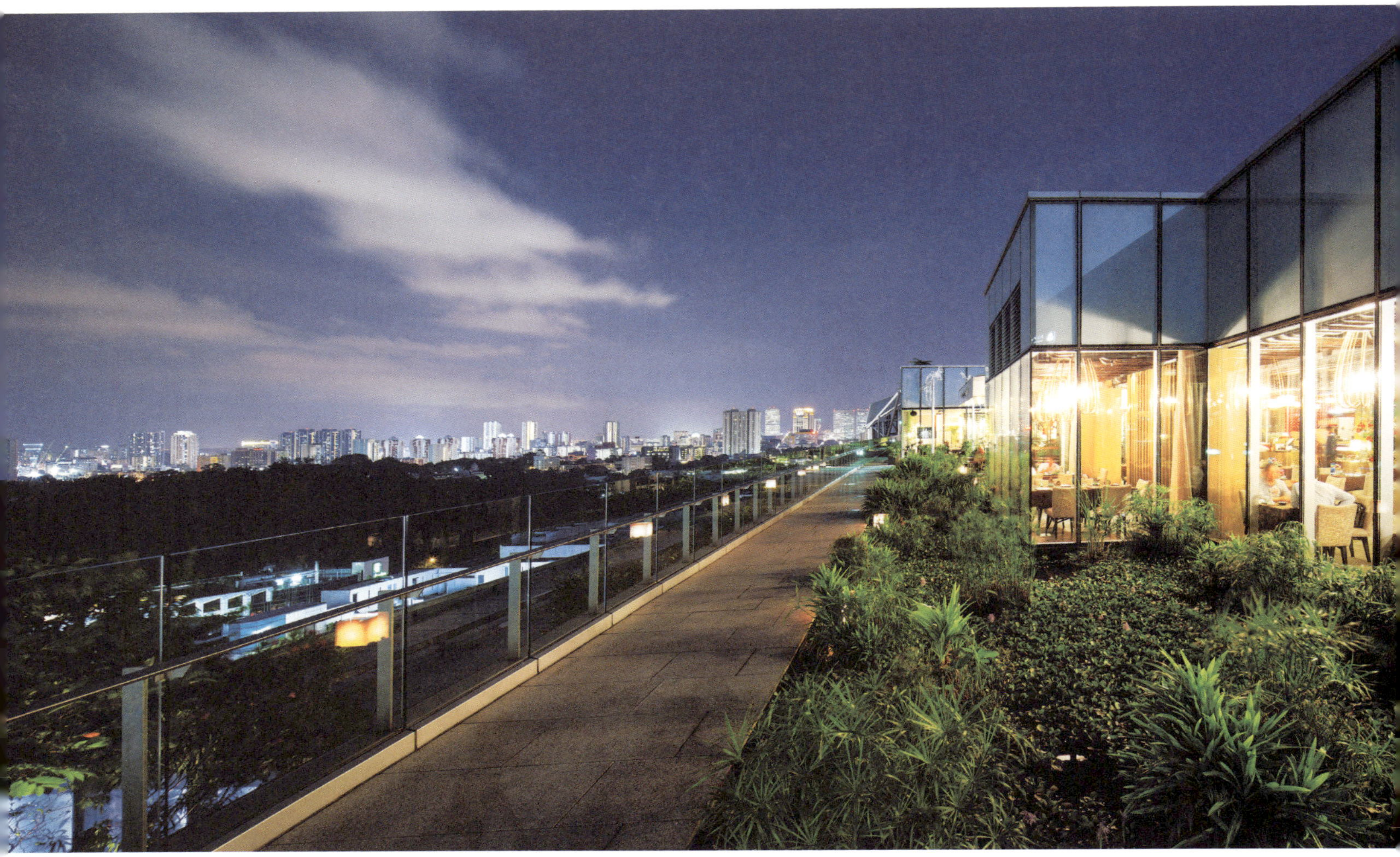

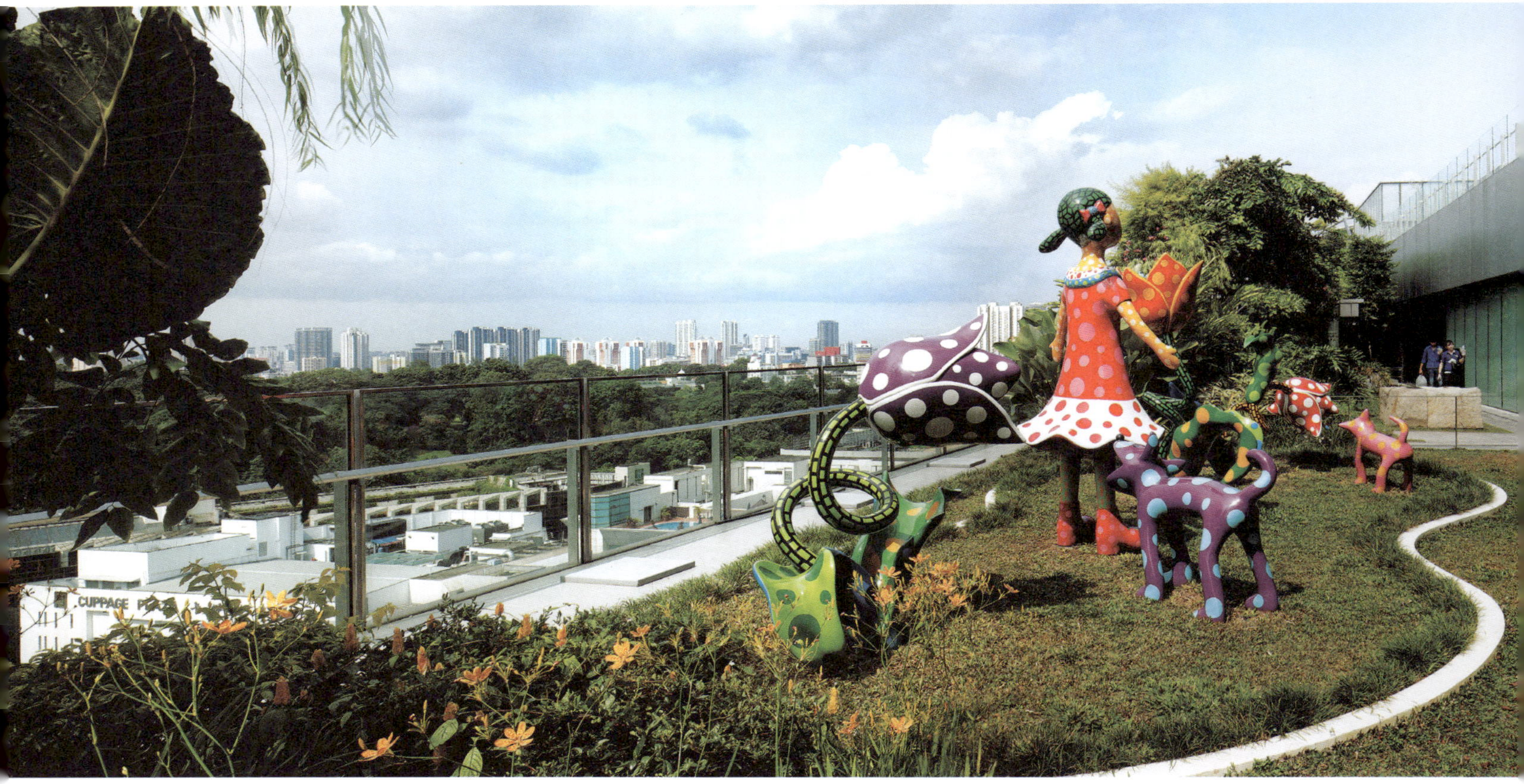

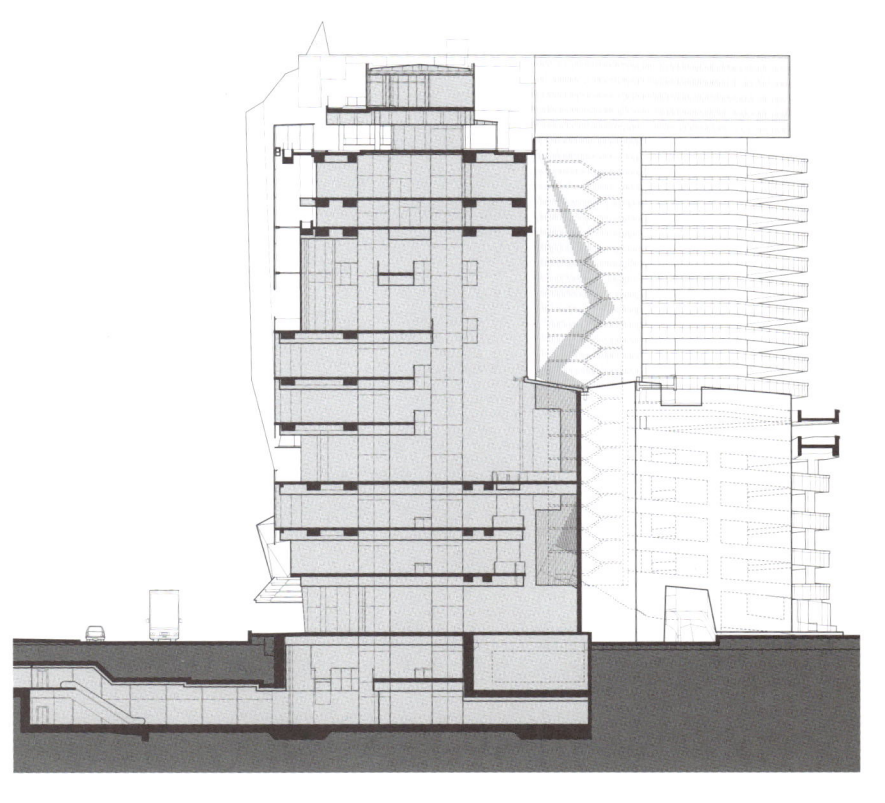

TOP LEFT
Rooftop dining offers views onto the city.
BOTTOM LEFT
The roof deck is landscaped with gardens and artwork.
RIGHT
Section through the atrium and Orchard Road underpass.

A A rock-climbing wall activates the atrium.
B & C The atrium extends eight storeys.
D Façade glazing detail.
E & F External escalators connect each level with the street.

FEATURE PROJECTS – ORCHARD CENTRAL　　　CHAPTER TWO　　177

Core activated spaces – a five-storey rock-climbing wall in the atrium, transparent elevators and US$10 million worth of public art displays – form a clear internal hierarchy and fuel the building with life.

ORCHARD CENTRAL
- New build, 2009

1 **Roof decks** are programmed with restaurants and landscaped gardens, offering views of Orchard Road and downtown Singapore.

2 **Outdoor escalators** connect the sidewalk to landings and entrances on all 12 storeys.

3 **An internal atrium** extends eight storeys to activate and visually connect each level of retail. It contains a five-storey rock-climbing wall.

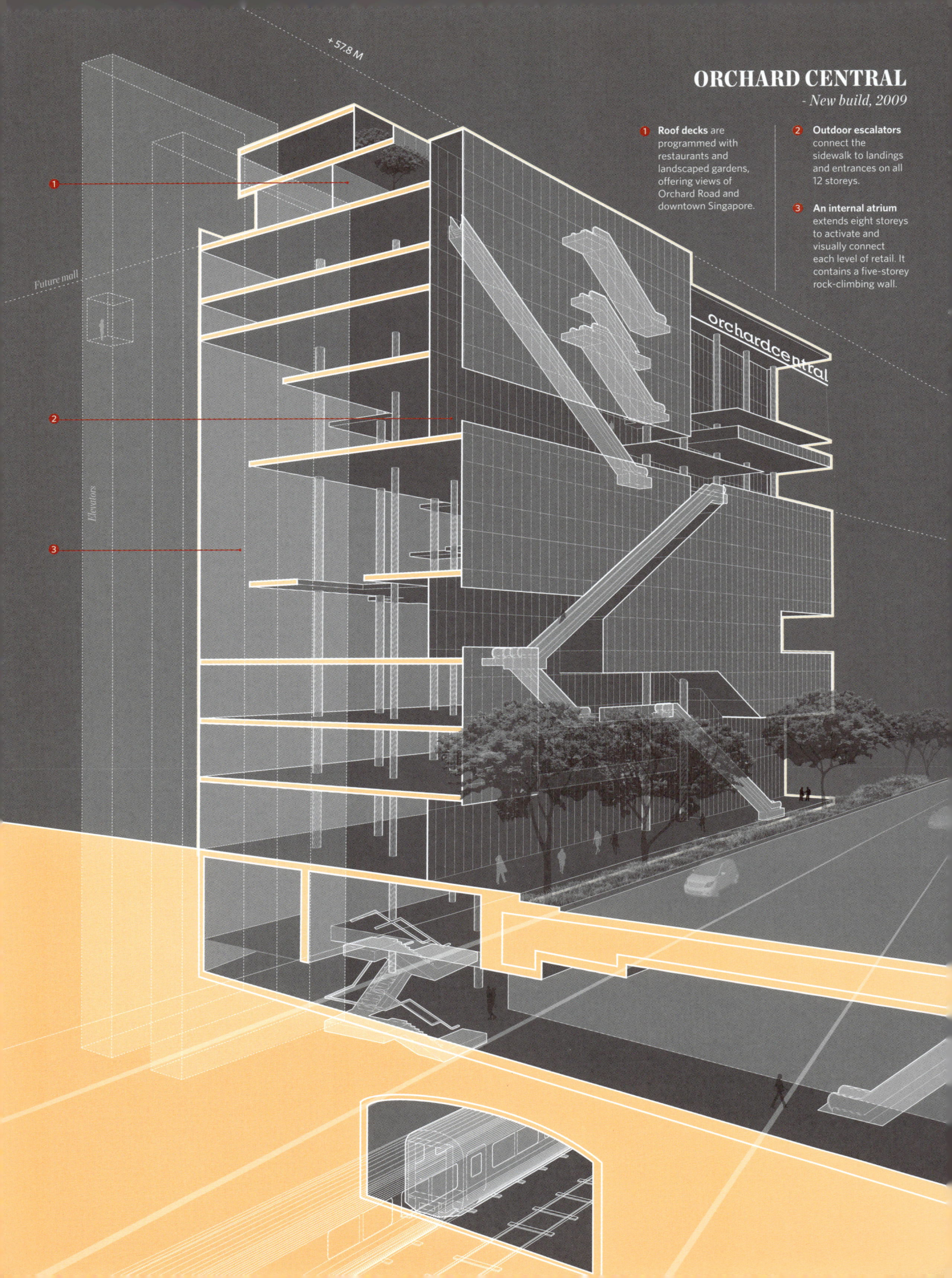

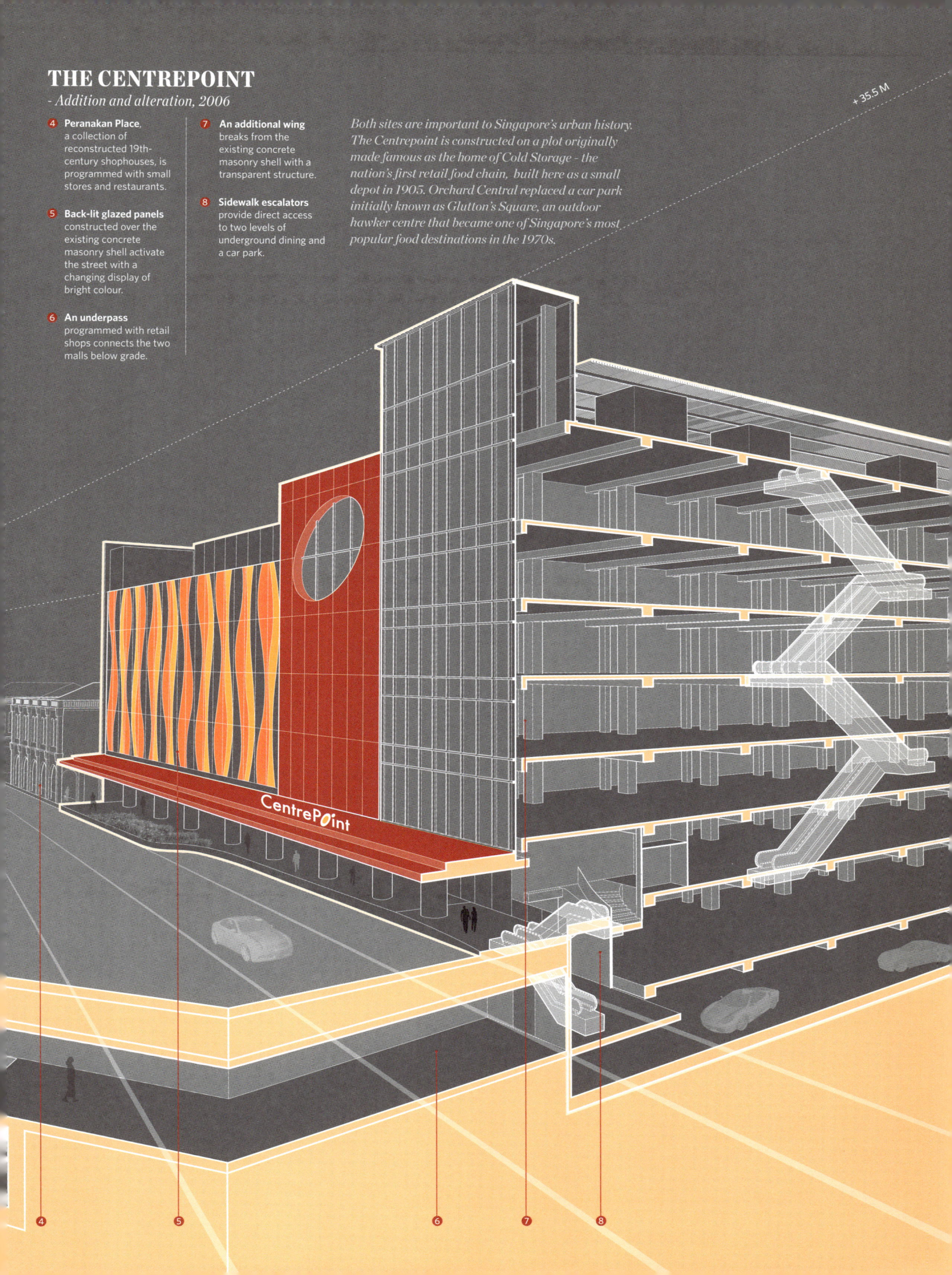

THE CENTREPOINT
- Addition and alteration, 2006

4 **Peranakan Place**, a collection of reconstructed 19th-century shophouses, is programmed with small stores and restaurants.

5 **Back-lit glazed panels** constructed over the existing concrete masonry shell activate the street with a changing display of bright colour.

6 **An underpass** programmed with retail shops connects the two malls below grade.

7 **An additional wing** breaks from the existing concrete masonry shell with a transparent structure.

8 **Sidewalk escalators** provide direct access to two levels of underground dining and a car park.

Both sites are important to Singapore's urban history. The Centrepoint is constructed on a plot originally made famous as the home of Cold Storage - the nation's first retail food chain, built here as a small depot in 1905. Orchard Central replaced a car park initially known as Glutton's Square, an outdoor hawker centre that became one of Singapore's most popular food destinations in the 1970s.

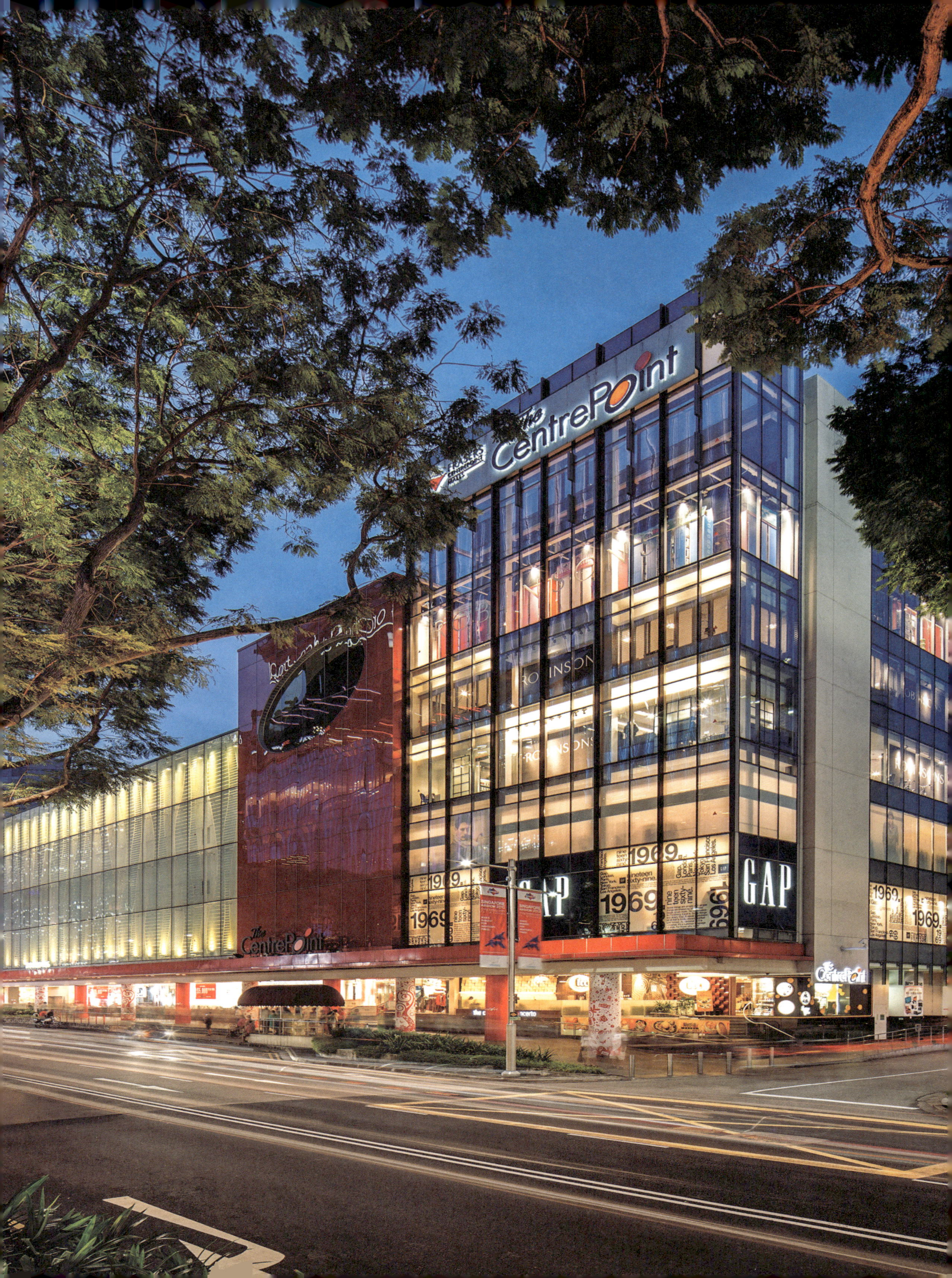
The CentrePoint
GAP
GAP

Feature Projects
The Centrepoint

Year Completed : 2006
Project Type : Addition and alteration
Area : 7800 square metres

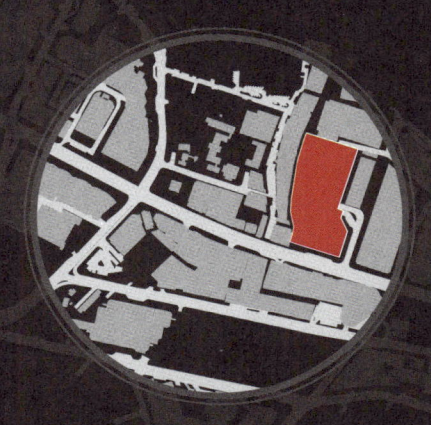

The establishment of Singapore Cold Storage Company in 1905 on Orchard Road marked a significant turning point for the region in the direction of commercial development. A storage and distribution business for perishable food products from Australia, Cold Storage was the nation's first supermarket, built alongside what was in the early 1900s a Malaysia-bound railway.

The current structure for The Centrepoint was the company's first major property development, and was opened in 1983, then refurbished and expanded with a new wing by DP Architects in 2006. Its architectural attributes respond to its immediate surroundings, which are a diverse mix of old and new. Site adjacencies include the 19th-century Peranakan shophouses of Emerald Hill and the modern Orchard Central mall. Designing within the existing building structure, the architecture reconsiders its surrounding context and portrays a modern building that achieves transparency and connectivity.

OPPOSITE
The Centrepoint's existing concrete shell is overlaid with a plane of back-lit glazing. Both this and an additional wing of transparent glass help to engage the retail mall with the street.

3.00 m

ESCALATORS TO BASEMENT
FOOD COURT

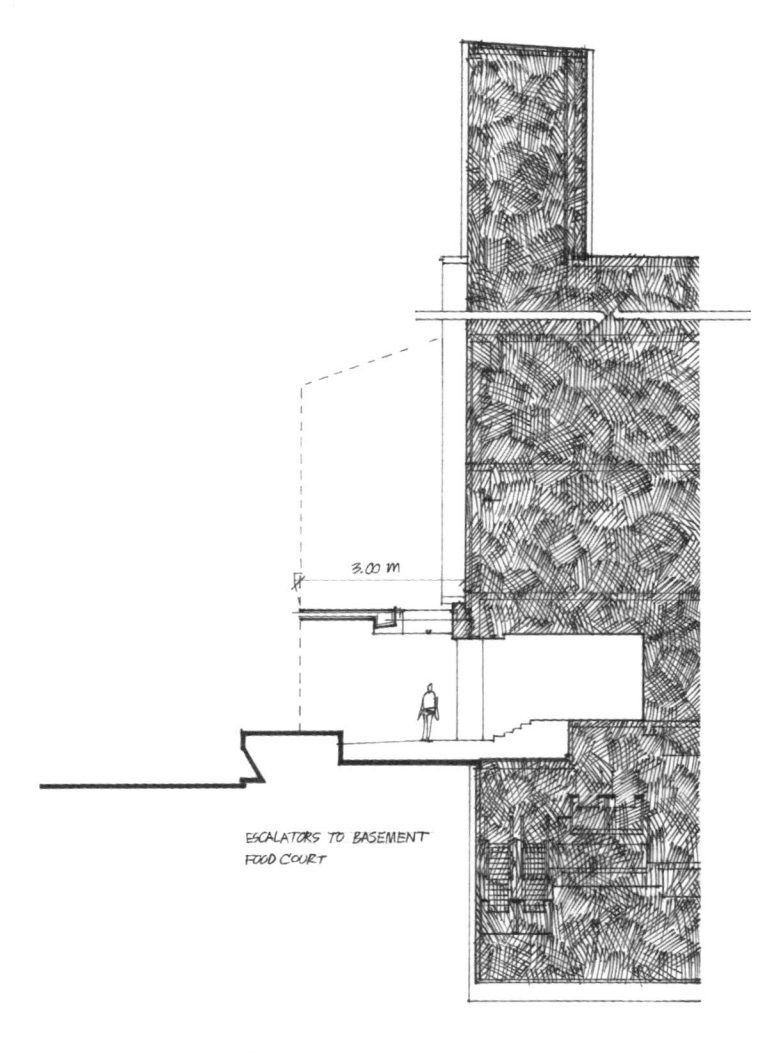

To the east, escalators connect the sidewalk to the basement-level food courts; to the west, the canopied frontage leads directly into the arched entrances of the shophouses of Emerald Hill; below-grade, an underground link runs from Orchard Road to establish connection with Orchard Central.

The Centrepoint's frontage is divided into three stepped-block forms. This composition segments the mall into three seemingly individual buildings overlaid by a consistent grid of glazing units, a shared canopy and a regulated set of columns at the level of the sidewalk. This massing technique drops the scale of the structure to complement the abutting century-old shophouses to the west while accentuating the seven-storey transparent extension at the building's prominent corner to the east. The three block forms are treated with individualised façade systems that relate to internal function. A layering technique is implemented to soften the building's existing concrete masonry shell: a back-lit, fritted glazing system comprising of 1.5-metre by 4.3-metre panels is mounted with a 0.6-metre offset from the existing concrete face. This fronts the large department store and seven-storey, full-height atrium beyond.

A central red glazing block is punctured by an oval opening that signals the entrance, and fronts a ground-storey corridor that leads into the atrium at the heart of the building; its red colour is associated with the mall's company brand. Meanwhile, a transparent curtainwall is designed to front the mall's extension wing, opening up internal programme to the Orchard–Cuppage intersection.

Unlike the majority of Orchard Road's malls, which have been developed in a linear fashion with internal programming aligned parallel to the street, the development of The Centrepoint has conformed to the plan of the adjacent Emerald Hill shophouses, with a comparatively deep section that requires an internal arrangement perpendicular to Orchard Road, its atrium set deep within the building, some 100 metres from the sidewalk. The additional wing also works linearly in this fashion, providing an additional ground-level corridor.

In plan and section, Orchard Road can be thought to have two main segments. While the majority of its malls are set back significantly from the vehicular streets, The Centrepoint has been developed in a manner that hugs the road more closely, in alignment with the older shophouse structures. Unlike its counterparts, the pedestrian promenade does not run in front of the building and the site is not buffered from the road by the thick layer of Angsana trees. Rather, the building's overhanging upper levels allow the promenade to continue at the building's base; a raised sidewalk performs as the cushion between sidewalk and vehicular street.

The renovation linked the building below-grade to Orchard Central opposite; this is the only cross-road link in the lower region of the Orchard Road corridor. A proposed link bridge will eventually connect The Centrepoint with Orchard Point mall at the second storey.

ABOVE
A partial section through the storefront and main entrance.

OPPOSITE
The mall's additional wing illuminated at night.

FRASERS CENTREPOINT MALLS
The CentrePoint
ROBINSONS
ROBINSONS
1969
1969
The CentrePoint

The Centrepoint's frontage is divided into three stepped-block forms. This composition segments the mall into three seemingly individualised buildings overlaid by a consistent grid of glazing units, a shared canopy and a regulated set of columns at the level of the sidewalk.

ABOVE
The back-lit, fritted glazing system is overlaid onto the existing building's concrete shell. It provides the mall with a vibrant display of shifting light and colours.

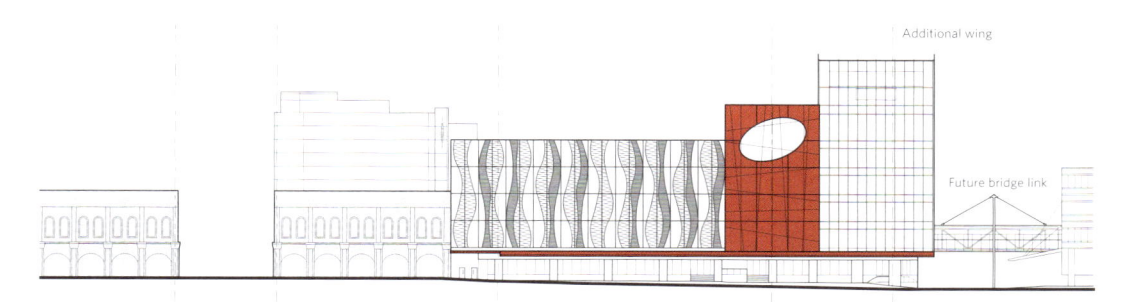

FEATURE PROJECTS THE CENTREPOINT — CHAPTER TWO — 185

Elevation fronting Orchard Road. The Centrepoint's form has stepped roof heights to mediate between its own scale and the scale of the adjacent Peranakan shophouses.

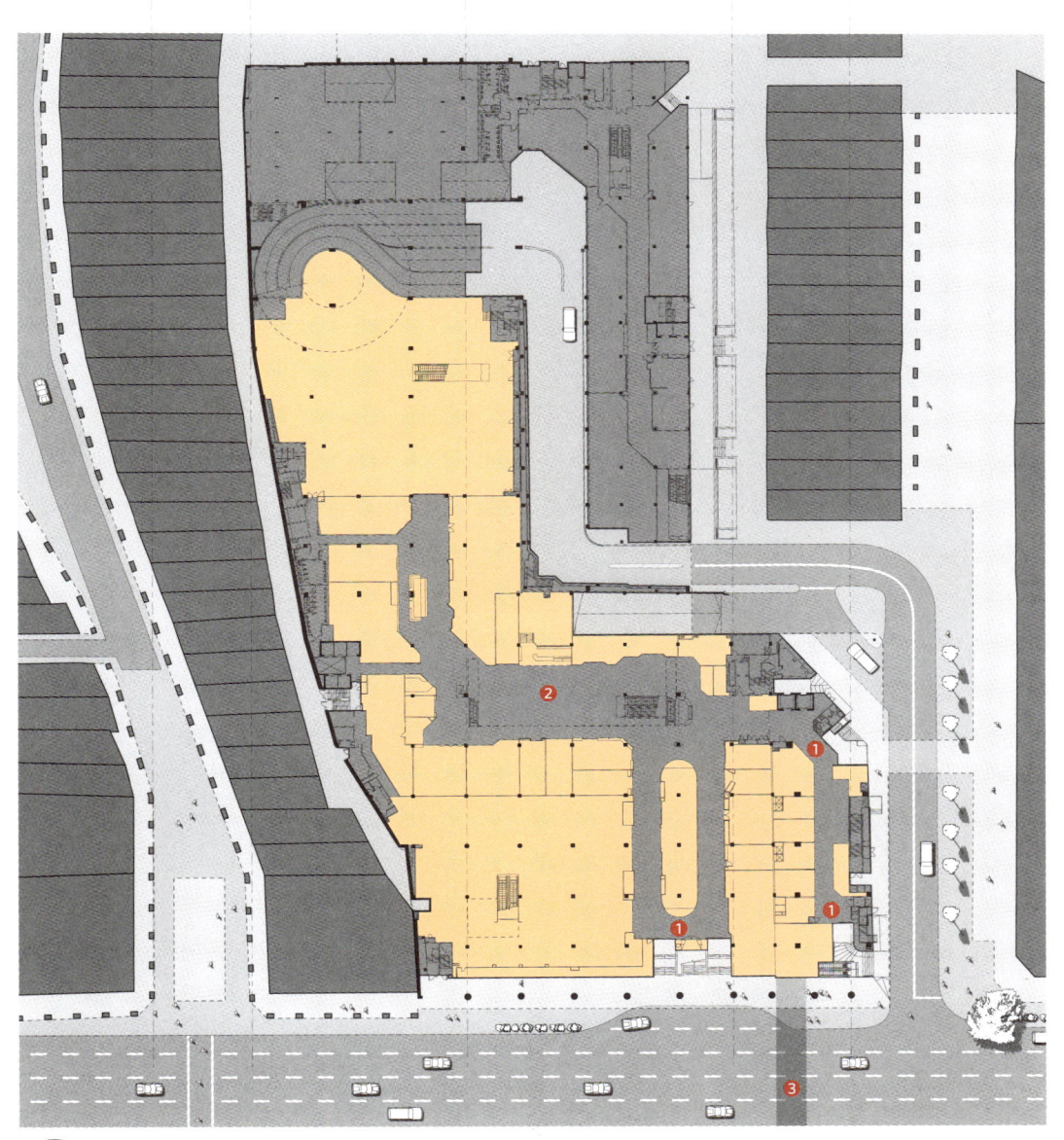

- Retail, Food & Beverage
- ❶ Mall entrance
- ❷ Atrium
- ❸ Underground link

Ground level and site plan

A Global Presence:
RETAIL PROJECTS WORLDWIDE

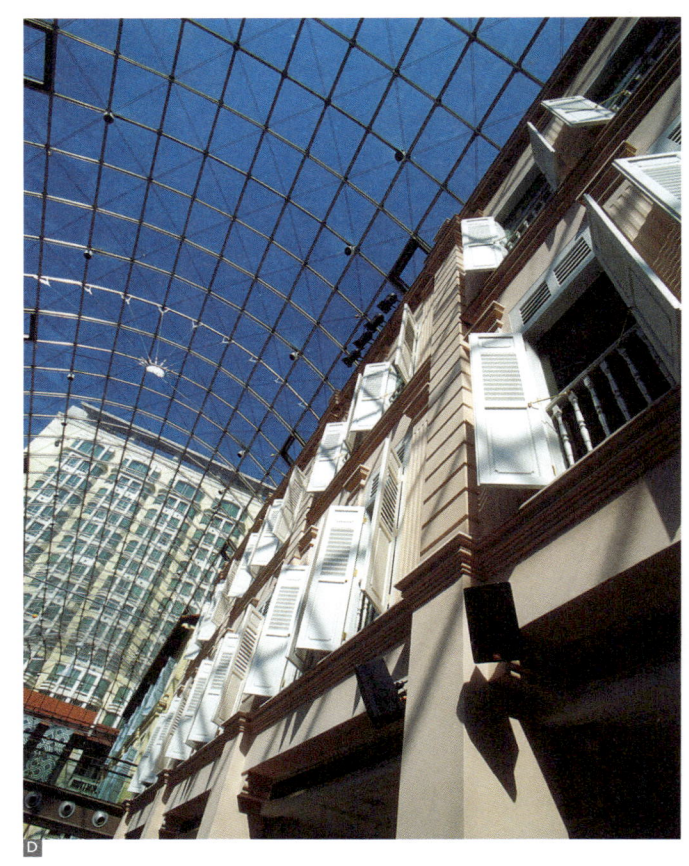

A GLOBAL PRESENCE: RETAIL PROJECTS WORLDWIDE

A **SENAYAN CITY, INDONESIA**
2006 | 193,600 square metres
Retail, Hotel, Office, Residential

B **CENTRAL PARK, INDONESIA**
2010 | 388,600 square metres
Retail, Hotel, Office, Residential

C **THE DUBAI MALL, UAE**
2008 | 555,600 square metres
Retail, Hotel

D **BUGIS JUNCTION, SINGAPORE**
1994 | 119,220 square metres
Retail, Hotel

E **SUNTEC CITY, SINGAPORE**
1997 | 490,000 square metres
Retail, Office

F **NOON SQUARE, SOUTH KOREA**
2007 | 24,000 square metres | Retail

G **MY VILLAGE@SERANGOON GARDEN, SINGAPORE**
2011 | 5,515 square metres | Retail

H **VELOCITY@NOVENA SQUARE, SINGAPORE**
2007 | 70,000 square metres
Retail, Office

I **VIVOCITY, SINGAPORE**
2006 | 137,000 square metres | Retail
In association with Toyo Ito Associates, Japan.

J **I12 KATONG, SINGAPORE**
2011 | 26,200 square metres | Retail

OUR PEOPLE

DP Architects is one of Asia's strongest design firms, and employs over 1200 staff working on projects worldwide. Its architects operate from twelve global offices in Singapore, China, India, Indonesia, Malaysia, Thailand, Vietnam and the United Arab Emirates.

The multi-disciplinary practice first took root in post-independence Singapore, and prides itself on having strongly contributed to writing the young nation's architectural language. Since 1967 DP Architects has been driven by a deep-seated philosophy devoted to improving the civic quality of the city. Each generation of the firm's leadership has shared a design approach focused on enriching the experiences of people, and each project has been treated as part of an ongoing exploration in shaping the public domain.

LEFT TO RIGHT
Chin Thoe Chong, Wu Tzu Chiang, Angelene Chan, Francis Lee (CEO), Ti Lian Seng, Vikas M Gore, Chan Sui Him (Chairman), Teoh Hai Pin, Lesley Lim and Dadi Surya.

Board of Directors

FEATURE PROJECTS STAFF

Wisma Atria

1986
Gan Eng Oon*
Francis Lee

Dave Riviera
Elsie Ong
Peter Lee
Yong Chin Hwei

2004
Angelene Chan
Cheang Mei Ling
Clyde Uriarte

Elsie Ong
Jacqueline Pong

2012
Angelene Chan
Mike Lim

Alvin Arre
Chai Ming Kuang
Claudia Nam
Elsie Ong
Tan Ting Chun

Paragon Shopping Centre

1999
Francis Lee
Ti Lian Seng
Tong Bin Sin

Jenny Cheng
Karen Yeo
Zairi bin Ismail

2003
Ti Lian Seng
Mike Lim
Tong Bin Sin
Wang Tse Lip

Jacqueline Pong
Jenny Cheng
Karen Yeo
Zairi bin Ismail

2009
Ti Lian Seng
Tong Bin Sin

Dominique Gotangco
Jeffrey Ang
Roland Pinpin
Toh Li Chuin

Grand Park Orchard

2010
Chan Sui Him
Steven Gan

Charmaine Wong Hui Jun
Cleofer Malijan
Edwin Lim Liak Zheng
Eric Yau
John Ting
Lionel Han Yuan Sann
Lionel Leow Teck Lee
Ng Bee Chen
Nur Hidayah Binte Kasturi
Pao Ven Yuen
Varit Charoenveingvechkit
Yong Chin Hwei

Mandarin Gallery

2009
Ti Lian Seng
Lee Siat Kiat

Ghufron Yudhaskoro
Khalil Bin Mohamed Yusof
Luo Hao
Nancy Natalia Eliem
Ng Swee Hong
Ong Pei Ye
Paul Appasamy
Roslinah Ahmad

The Heeren

2010
Francis Lee
Ti Lian Seng
Mike Lim
Toh Sze Chong

Alex Wang
Calliope Lee Ning Ying
Derrick Lee Chee Kau
Laura Phay Su-Min
Leong Wei Lin
Lisa Teo
Nurul Farhana Bte Baharom
Roslinah Ahmad
Sirirat Cheawsirikul
Theresia Widyasari
Thomas Manthovani

TripleOne Somerset

2010
Angelene Chan
Mike Lim

Alvin Arre
Alvin Sugiyanto
Amit Pathak
Angela Tseng
Chai Ming Kuang
Chailerd Siripongtikanon
Taweechok Kumklud
Wellington Kuswanto

Orchard Central

2009
Chan Sui Him
Ng San Son

Angela Ng
Eric Yau
Lim Sheau Miin
Maria Rizalina L Laforteza
Mary Grace David Judar
Sebastian Tong

The Centrepoint

2006
Wu Tzu Chiang
Dadi Surya
Suneeth CN

Chia Wee Hou
Seow Lee Koon
Tan Chung Keong
Tan Swat Tin

Master Plan

2001
Chan Sui Him
Jeremy Tan
Loh Hai Yew

Chow Lai Fun
Villy Tampi

* Project Directors in bold

ENDNOTES

Introduction | *DP Architects on Orchard Road* (pages 11-19)

1. See Singapore Ministry of Trade and Industry, 'Economic Survey of Singapore Second Quarter 2010: Recent Trends in Singapore's Retail Sector', in *Economic Survey of Singapore, Second Quarter 2010*, August 2010. Orchard Road is recorded as home to 450,000 square metres of privately owned, leasable retail space. Retrieved from http://app.mti.gov.sg/default.asp?id=148&articleID=22541.

PART 1 – A CONTEXTUAL HISTORY

Chapter One | *Situating Orchard Road's Malls: a History of Retail Form* (pages 22-31)

1. Segard and François Martin Testard, *Picturesque Views of Public Edifices in Paris. Aquatinted in Imitation of the Drawings by Mr. Rosenberg* (London: Printed for Samuel Leigh, 1814), 10.

2. Walter Benjamin, 'Paris - Capital of the Nineteenth Century, Exposé of 1939', in *The Arcades Project*, trans. Howard Eiland and Kevin McLaughlin (Cambridge: Belknap Press of Harvard University Press, 1999), 3.

3. Michael B Miller, *The Bon Marché: Bourgeois Culture And The Department Store, 1869-1920* (Princeton: Princeton University Press, 1994), 166.

4. Anthony Sutcliffe, *Paris: An Architectural History* (New Haven: Yale University Press, 1993), 132.

5. Miller, *The Bon Marché*, 42.

6. Robert Hendrickson, *The Grand Emporiums: The Illustrated History Of America's Great Department Stores* (New York: Stein and Day, 1979), 66.

7. Victor Gruen was born Viktor David Grünbaum (18 July, 1903 – 14 February, 1980).

8. Tom Van Riper, 'World's Largest Malls', on *Forbes*, 18 January 2008, retrieved from http://www.forbes.com/2008/01/17/retail-malls-shopping-biz-commerce-cx_tvr_0118malls.html.

Chapter Two | *A Comparison: Global Retail Streetscapes* (pages 32-45)

1. 'Orchard Road One Way All Along Soon', in *Straits Times*, 8 February 1974, 8. See also 'Orchard Road Project', in Straits Times, 31 January 1984, 10.

Champs-Élysées, Paris

2. J M Pérouse de Montclos, *Histoire de l'architecture française de la Renaissance* (Paris: Ménges, 1989), 80.

3. Anthony Sutcliffe, *Paris: An Architectural History* (New Haven: Yale University Press, 1993), 154.

4. Sutcliffe, *Paris: An Architectural History*, 132.

5. 'Mission', on *The Champs-Élysées Committee*, retrieved from http://www.champselysees.org/champselysees/committee.

6. 'Global Retail Markets Rebound Strongly', on *Cushman & Wakefield*, 1 September 2011, retrieved from http://www.cushwake.com/cwglobal/jsp/newsDetail.jsp?Country=FR&Language=EN&repId=c43900010p. The report lists the top ten most expensive shopping streets in the world based on rental rates.

Fifth Avenue, New York

7. 'The Kress Legacy', on *Samuel H Kress Foundation*, 15 October 2011, retrieved from http://www.kressfoundation.org/about/kress_legacy/.

8. Jerry Patterson, *Fifth Avenue: The Best Address* (New York: Rizzoli, 1998), 255.

9. Peter Hellman, 'Real Estate Power - Private and Public', *New York Magazine* (January 1, 1973), 39-41.

10. Ibid.

11. New York Department of City Planning, 'Article 81-80, Special Regulations for Fifth Avenue Subdistrict', *Zoning Resolution, The City of New York* (New York: City of New York, 1982).

Omotesandō, Tokyo

12. Edward Seidensticker, *Low City, High City: Tokyo from Edo to the Earthquake: How the Shogun's Ancient Capital Became a Great Modern City, 1867–1923* (Cambridge, MA: Harvard University Press, 1991), 108-113.

13. Edward Seidensticker, *Tokyo from Edo to Showa 1867 - 1989: the Emergence of the World's Greatest City* (Tokyo: Tuttle Publishing, 2010), 509.

Key Ingredients

14. Jane Jacobs, *The Death and Life of Great American Cities* (New York: Random House, 1961), 29.

15. Howard Saalman, *Haussman: Paris Transformed* (New York: George Braziller, 1971), 44.

Chapter Three | *A Contextual History of Singapore* (pages 46-53)

1. The 'Jackson Plan' was implemented under the supervision of Philip Jackson, a Lieutenant of the British Royal Navy. See P Motha and BKP Yuen, *Singapore Real Property Guide*, 3rd ed. (Singapore: Singapore University Press Singapore, 1989), 99.

2. Ole Johan Dale, *Urban Planning in Singapore: The Transformation of a City* (London: Oxford University Press, 1999), 22.

3. Motha, *Real Property Guide*, 99.

4. Dale, *Urban Planning*, 15.

5. Functional and programmatic comparisons can be made between the 19th-century shophouses and Orchard Road's present malls, for instance in the ground-level arcades. For notes on the 1984 Emerald Hill restoration see Kweck Luck, 'Singapore: A Skyline of Pragmatism', *Beyond Description: Singapore Space Historicity*, Ryan Bishop, ed. (New York: Routledge, 2004), 112-124.

6. For early population statistics, see Swee Hock Saw, 'Population Trends in Singapore, 1819-1967', *Journal of Southeast Asian History* (March 1969), 36-49. For post-independence data, visit Singapore Department of Statistics, 'Time Series on Population (Mid-Year Estimates)', retrieved from http://www.singstat.gov.sg.

7. Mah Bow Tan, 'Speech by Mah Bow Tan, Minister for National Development, at the official opening of the URA Centre', 20 November 1999, retrieved from http://www.ura.gov.sg.

8. Singapore Housing and Development Board, *Facts on Public Housing in Singapore* (Singapore: Housing Development Board, 1997).

9. N Khublall and B Yuen, *Development Control and Planning Law in Singapore* (Singapore: Longman Singapore, 1991), 42.

10. 'Concept Plan 2001', Urban Redevelopment Authority, retrieved from http://www.ura.gov.sg/conceptplan2001/index.html.

11. See Singapore Ministry of Trade and Industry, 'Economic Survey of Singapore Second Quarter 2010: Recent Trends in Singapore's Retail Sector', in *Economic Survey of Singapore, Second Quarter 2010*, August 2010. Orchard Road is recorded as home to 450,000 square metres of privately owned, leasable retail space. Retrieved from http://app.mti.gov.sg/default.asp?id=148&articleID=22541.

12. Dale, *Urban Planning*, 57. The source states *Tourism 21* as targeting S$16 billion of investment. SGD converted to USD according to a 1995 average conversion rate estimated at 1.4.

13. 'Industry News September 2006', on *Singapore Tourism Board*, retrieved from http://www.stbpassport.com/archives/298.htm. All dollar amounts converted from SGD to USD.

14. Belinda Yuen, 'Urban Heritage in Singapore', in *Global Urban Development Magazine* 1:1 (May 2005). Retrieved from http://www.globalurban.org/IssuelPIMag05/Yuen%20article.htm.

Chapter Four | *The Evolution of Orchard Road* (pages 54-69)

1 Kalpana Rashiwala, 'Mega property sales on the cards in Orchard area', in *The Business Times*, 20 May 2011. For Orchard Road retail rental rates, valued at $40 / sq ft / month in the second quarter of 2011, see Carine Lee, 'Prime retail rentals up 0.5% in Q2', in *The Business Times, Singapore*, 24 June 2011.

2 'A Preview of the Orchard Road Mall', in *Straits Times*, 3 December 1973, 7. See also 'Stamford Canal Being Re-built', in *Straits Times*, 9 February 1979, 13.

3 Peter K G Dunlop, *Street Names of Singapore* (Singapore: Who's Who Publishing, 2000).

4 Edwin Lee, *Historic Buildings of Singapore* (Singapore: Preservation of Monuments Board) 13.

5 Bus Doomed and Rikida Doomed, 'Singapore-Jahore Railway Opened to 'Woodlands' Yesterday', in *Straits Times*, 11 April 1903, 5.

6 Ole Johan Dale, *Urban Planning in Singapore: The Transformation of a City* (London: Oxford University Press, 1999) 24.

7 G A Chatfield, *Shops and Shopping in Singapore* (Singapore: Eastern Universities Press, 1962) 10.

8 Lynda Hong, 'Orchard Road to undergo S$40m rejuvenation: STB' on *Channel NewsAsia*, 29 October 2007, retrieved from http://www.channelnewsasia.com/stories/singaporelocalnews/view/308356/1/.html. SGD converted to USD, estimated using 2007 average conversion rate of 1.5.

PART 2 - CONTRIBUTIONS OF DP ARCHITECTS

Chapter One | *Designing Orchard Road's Street-Integrated Malls* (pages 72-83)

1 The merger of buildings with landscape is embodied in projects such as Weiss Manfredi's Seattle Olympic Sculpture Park. Buildings can themselves act as landscapes, as does the Yokohama Ferry Terminal designed by Foreign Office Architects. For a comprehensive discussion on the subject of relating building to landscape, see Stan Allen and Marc McQuade, eds., *Landform Building: Architecture's New Terrain* (Baden: Lars Müller Publishers, 2011).

2 See Circular to Professional Institutes 'Urban Design Plans and Guidelines for the Orchard Planning Area, Circular No: URA/PB/2002/02-CUDD', retrieved from http://www.ura.gov.sg/circulars/text/dc02-02.html. For the 2009 amendment, see 'Circular No: URA/PB/2009/14-CUDG', retrieved from http://www.ura.gov.sg/circulars/text/dc09-14.pdf.

3 'Sale of Site for Commercial Development on Land Parcel at Orchard Road / Somerset Road', *Urban Redevelopment Authority*, 28 March 2006, retrieved from http://www.ura.gov.sg/sales/Somerset(28Mar06)/tender%20docs/tcot-Somerset.pdf.

Chapter Two | *Feature Projects* (pages 84-185)

1 G A Chatfield, *Shops and Shopping in Singapore* (Singapore: Eastern Universities Press, Singapore, 1962), 19.

INFORMATIONAL GRAPHICS

Orchard Road Facts and Figures (page 50)

Mall listings, square metre counts, and outlet numbers recorded by Singapore Tourism Board, retrieved from https://app.stb.gov.sg/asp/index.asp.

Tourism and Shopping in Singapore (page 61)

Annual Tourism Reports compiled by the Research and Incentives Division, Singapore Tourism Board, retrieved from https://app.stb.gov.sg/asp/tou/tou03.asp. All dollar values converted to USD from values recorded in SGD, based on average annual exchange rates.

2011 Rental Rates World Map (page 69)

A listing of rental rates in USD/square foot/year is compiled quarterly by Colliers International. For Spring 2011 figures, see Ross J Moore, 'Premier Retail Streets Bounce-Back', *Colliers International Spring Highlights 2011 Retail*, retrieved from http://www.colliers.com/content/globalretailhighlightsspring2011.pdf.

Urban Redevelopment Authority Building Codes (pages 76-77)

See Circular to Professional Institutes 'Urban Design Plans and Guidelines for the Orchard Planning Area, Circular No: URA/PB/2002/02-CUDD', retrieved from http://www.ura.gov.sg/circulars/text/dc02-02.html.

ADDITIONAL REFERENCES

Bridges, William. *Map Of The City Of New York And Island Of Manhattan With Explanatory Remarks And References*. New York: William Bridges, 1811.

Gruen, Victor and Larry Smith. *Shopping Towns USA: The Planning of Shopping Centers*. New York: Reinhold, 1960.

Hack, Karl and Jean-Louis Margolin, eds. *Singapore from Temasek to the 21st Century: Reinventing the Global City*. Singapore: NUS Press, 2010.

Jacobs, Allan B. *Great Streets*. Cambridge, MA: The MIT Press, 1995.

Le Corbusier. *The Athens Charter*. Translated by Anthony Eardley. New York: Grossman, 1973. First published in 1943.

Lim, Jon S H. 'The Shophouse Rafflesia: An Outline of its Malaysian Pedigree and its Subsequent Diffusion in Asia', in *Journal of the Royal Asiatic Society* LXVI:1 (1993): 47-66.

Lim, William S W. *Cities for People: Reflections of a Southeast Asian Architect*. Singapore: Select Books, 1990.

Lim, William S W. *Asian Alterity: With Special Reference to Architecture and Urbanism through the Lens of Cultural Studies*. Singapore: World Scientific Publishing, 2007.

Lynch, Kevin. *A Theory of Good City Form*. Cambridge, MA: The MIT Press, 1981.

Page, Max. *The Creative Destruction of Manhattan, 1900-1940*. Chicago: University Of Chicago Press, 2000.

Slater, Don. 'Going Shopping: Markets, Crowds and Consumption', in *Cultural Reproduction*, ed. Chris Jencks. London: Routledge, 1993.

Turnbull, Constance M. *A History of Singapore: 1819-1975*. Kuala Lumpur: Oxford University Press, 1977.

Urban Redevelopment Authority. *Planning Report 114: Orchard Planning Area*. Singapore: Select Books, 1994.

Urban Redevelopment Authority, 'Our History'. Retrieved from http://www.ura.gov.sg/about/ura-history.htm.

Yuen, Belinda. *Planning Singapore: From Plan to Implementation*. Hawaii: University of Hawaii Press, 1998.

CREDITS

IMAGE CREDITS

PHOTOGRAPHERS Jeremy San
Mori Hidetaka
Ng San Son
Rory Daniel

Except otherwise noted, all photos and drawings are owned by DP Architects Pte Ltd:

Page 24 Galleria Vittorio Emanuele II. Courtesy of the University of New Hampshire, Historical European Photographs Collection, 1892-1894.

Page 46 Map of the Town and Environs of Singapore 1878. Courtesy of the Chief Surveyor, Singapore Land Authority, and the National Archives of Singapore.

Page 58 Orchard Road Shophouse, Courtesy of the National Archives of Singapore.

Page 64 'Car Park' Hawker Centre at Orchard Road. Courtesy of the Ministry of Information, Communications and the Arts (MICA), and the National Archives of Singapore.

Page 186 Photo credits: PT. Agung Podomoro Land (Central Park); Wonyang Kim, Baum Architects (Noon Square).

Historical Sketches
The sketches included in chapters 1 through 4 are drawn by the staff of DP Architects, and each has been adapted or interpreted from photograph collections. Historical Orchard Road sketches are compiled from a collection of photographs owned by the National Archives of Singapore.

Page 25 Sketch adapted from Passage des Princes, Paris, published in L'Illustration, Journal Universel, Paris, 1860.

Page 26 Sketch adapted from Alexander Laplanche and Hector Boileau, Au Bon Marché, Paris, 1872; and the new staircase at Au Bon Marché Illustration from Le Monde illustré (ca. 1875).

Every effort has been made to trace the original source of copyrights material contained in this book. The publishers would be pleased to hear from copyrights holders to rectify any errors or omissions.

The information and illustrations in this publication have been prepared and supplied by DP Architects Pte Ltd. While all reasonable efforts have been made to ensure accuracy, the publishers do not, under any circumstances, accept responsibility for errors, omissions and representations express or implied.

ACKNOWLEDGEMENTS

EDITOR-IN-CHIEF Angelene Chan

EDITORIAL TEAM Chan Hui Min
David Liauw
Jackie Poh
Nartano Lim

AUTHOR Collin Anderson

GRAPHICS EDITORS Collin Anderson
Fu Tingting

GRAPHICS TEAM Loh Yew Cheng
Low Si Ni

LAYOUT Fu Tingting

COVER DESIGN Fu Tingting

ILLUSTRATIONS Anusan Angkuna
Eugene Foong
Lek Chalermchart Noonchoo

CONTRIBUTORS Fumihiko Maki
Maki and Associates
Kenneth Frampton
Columbia University

DESIGN CONSULTATION The Press Room
Kelley Cheng and Celestine Tan

ABOUT THE AUTHOR

Collin Anderson was trained as an engineer at Duke University's Pratt School of Engineering and as an architect at Columbia University's Graduate School of Architecture, Planning and Preservation. He has worked as a designer in the offices of Michael Graves & Associates and Ove Arup & Partners.

CONTACT DETAILS

SINGAPORE
6 RAFFLES BOULEVARD
#04-100
MARINA SQUARE
SINGAPORE 039594

DP ARCHITECTS PTE LTD
dparchitects@dpa.com.sg

DP CONSULTANTS PTE LTD
dpconsultants@dpc.com.sg

DP ENGINEERS PTE LTD
dpengineers@dpe.com.sg

DP GREEN PTE LTD
dpgreen@dpg.com.sg

DPD INTERNATIONAL PTE LTD
dpdi@dpdinternational.asia

DPD+ PTE LTD
general@dpdplus.com

CHINA
UNIT 3201 WHEELOCK SQUARE NO 1717
NANJING ROAD WEST
JING AN DISTRICT
SHANGHAI 200040

DP ARCHITECTS PTE LTD (SHANGHAI)
dparchitects@dpa-cn.com

NO 5 GUANG HUA ROAD
PROSPER CENTRE
(EAST)
TOWER 1 UNIT 2202
CHAOYANG DISTRICT
BEIJING 100026

DP ARCHITECTS PTE LTD (BEIJING)
dpapek@dpa-cn.com

SUITE 1103
HAN TANG BUILDING
OVERSEA CHINESE TOWN
SHENZHEN 518053

DP ARCHITECTS PTE LTD (SHENZHEN)
dpasz@dpa-cn.com

UNIT 1801-1802
TOWER A
YAOZHONG SQUARE
NO 9 LINHE ROAD WEST
TIAN'HE DISTRICT
GUANGZHOU 510610

DP ARCHITECTS PTE LTD (GUANGZHOU)
dpagz@dpa-cn.com

INDIA
21/ VASWANI
MANSION 4TH FLOOR
120 DINSHAW
VACHHA ROAD
CHURCHGATE
MUMBAI 400 020

DP CONSULTANTS PVT LTD (MUMBAI)
dpindia@dpc-in.com

27/1 4TH CROSS
5TH MAIN
JAYAMAHAL
EXTENSION
BANGALORE 560046

DP CONSULTANTS PVT LTD (BANGALORE)
dpindia@dpc-in.com

INDONESIA
JALAN TARAKANITA
111 NO 34 RT 001/008
PATAL SENAYAN
JAKARTA 12210

PT DP ARCHITECTS INDONESIA
dpaindon@dparchitects.com

MALAYSIA
LEVEL 20 AMODA
22 JALAN IMBI
55100 KUALA LUMPUR

DP ARCHITECTS SDN BHD
dpa@dpa.com.my

THAILAND
NO 25 MOO 17
PAHOLYOTHIN ROAD
TAMBOL KUKOT
AMPHUR LAMLUKKA
CHANGWAT
PATHUMTHANI 12130
BANGKOK

DP ARCHITECTS PTE LTD
dparchitects@dpa.com.sg

UAE
P O BOX 211711
DUBAI

DP ARCHITECTS PTE LTD (DUBAI)
dparchitects@dpa-ae.com

VIETNAM
9TH FLOOR, IDD
BUILDING NO 111
LY CHINH THANG
STREET WARD 7
DISTRICT 3
HO CHI MINH CITY

DP ARCHITECTS VIETNAM CO., LTD
dparchitects@dpa-vn.com